AWS Administration Definitive Guide

Learn to design, build, and manage your infrastructure on the most popular of all the Cloud platforms—Amazon Web Services

Yohan Wadia

BIRMINGHAM - MUMBAI

AWS Administration – The Definitive Guide

First published: February 2016

Production reference: 1080216

Published by Packt Publishing Ltd.
Livery Place
35 Livery Street
Birmingham B3 2PB, UK.

ISBN 978-1-78217-375-5

www.packtpub.com

Credits

Author
Yohan Wadia

Reviewer
Paul Deng

Commissioning Editor
Kunal Parikh

Acquisition Editor
Rahul Nair

Content Development Editor
Anish Dhurat

Technical Editor
Pranjali Mistry

Copy Editor
Charlotte Carneiro

Project Coordinator
Bijal Patel

Proofreader
Safis Editing

Indexer
Monica Ajmera Mehta

Production Coordinator
Nilesh Mohite

Cover Work
Nilesh Mohite

About the Author

Yohan Wadia is a client-focused virtualization and cloud expert with 6 years of experience in the IT industry.

He has been involved in conceptualizing, designing, and implementing large-scale solutions for a variety of enterprise customers based on VMware vCloud, Amazon Web Services, and Eucalyptus Private Cloud.

His community-focused involvement also enables him to share his passion for virtualization and cloud technologies with peers through social media engagements, public speaking at industry events, and through his personal blog — yoyoclouds.com

He is currently working with an IT services and consultancy company as a Cloud Solutions Lead and is involved in designing and building enterprise-level cloud solutions for internal as well as external customers. He is also a VMware Certified Professional and a vExpert (2012 and 2013).

I wish to dedicate this book to both my loving parents, Ma and Paa. Thank you for all your love, support, encouragement, and patience. I would also like to thank the entire Packt Publishing team, especially Ruchita Bhansali, Athira Laji, and Gaurav Sharma, for their excellent guidance and support.

And finally, a special thanks to one of my favorite bunch of people: the amazing team of developers, support staff, and engineers who work at AWS for such an "AWSome" cloud platform!

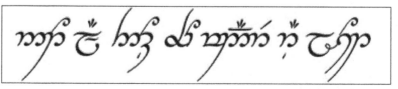

Not all those who wander are lost.

- J. R. R. Tolkien

About the Reviewer

Paul Deng is a senior software engineer with over 8 years of experience in end-to-end IoT app design and development, including embedded devices, large-scale machine learning, cloud, and web apps.

Paul holds software algorithm patents and was a finalist of Shell Australian Innovation Challenge 2011. He has authored several publications on IoT and cloud.

He lives in Melbourne, Australia, with his wife Cindy and son Leon. Visit his website at http://dengpeng.de to see what he is currently exploring and to learn more about him.

www.PacktPub.com

Support files, eBooks, discount offers, and more

For support files and downloads related to your book, please visit www.PacktPub.com.

Did you know that Packt offers eBook versions of every book published, with PDF and ePub files available? You can upgrade to the eBook version at www.PacktPub.com and as a print book customer, you are entitled to a discount on the eBook copy. Get in touch with us at service@packtpub.com for more details.

At www.PacktPub.com, you can also read a collection of free technical articles, sign up for a range of free newsletters and receive exclusive discounts and offers on Packt books and eBooks.

https://www2.packtpub.com/books/subscription/packtlib

Do you need instant solutions to your IT questions? PacktLib is Packt's online digital book library. Here, you can search, access, and read Packt's entire library of books.

Why subscribe?

- Fully searchable across every book published by Packt
- Copy and paste, print, and bookmark content
- On demand and accessible via a web browser

Free access for Packt account holders

If you have an account with Packt at www.PacktPub.com, you can use this to access PacktLib today and view 9 entirely free books. Simply use your login credentials for immediate access.

Instant updates on new Packt books

Get notified! Find out when new books are published by following @PacktEnterprise on Twitter or the *Packt Enterprise* Facebook page.

Table of Contents

Preface

Cloud computing has definitely matured and evolved a lot ever since its conception. Practically all major industries and top fortune 500 companies today run their application workloads on clouds to reap all sorts of benefits, ranging from reduced costs, better availability of their applications, and easier manageability to on-demand scalability, and much more! At the forefront of this cloud innovation is a market leader like no other: Amazon Web Services (AWS).

AWS provides a ton of easy-to-use products and services that you can leverage to build, host, deploy, and manage your applications on the cloud. It also provides a variety of ways to interact with these services, such as SDKs, APIs, CLIs, and even a web-based management console.

This book is a one stop shop where you can find all there is to getting started with the core AWS services, which include EC2, S3, RDS, VPCs, and a whole lot more! If you are a sysadmin or an architect or someone who just wants to learn and explore various aspects of administering AWS services, then this book is the right choice for you! Each chapter of this book is designed to help you understand the individual services' concepts as well as gain hands-on experience by practicing simple and easy to follow steps. The chapters also highlight some key best practices and recommendations that you ought to keep in mind when working with AWS.

What this book covers

Chapter 1, *Introducing Amazon Web Services*, covers the introductory concepts and general benefits of cloud computing along with an overview of Amazon Web Services and its overall platform. The chapter also walks you through your first AWS signup process, and finally ends with the configuration of the AWS CLI.

Chapter 2, Security and Access Management, discusses the overall importance of security and how you can achieve it using an AWS core service known as Identity and Access Management (IAM). The chapter walks you through the steps required to create and administer AWS users, groups, as well as how to create and assign permissions and policies to them.

Chapter 3, Images and Instances, provides hands-on knowledge about EC2 instances and images, and how you can create and manage them using both the AWS Management Console as well as the AWS CLI.

Chapter 4, Security, Storage, Networking and Lots More!, discusses some of the key aspects that you can leverage to provide added security for your applications and instances. The chapter also provides an in-depth overview of EC2 instance storage as well as networking options followed by some recommendations and best practices.

Chapter 5, Building Your Own Private Clouds Using Amazon VPC, introduces you to the concept and benefits provided by AWS Virtual Private Cloud (VPC) service. The chapter also provides an in-depth look at various VPC deployment strategies and how you can best leverage them for your own environments.

Chapter 6, Monitoring Your AWS Infrastructure, covers AWS's primary monitoring service, called as Amazon CloudWatch. In this chapter, you will learn how to effectively create and manage alerts, loggings, and notifications for your EC2 instances, as well as your AWS environment.

Chapter 7, Manage Your Applications with Auto Scaling and Elastic Load Balancing, discusses some of the key AWS services that you should leverage to create a dynamically scalable and highly available web application.

Chapter 8, Database-as-a-Service Using Amazon RDS, provides an in-depth look at how you can effectively design, create, manage, and monitor your RDS instances on AWS.

Chapter 9, Working with Simple Storage Service, provides practical knowledge and design considerations that you should keep in mind when working with Amazon's infinitely scalable and durable object storage known as Amazon S3.

Chapter 10, Extended AWS Services for Your Application, provides a brief overview of add-on AWS services that you can leverage for enhancing your applications' performance and availability.

What you need for this book

To start using this book, you will need the following set of software installed on your local desktop:

- An SSH client such as Putty, a key generator such as PuttyGen, and a file transferring tool such as WinSCP
- Any modern web browser, preferably Mozilla Firefox

Who this book is for

This book is intended for any and all IT professionals who wish to learn and implement AWS for their own environments and application hosting. Although no prior experience or knowledge is required, it will be beneficial for you to have basic Linux knowledge as well as some understanding of networking concepts and server virtualization.

Conventions

In this book, you will find a number of text styles that distinguish between different kinds of information. Here are some examples of these styles and an explanation of their meaning.

Code words in text, database table names, folder names, filenames, file extensions, pathnames, dummy URLs, user input, and Twitter handles are shown as follows: "We can include other contexts through the use of the `include` directive."

A block of code is set as follows:

```
{
"Id": "Policy1448937262025",
"Version": "2012-10-17",
"Statement": [
  {
"Sid": "Stmt1448937260611",
"Effect": "Allow",
"Principal": "*",
  }
}
```

Any command-line input or output is written as follows:

```
CREATE TABLE doge
(
idint(11) NOT NULL auto_increment,
namevarchar(255),
description text,
```

New terms and **important words** are shown in bold. Words that you see on the screen, for example, in menus or dialog boxes, appear in the text like this: "Next, select the **Launch DB Instance** button to bring up the DB Launch Wizard:"

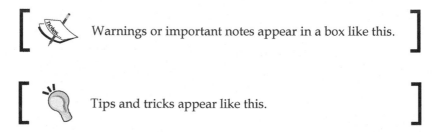

> Warnings or important notes appear in a box like this.

> Tips and tricks appear like this.

Reader feedback

Feedback from our readers is always welcome. Let us know what you think about this book—what you liked or disliked. Reader feedback is important for us as it helps us develop titles that you will really get the most out of.

To send us general feedback, simply e-mail feedback@packtpub.com, and mention the book's title in the subject of your message.

If there is a topic that you have expertise in and you are interested in either writing or contributing to a book, see our author guide at www.packtpub.com/authors.

Customer support

Now that you are the proud owner of a Packt book, we have a number of things to help you to get the most from your purchase.

Downloading the example code

You can download the example code files from your account at http://www.packtpub.com for all the Packt Publishing books you have purchased. If you purchased this book elsewhere, you can visit http://www.packtpub.com/support and register to have the files e-mailed directly to you.

Errata

Although we have taken every care to ensure the accuracy of our content, mistakes do happen. If you find a mistake in one of our books—maybe a mistake in the text or the code—we would be grateful if you could report this to us. By doing so, you can save other readers from frustration and help us improve subsequent versions of this book. If you find any errata, please report them by visiting http://www.packtpub.com/submit-errata, selecting your book, clicking on the **Errata Submission Form** link, and entering the details of your errata. Once your errata are verified, your submission will be accepted and the errata will be uploaded to our website or added to any list of existing errata under the Errata section of that title.

To view the previously submitted errata, go to https://www.packtpub.com/books/content/support and enter the name of the book in the search field. The required information will appear under the **Errata** section.

Piracy

Piracy of copyrighted material on the Internet is an ongoing problem across all media. At Packt, we take the protection of our copyright and licenses very seriously. If you come across any illegal copies of our works in any form on the Internet, please provide us with the location address or website name immediately so that we can pursue a remedy.

Please contact us at copyright@packtpub.com with a link to the suspected pirated material.

We appreciate your help in protecting our authors and our ability to bring you valuable content.

Questions

If you have a problem with any aspect of this book, you can contact us at questions@packtpub.com, and we will do our best to address the problem.

1
Introducing Amazon Web Services

Being in the IT industry, we all have gone through the long and tedious process of procuring new infrastructure for our data centers at one time or another. Let's be honest, it is not a task for the faint-hearted At a minimum, a brand new server can take weeks if not months to get delivered from its date of ordering, and this is too heavily dependent on a lot of external factors which, most of the time, are not in our control. Even if the new server comes in on time, there is the additional burden of prepping the rack, clearing space for the new resources, cabling, cooling, mounting, installation of software, configuration, and the list just keeps on going on for another mile. Putting the server and storage on one side, the same can also apply for networking, applications, software, and a whole lot of other things. But what if all this was to change? What if tomorrow, you could simply jump start your business or scale your application to thousands of servers, all with the simple click of a button? Seems farfetched, doesn't it, but in reality, this is possible today with a little help from something called as cloud computing.

Cloud computing has definitely evolved a lot over the years, and today it has become almost a mainstream part of our lives. Everything from storing large amounts of data, to having burst compute capacity at your fingertips and having enterprise software applications available on demand any time anywhere are just some of the key benefits that clouds provide today. At the helm of this new way of computing is **Amazon Web Services (AWS)**.

In this chapter, we are going to look at some of the key features and benefits provided by cloud computing in general along with few interesting enterprise use cases. Later on, you will learn a bit more about Amazon Web Services and its core components, and finally have a look at how to sign up and get started with AWS.

What is cloud computing?

Cloud computing has become one of the most discussed topics over the last few years, but what does it actually mean? Why is it important for you and your business? Let's take a quick look at what cloud computing actually is and how you as an end user can benefit from it.

NIST defines cloud computing as a model for enabling ubiquitous, convenient, on-demand network access to a shared pool of configurable computing resources (for example, networks, servers, storage, applications, and services) that can be rapidly provisioned and released with minimal management effort or service provider interaction. Was that a bit confusing? Let's break it down to understand it a little bit better:

- **On demand**: Contrary to traditional IT data centers where requesting and obtaining resources for your applications used to take weeks, the same resources can be made available on an on-demand basis in the cloud, without requiring any human interventions at all.

- **Network access**: One of the key features of any cloud is that all of its resources can be accessed over the Internet or a network in general. This makes it really easy for the end user to access and leverage cloud from heterogeneous devices such as laptops, workstations, mobile phones, and so on.

- **Shared pool**: We must have all experienced the *silo*-based infrastructure setup in our traditional IT data centers. Silos of resources are often created by individual departments where each application gets overcommitted resources, which are more than often wasted. In case of the cloud, IT resources such as compute, storage, and network are pooled and abstracted together from the end user. This pooling enables the cloud to dynamically provide resources to its tenants as and when required without the end user having any knowledge of where their application will actually reside in a cluster or a rack.

- **Rapid provisioning**: Rapid provisioning or elasticity as it is referred to nowadays, is the ability of a cloud to scale its resources either horizontally (scale out) or vertically (scale up) on an automated basis. This elasticity provides end users with a lot of flexibility and control over their resources and how they get consumed.

Cloud computing features and benefits

Okay, so now we know what cloud computing really means, but why should you as an end user use it? How are you and your organization going to benefit from it? Let's look at some of the key benefits and features cloud computing has to offer:

- **Lower costs**: Cloud computing does not have any upfront costs. Capital expenditure is virtually zero as the entire necessary infrastructure and resources are already made available and ready for use by the Cloud provider. All the end user has to do is consume these resources and pay only for what they use.

  This also reduces the overall maintenance costs as well. Since the organization now has less hardware to manage, it doesn't necessarily have to bother about its server, network, and storage capacity or have a full time staff to manage them.

- **Self-service**: Cloud computing provides a simple, centralized, self-service-based model that end users can use to interact with the cloud platform. The interaction can be in terms of performing simple tasks, such as spinning up new compute resources, adding more storage resources at runtime, or more complex ones, such as scheduling resources and so on. This ensures that the end user can leverage and consume any of the cloud's resources on an on-demand basis.

- **Faster time to markets**: Unlike traditional IT, compute resources can be brought up in a cloud in a matter of minutes as compared to the weeks it used to take. This provides the end users with the ability to deploy new applications much faster, thus decreasing overall time to markets and reducing management overheads and costs.

- **Scale as required:** The best part of using the cloud is that your backend resources can grow as your application grows. This means that you are never lagging behind with your application's needs and demands, you are always scaling with your application's needs.

Cloud computing use cases

With such features and benefits it is easy to see why there has been such a boom in the overall adoption and utilization of the cloud. Let's take a quick look at some interesting real-world use cases where your organization can leverage clouds:

- **Website hosting**: Perhaps the most common of the use cases, you as an end user can leverage cloud to build and host your websites with relative ease. The cloud enables your website to scale up and down dynamically as per its demands.

- **Storage and sharing**: The cloud offers virtually unlimited storage capacity that can used to store and share anything, from documents, media, files, and so on. Dropbox and Google Drive are classic examples of cloud being used as a storage and sharing medium.

- **Disaster recovery (DR)**: This is a more upcoming use case with clouds as more and more companies are now realizing that it is way easier and cost efficient to host a disaster recovery environment on the cloud, rather than hosting and managing a DR site of its own. Organizations can spin up failover environments on the cloud in a matter of minutes, test the failover and then shut down the entire stack. This helps save on the costs and also reduces overall management overheads and failover time.

- **Dev/test**: Dev and test are way easier to set up and run on clouds as the entire development and test environments can be built up, tested, and torn back down quickly as per requirements.

- **Short term projects/ advertising**: Similar to the Dev/test scenario, the cloud can also be leveraged to perform a variety of short-term projects/proof of concepts. A classic example is the advertising campaigns hosted on the cloud that are created for a very short duration of time, however, they need a global presence to reach out to a wider set of audiences.

- **Big data analytics**: Organizations leverage the cloud's scalability and on-demand infrastructure to capture and perform real-time analytics and data mining on extremely large datasets (big data).

Introducing Amazon Web Services

Now, that you clearly understand what cloud computing is all about and what it can do for you, let's get to know the main topic of this book—Amazon Web Services—a little better.

Amazon Web Services or AWS is a comprehensive public cloud computing platform that offers a variety of web-based products and services on an on-demand and pay-per-use basis. AWS was earlier a part of the e-commerce giant Amazon.com, and it wasn't until 2006 that AWS became a separate entity of its own. Today, AWS operates globally with data centers located in USA, Europe, Brazil, Singapore, Japan, China, and Australia. AWS provides a variety of mechanisms, using which the end users can connect to and leverage its services, the most common form of interaction being the web-based dashboard also called as AWS Management Console.

So how does the whole thing work? Well, it is very easy to understand when you compare the way AWS works with a power and utilities company. AWS offers its customers certain services just as a power company would to its consumers. You as an end user simply consume the electricity without having to worry about the underlying necessities such as generator costs, cabling, and so on. At the end of the month, all you get is a bill based on your electricity consumption and that's it! In a similar way, AWS provides its products such as compute, storage, and networking all as a service, and you only have to pay for the amount of service that you use. No upfront costs or heavy investments whatsoever!

The other important thing worth mentioning here is that AWS allows organizations to use their own operating systems, databases, and programming/architecting models as well, without requiring any major re-engineering. This provides a lot of flexibility and cost optimization to organizations as they get to operate and work with platforms that they are familiar with. This, accompanied with AWS's massively scalable and highly available infrastructure, ensures that your applications and data remain secure and available for use no matter what.

AWS architecture and components

Before we begin with the actual signup process, it is important to take a look at some of the key architecture and core components of services offered by AWS.

Regions and availability zones

We do know that AWS is spread out globally and has its presence across USA, Europe, Asia, Australia, and so on. Each of these areas is termed as a region. AWS currently has about 10 regions, each containing multiple data centers within themselves. So what's with all these regions and why do they matter? In simple terms, the resources that are geographically close to your organization are served much faster! For example, an organization running predominantly from USA can leverage the USA's regions to host their resources and gain access to them must faster.

For most of the AWS services that you use, you will be prompted to select a region in which you want to deploy the service. Each region is completely isolated from the other and runs independently as well.

 AWS does not replicate resources across regions automatically. It is up to the end user to set up the replication process.

A list of regions and their corresponding codes is provided here for your reference. The code is basically how AWS refers to its multiple regions:

Region	Name	Code
North America	US East (N. Virginia)	us-east-1
	US West (N. California)	us-west-1
	US West (Oregon)	us-west-2
South America	Sao Paulo	sa-east-1
Europe	EU (Frankfurt)	eu-central-1
	EU (Ireland)	eu-west-1
Asia	Asia Pacific (Tokyo)	ap-northeast-1
	Asia Pacific (Singapore)	ap-southeast-1
	Asia Pacific (Sydney)	ap-southeast-2
	Asia Pacific (Beijing)	cn-north-1

Each region is split up into one or more **Availability Zones** (**AZs**) and pronounced as A-Zees. An A Z is an isolated location inside a region. AZs within a particular region connect to other AZs via low-latency links. What do these AZs contain? Well, ideally they are made up of one or more physical data centers that host AWS services on them. Just as with regions, even AZs have corresponding codes to identify them, generally they are regional names followed by a numerical value. For example, if you select and use us-east-1, which is the North Virginia region, then it would have AZs listed as us-east-1b, us-east-1c, us-east-1d, and so on:

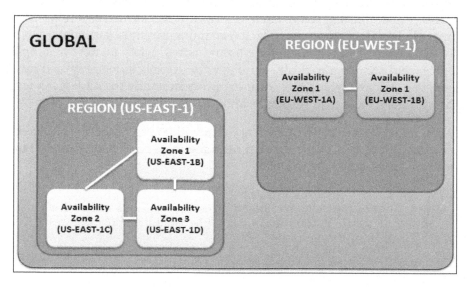

AZs are very important from a design and deployment point of view. Being data centers, they are more than capable of failure and downtime, so it is always good practice to distribute your resources across multiple AZs and design your applications such that they can remain available even if one AZ goes completely offline.

An important point to note here is that AWS will always provide the services and products to you as a customer; however, it is your duty to design and distribute your applications so that they do not suffer any potential outages or failures.

RULE OF THUMB: Design for failure and nothing will fail! This is what we will be sticking with for the remainder of this book as we go along the different AWS services and products; so keep this in mind, always!

 AWS provides a health dashboard of all its services running across each of the regions. You can view the current status and availability of each AWS service by visiting the following link: http://status.aws.amazon.com/.

AWS platform overview

The AWS platform consists of a variety of services that you can use either in isolation or in combination based on your organization's needs. This section will introduce you to some of the most commonly used services as well as some newly launched ones. To begin with, let's divide the services into three major classes:

- **Foundation services**: This is generally the pillars on which the entire AWS infrastructure commonly runs on, including the compute, storage, network, and databases.

- **Application services**: This class of services is usually more specific and generally used in conjunction with the foundation services to add functionality to your applications. For example, services such as distributed computing, messaging and Media Transcoding, and other services fall under this class.

- **Administration services**: This class deals with all aspects of your AWS environment, primarily with identity and access management tools, monitoring your AWS services and resources, application deployments, and automation.

Let's take a quick look at some of the key services provided by AWS. However, do note that this is not an exhaustive list:

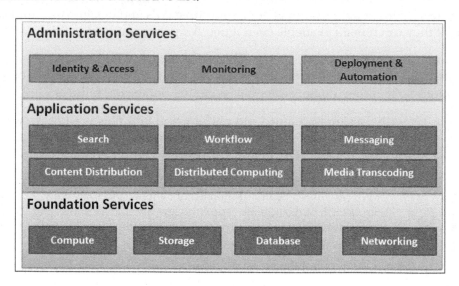

We will discuss each of the foundation services.

Compute

This includes the following services:

- **Elastic Compute Cloud (EC2)**: When it comes to brute computation power and scalability, there must be very few cloud providers out there in the market that can match AWS's EC2 service. EC2 or Elastic Compute Cloud is a web service that provides flexible, resizable, and secure compute capacity on an on-demand basis. AWS started off with EC2 as one of its core services way back in 2006 and has not stopped bringing changes and expanding the platform ever since. The compute infrastructure runs on a virtualized platform that predominantly consists of the open sourced Xen virtualization engine. We will be exploring EC2 and its subsequent services in detail in the coming chapters.

- **EC2 Container Service**: A recently launched service, the EC2 Container Service, allows you to easily run and manage docker containers across a cluster of specially created EC2 instances.

- **Amazon Virtual Private Cloud (VPC)**: VPC enables you to create secure, fully customizable, and isolated private clouds within AWS's premises. They provide additional security and control than your standard EC2 along with connectivity options to on premise data centers.

Storage

This includes the following services:

- **Simple Storage Service (S3)**: S3 is a highly reliable, fault tolerant, and fully redundant data storage infrastructure provided by AWS. It was one of the first services offered by AWS way back in 2006, and it has not stopped growing since. As of April 2013, an approximate 2 trillion objects have been uploaded to S3, and these numbers are growing exponentially each year.

- **Elastic Block Storage (EBS)**: EBS is a raw block device that can be attached to your compute EC2 instances to provide them with persistent storage capabilities.

- **Amazon Glacier**: It is a similar service offering to S3. Amazon Glacier offers long-term data storage, archival, and backup services to its customers.

- **Amazon Elastic File System**: Yet another very recent service offering introduced by AWS, **Elastic File System** (**EFS**) provides scalable and high-performance storage to EC2 compute instances in the form of an NFS filesystem.

Databases

This includes the following services:

- **Amazon Relational Database Service (RDS)**: RDS provides a scalable, high-performance relational database system such as MySQL, SQL Server, PostgreSQL, and Oracle in the cloud. RDS is a completely managed solution provided by AWS where all the database heavy lifting work is taken care of by AWS.

- **Amazon DynamoDB**: DynamoDB is a highly scalable NoSQL database as a service offering provided by AWS.

- **Amazon Redshift**: Amazon Redshift is a data warehouse service that is designed to handle and scale to petabytes of data. It is primarily used by organizations to perform real-time analytics and data mining.

Networking

This includes the following services:

- **Elastic Load Balancer (ELB)**: ELB is a dynamic load balancing service provided by AWS used to distribute traffic among EC2 instances. You will be learning about ELB a bit more in detail in subsequent chapters.

- **Amazon Route 53**: Route 53 is a highly scalable and available DNS web service provided by AWS. Rather than configuring DNS names and settings for your domain provider, you can leverage Route 53 to do the heavy lifting work for you.

These are just few of the most commonly used AWS foundational services that we listed out here. There are a lot more services and products that you can leverage to add functionality or use to manage your applications. A few of these important services are briefly described in the next section.

Distributed computing and analytics

This includes the following services:

- **Amazon Elastic MapReduce (EMR)**: As the name suggests, this service provides users with a highly scalable and easy way to distribute and process large amounts of data using Apache's Hadoop. You can integrate the functionalities of EMR with Amazon S3 to store your large data or with Amazon DynamoDB as well.

- **Amazon Redshift**: This is a massive data warehouse that users can use to store, analyze, and query petabytes of data.

Content distribution and delivery

Amazon CloudFront is basically a content delivery web service that can be used to distribute various types of content, such as media, files, and so on, with high data transfer speeds to end users globally. You can use CloudFront in conjunction with other AWS services such as EC2 and ELB as well.

Workflow and messaging

This includes the following services:

- **Amazon Simple Notification Service (SNS)**: SNS is a simple, fully managed push messaging service provided by AWS. You can use it to push your messages to mobile devices (SMS service) and even to other AWS services as API calls to trigger or notify certain activities.

- **Amazon Simple Email Service (SES)**: As the name suggests, SES is used to send bulk e-mails to various recipients. These e-mails can be anything, from simple notifications to transactions messages, and so on. Think of it as a really large mail server that can scale as per your requirements and is completely managed by AWS! Awesome, isn't it!

Monitoring

Amazon CloudWatch is a monitoring tool provided by AWS that you can use to monitor any and all aspects of your AWS environment, from EC2 instances to your RDS services to the load on your ELBs, and so on. You can even create your own metrics, set thresholds, create alarms, and a whole lot of other activities as well.

Identity and access management

AWS provides a rich set of tools and services to secure and control your infrastructure on the cloud. The most important and commonly used service for this is **identity and access management (IAM)**. Using IAM, you can, as an organizational administrator, create and manage users, assign them specific roles and permissions, and manage active directory federations as well. We will be using a lot of IAM in the next chapter, which covers this topic in greater depth.

Getting started with AWS

So far, you have learned a lot about AWS, its architecture, and core components. Now, let's get started with the fun part—the signup process.

For all first time users, signing up for AWS is a very simple and straightforward process. We will go through this shortly, but first let's take a quick look at something called as a Free Tier! Yes, you heard it right… FREE!

So, AWS basically offers usage of certain of its products at no charge for a period of 12 months from the date of the actual signup. A brief list of a few products along with their description is listed here for your reference. Note that some of the description text may not make much sense now, but that's ok as this is just for your reference, and we will be bringing this up from time to time as we progress through the book.

AWS Product	What's free?
Amazon EC2	750 hours per month of Linux micro instance usage
	750 hours per month of Windows micro instance usage
Amazon S3	5 GB of standard storage
	20,000 get requests
	2,000 put requests
Amazon RDS	750 Hours of Amazon RDS Single-AZ micro instance usage
	20 GB of DB Storage: any combination of general purpose (SSD) or magnetic
	20 GB for backups
	10,000,000 I/Os

AWS Product	What's free?
Amazon ELB	750 hours per month
	15 GB of data processing

 For a complete insight into the free tier usage, check `http://aws.amazon.com/free/`.

Awesome! So when we have free stuff for us right from the word go, why wait? Let's sign up for AWS. To begin with, launch your favorite web browser and type in the following URL in the address bar: `http://aws.amazon.com/`.

You should see the AWS landing page similar to one shown here. Here, select either the **Create an AWS Account** option or the **Create a Free Account** option to get started:

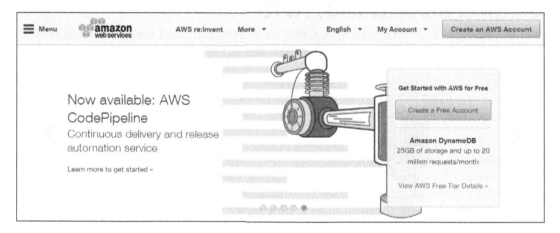

The next screen will help you with the initial signup process. Provide a suitable e-mail address or your contact number in the **E-mail or mobile number** field. Select the **I am a new user** option and select the **Sign in using our secure server** button to proceed:

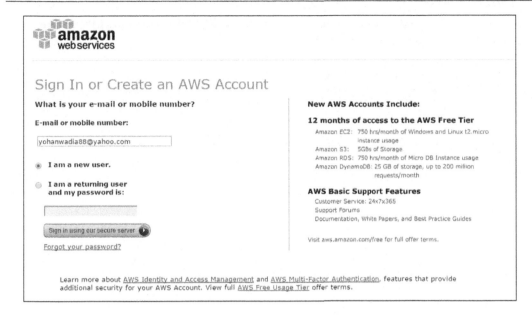

 You can alternatively sign in using your Amazon.com credentials as well; however, its best to use separate credentials for working with AWS.

The next couple of screens will be used to provide your basic details along with the billing information. In the **Login Credentials** page, enter your **Name**, your **E-mail address** along with a suitable **Password**. This password will be used by you to login to the AWS Management Console, so ideally provide a strong password here. Click on **Create account** when done.

The next screen is the **Contact Information** page. Provide your **Full Name**, **Company Name**, **Country**, **Address**, **City**, **Postal Code**, and **Phone Number** as requested. Check the **Amazon Internet Service Pvt. Ltd. Customer Agreement** checkbox and select the **Create Account** and **continue** options.

Enter a suitable **Cardholder's Name** and your **Credit/Debit Card Number** in the **Payment Information** page as shown:

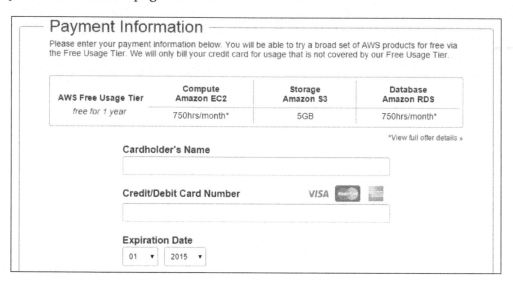

The last part of the signup process is the **Identity Verification** process where you will receive an automated call from AWS as a part of the verification process. You will have to enter the displayed four digit **PIN code** on your telephone's keypad during the call. Once the verification is completed, you can click on the **Continue to select your Support Plan** tab:

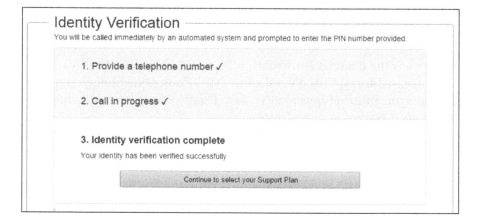

The final step in the signup process involves the selection of the Support Plan. AWS provides four support options to customers, each having their own SLAs and costs associated with it. Here is a quick look at the support plans provided by AWS:

- **Basic Support**: As the name suggests, this is the most basic level of support provided by AWS. This support level provides you with access to the AWS community forums. You can additionally contact customer services for any queries related to your account and bill generation.

> The Basic Support plan is free of charge and all customers are entitled to it.

- **Developer Support**: This is a paid support service ($49 per month). You can create and raise tickets for your support case, which is generally answered within 12 working hours.

- **Business Support**: This is a paid support service as well and is generally meant for enterprise-level customers running production workloads on AWS. The SLAs for this support are much higher as a case has to be answered within an hour from its creation. Additional support is provided 24/7, 365 days a year via phone and chat.

- **Enterprise Support**: A paid support service with the highest SLA available (15 minutes); these cases are generally handled by a separate team at AWS called the **Technical Account Manager** (**TAM**) who are subject matter experts in their own fields.

In our case, we opted to go with **Basic Support** for the time being. You can change the support levels later on as well according to your needs. Click on **Continue** to complete the signup process. You should receive a couple of e-mails on your supplied e-mail address as well. These are introductory e-mails that will provide you with important links such as how to get started with AWS, billing page, account information, and so on.

With these steps completed, you are now ready to sign in to the AWS Management Console!

Introducing the AWS Management Console

So here we are, all ready to get started with the AWS Management Console! This is the most commonly used method to access, manage, and work with AWS services. We shall be looking more closely at the different AWS access mechanisms in the next chapter; however for now, let's quickly look at what the AWS Management Console is all about.

First off, sign in to the Management Console by launching your favorite browser and typing in http://aws.amazon.com. Click on the **Sign in to the Console** option and provide your **Email Address** and **password** as set during our signup process. Once you sign in, you will be welcomed to the AWS Management Console main landing page as shown here. Wow! That's a lot of products and services, right? The products are classified into their main classes such as compute, storage and content delivery, administration and security, and so on so forth. Take a moment and just browse through the dashboard. Get a good feel for it.

Navigating through the dashboard is also pretty straightforward. Let's look at the top navigation bar first. To the right-hand side you should be able to see three drop-down menus. The first should display your name as an end user. This option consists of three submenus that will help you with configuring your account details, security credentials, and billing management. The next tab lists the **Region** from where you will currently be operating. In our case, we have been placed in the US West (**Oregon**) region. Remember you can change these regions as and when you require, so feel free to change as per your current global presence:

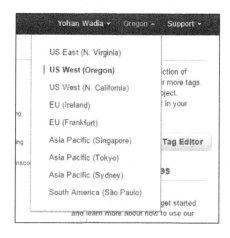

The US East (North Virginia) region is the cheapest region in AWS as it was one of the first regions to get set up and started.

The final tab in the list is the **Support** tab, and you can use it to login to the **Support Center, AWS Forums**, and view the latest set of **AWS Documentation** as well. Moving to the left-hand side of the tool bar, you will see four main icons listed there. Among these is a **Home Screen** icon, which when clicked on will bring you back to the AWS dashboard screen irrespective of where you currently are.

The next drop-down option in the list is named as **AWS**, but what it really contains is called as **Resource Groups**. These are a collection of AWS resources that can be organized and viewed as per your requirements. Think of these resource groups as a customized console where you as an end user can view all your required information about various AWS services in a single pane. How do resource groups work? Don't worry. We will be looking into this in more detail in the upcoming chapter.

Adjoining the **Resource Groups** is the **Services** tab, which lists the AWS services according to their class. It also has a history option that can be used to list and view your recently used AWS services.

The final tab is the **Edit** tab. This tab is used to customize your toolbar by filling it with those AWS services that you use frequently, kind of like a quick access bar. To add a particular AWS service to the toolbar, simply select the AWS service, drag and place it on the toolbar:

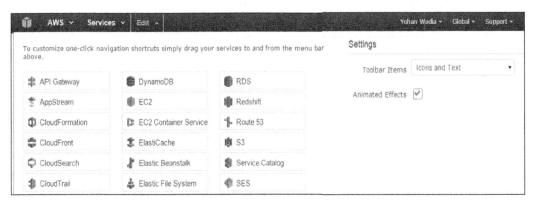

You can add multiple services as you see fit, and arrange them according to your needs as well. To save the changes to the toolbar, simply select the **Edit** option once again. You should see your AWS services listed out on the toolbar now. Feel free to dig around and check out the various options under each menu.

Getting started with AWS CLI

Now that you have a hang of the AWS Management Console, this would be a good time to take a quick look at the AWS CLI as well. Yes, you heard it right, apart from the standard web user interface, AWS provides a host of other mechanisms as well to help you gain access and use the various AWS resources. But why use a CLI in the first place? Isn't the AWS Management Console more than enough? Well, no. CLIs are more than just simple access and management tools. Using CLIs, you can automate the deployment and management of your AWS services using simple code and script, much like how you would use bash and shell scripting. This provides you with a lot of flexibility and customizability that a standard GUI simply won't provide!

The AWS CLI can be either installed on a Windows or a Linux machine. In case of Windows, AWS provides an easy-to-use installer, which can be downloaded directly from the AWS site. Once downloaded, all you need to do is run the installer, and voila, your Windows server should have the CLI installed and ready for use. But I'm not a Windows guy, so we will be walking you through the installation procedure on a standard Linux system.

 The 64-bit AWS CLI installer for Windows can be downloaded from https://s3.amazonaws.com/aws-cli/AWSCLI64. msi. The 32-bit installer can be downloaded from https:// s3.amazonaws.com/aws-cli/AWSCLI32.msi.

In this case, we will be installing the AWS CLI on a CentOS 6.5 64-bit OS. The Linux distribution can be anything, from a Debian such as Ubuntu to a RedHat system; so long as it has Python installed and running off the latest version.

 Python versions supported are Python 2 version 2.6.5 and above or Python 3 version 3.3 and above.

You will also need sudo or root privileges to install and execute the commands, so make sure you have an appropriate user already created on your Linux system.

The installation of the CLI involves two major steps; the first involves the installation of Python setuptools, which is a prerequisite of installing Python's pip.

Run the following commands from your Linux terminal:

1. Download the setuptools tar file from the Python source repo:

    ```
    wget https://pypi.python.org/packages/source/s/setuptools/
    setuptools-7.0.tar.gz
    ```

2. Next, untar the setuptools installer using the `tar` command:

   ```
   tar xvf setuptools-7.0.tar.gz
   ```

3. Once the contents of the tar file are extracted, change the directory to the `setuptools` directory:

   ```
   cd setuptools-7.0
   ```

4. Finally, run the `setup.py` script to install the setuptools package:

   ```
   python setup.py install
   ```

The following is the screenshot of preceding commands of the install process:

```
[root@YoYoNUX ~]#
[root@YoYoNUX ~]# wget https://pypi.python.org/packages/source/s/setuptools/setuptools-7.0.tar.gz
[root@YoYoNUX ~]#
[root@YoYoNUX ~]# tar xvf setuptools-7.0.tar.gz
[root@YoYoNUX ~]#
[root@YoYoNUX ~]# cd setuptools-7.0
[root@YoYoNUX setuptools-7.0]#
[root@YoYoNUX setuptools-7.0]# python setup.py install
[root@YoYoNUX setuptools-7.0]#
[root@YoYoNUX setuptools-7.0]#
```

This completes the first part of the install process. The next process is very simple as well. We now install the Python pip package. Python pip is generally recommended when installing Python packages.

Run the following commands from your Linux terminal to install the Python pip package:

1. Download the Python pip installer script from Python's repo:

   ```
   wget https://bootstrap.pypa.io/get-pip.py
   ```

2. Install the pip package:

   ```
   python get-pip.py
   ```

3. Once pip is installed, you can now easily install the AWS CLI by executing the following command:

   ```
   pip install awscli
   ```

Refer to the following screenshot showing the output of the installation process:

```
[root@YoYoNUX setuptools-7.0]#
[root@YoYoNUX setuptools-7.0]# wget https://bootstrap.pypa.io/get-pip.py
[root@YoYoNUX setuptools-7.0]#
[root@YoYoNUX setuptools-7.0]# python get-pip.py
[root@YoYoNUX setuptools-7.0]#
[root@YoYoNUX setuptools-7.0]# pip install awscli
[root@YoYoNUX setuptools-7.0]#
[root@YoYoNUX setuptools-7.0]# aws --version
aws-cli/1.7.37 Python/2.6.6 Linux/2.6.32-431.el6.x86_64
```

4. Simple, wasn't it! You can test your AWS CLI by executing few simple commands, for example, check the AWS CLI version using the following command:

```
aws -version
```

That's just for starters! There is a whole lot more that you can achieve with the AWS CLI, and we will make sure to utilize it in each of our chapters, just to get a good feel for it.

Plan of attack!

For the purpose of this book, let's assume a simple use case in which a hypothetical company called as All About Dogs (not the best of names I could find) wants to host and manage their e-commerce website on the cloud. As a part of the hosting, the company would like to have the following feature set provided to them by the cloud provider:

- High availability and fault tolerance
- On-demand scalability
- Security
- Reduced management overheads and costs

Here is a simple, traditional architecture of the proposed website, which basically is a two-tier application primarily consisting of web servers and a backend database, something most IT admins will be familiar with, right? Let's look at the following figure of tradition web service architecture:

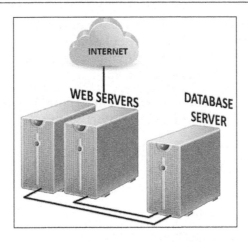

This traditional architecture has obvious drawbacks, such as poor scalability, little or no fault tolerance, more management overheads, and so on. Our goal is to leverage AWS's core services and make this obsolete architecture better! Each of the subsequent chapters will show you how to work with and administer these core AWS services keeping our use case in mind. By the end of this book, you should have a fully scalable, resilient, and secure website hosted on the AWS cloud with a design similar to this! Here is the AWS architecture:

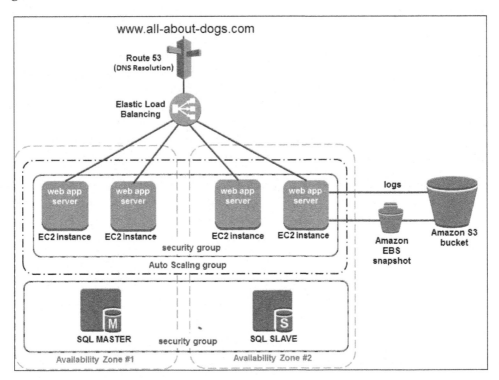

Awesome, isn't it! Believe it or not, this is a bare minimum website hosting architecture on AWS. There are still many enhancements and AWS services that you could incorporate here, but I like to keep things nice and clean, so this is what we will stick with for the remainder of this book.

Here's a list of AWS products that we will be incorporating and primarily learning about throughout the book, apart from few other services:

- Identity and Access Management (IAM)
- Elastic Compute Cloud (EC2)
- Elastic Container Service (ECS)
- Elastic Block Storage (EBS)
- Amazon Virtual Private Cloud (VPC)
- Amazon Cloudwatch
- Autoscaling and Elastic Load Balancing (ELB)
- Amazon Relational Database Service (RDS)
- Amazon Simple Storage Service (S3)

Summary

Let's quickly recap what all we accomplished so far in this chapter. To begin with, you learned a bit about what cloud computing is all about and saw a few features and benefits that it has to offer. Next, we drove straight into our core topic, that is, Amazon Web Services. You learned what Amazon Web Services is all about by understanding its architecture and core service offering. We then saw how easy and straightforward it is to sign up for AWS along with a brief walkthrough of the AWS Management Console. Towards the end, you also learned the importance of a command line interface and saw how to install the AWS CLI on a simple Linux server.

In the next chapter, you will learn a bit more about the CLI and see how to leverage it to manage and work with the AWS services. We will also be looking at few easy to use access management tools and techniques to safeguard and secure your AWS environment, so stick around! We are just getting started!

2
Security and Access Management

In the previous chapter, we accomplished a lot of things. To begin with, we got a better understanding of what cloud computing actually is all about and how you as an end user can benefit by leveraging it. Later on in the chapter, you had a brief overview of AWS, its architecture, and its core service offerings and also learned how to sign up for it.

In this chapter, you are going to learn a bit more about how to secure and provide users access to your AWS infrastructure and services. The chapter will first talk about security in general, and how AWS provides some of the best security there is. Later on, we will look at an AWS core service called as **Identity and Access Management (IAM)** and find out how to create, manage, and administer users using it.

Security and clouds

Security is a core requirement for any application whether it is hosted on an on-premise data center or a cloud such as AWS. It is a fundamental service that protects your applications and data from a variety of cyber-attacks, security breaches, accidental or deliberate data deletions, theft, and much more.

Most modern cloud providers offer security in a very similar way to traditional on-premise data centers with the same amount of control and compliance. The only difference is that in a traditional data center, you would have to deal with the complexities and costs of securing the hardware, whereas on the cloud, this task is performed by the cloud provider itself. This difference not only saves on overhead costs that every organization has to bear, but also reduces the time and effort it takes to monitor and protect all those resources.

Is AWS really secure

So the obvious question lingering in your mind right now must be, ok, we signed up for AWS and now are going to run our applications and store all our data on it, but is all that really secure? Is it safe to use AWS? The answer is a big yes!

Let's take a quick look at some of the different layers of security that AWS uses to safeguard and protect its resources:

- **Physical data center security**: The AWS infrastructure, which includes the data centers, the physical hardware, and networks, is designed and managed according to security best practices and compliance guides. The data centers themselves are housed at non-disclosed locations and entry to them is strictly controlled, managed, logged, and audited on a regular basis.

- **Virtualization and OS security**: AWS regularly patches and updates virtualization and operating systems against a variety of attacks such as DDoS, and so on.

- **Regulatory compliances**: The AWS infrastructure is certified against security and data protection in accordance with various industry and government requirements. Here are a few compliances that AWS is certified against:
  - SOC 1 (formerly SAS 70 Type II), SOC 2, and SOC 3
  - FISMA, DIACAP, and FedRAMP
  - ISO 27001
  - HIPAA

To read the complete list, visit the AWSrisk and compliance whitepaper at `http://aws.amazon.com/security/`.

Shared responsibility model

As you must have noticed by now, AWS provides a lot of security and protection for its hardware and its virtualization layers by providing patches, updates, performing regular audits and so on, but what about your applications and data? Who protects that? That's where AWS introduced the shared responsibility model.

According to this model, AWS provides secure infrastructure, services, and building blocks required while you, as an end user, are responsible for securing your operating system's data and applications. Think of it as a joint operation where you and AWS together ensure the security objectives are met.

Here is a simple depiction showing the shared responsibility model for AWS's infrastructure services:

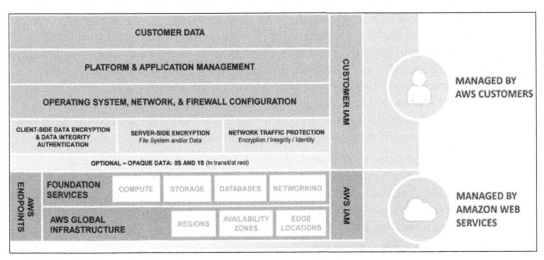

Image Source: AWS security best practices whitepaper.

Remember, that this is a basic shared responsibility model, which is only valid for AWS's core infrastructure services such as EC2 and Amazon VPC. The model tends to change as you start using more abstracted services such as Amazon S3, Amazon DynamoDB, Amazon SES, and so on. Why? Well that's simple! The more abstracted services you use, the less control you have over them. For example, if you are using SES as a bulk e-mail-sending tool, you don't have to set up the infrastructure, the operating systems, and the platforms on which the SES service works. It's already done for you. So as an end user, all you need to worry about from the security point of view is how is your data going to be protected at rest or in transit, whether you are going to use encryption/decryption techniques, and so on; this is your part of the responsibility now.

AWS provides a few services and products that are specifically designed to help you secure your infrastructure on the cloud, such as IAM, **AWS Multi-Factor Authentication** (**AWS MFA**), AWSCloudTrail, and much more. In the next section, we will look into IAM and see how we can leverage it for ourselves.

Identity and Access Management

AWS Identity and Access Management or IAM is a web service that provides secured access control mechanisms for all AWS services. You can use IAM to create users and groups, assigning users specific permissions and policies, and a lot more. The best part of all this is that IAM is completely FREE. Yup! Not a penny is required to use it.

Let's quickly look at some interesting IAM features in order to understand it a bit better:

- **Shared access to a single account**: With the sign in process completed, you currently are the sole owner and user of your AWS account. But what if you wanted to give access to few other users from within your organization to this account? You cannot just provide them with your username and password, right? Neither will you go and create a separate account for each user, as it is too tedious and not good practice. However, with IAM, you can create and provide users with shared access to your single account with real ease. It is something we will be looking into shortly.

- **Multi-factor authentication**: IAM allows you to provide two-factor authentications to users for added security. This means that now, along with your password, you will also have to provide a secret key/pin from a special hardware device, such as a hard token, or even from software apps such as Google Authenticator.

- **Integration with other AWS products**: IAM integrates with almost all AWS products and services and can be used to provide granular access rights and permissions to each service as required.

- **Identity federation**: Do you have an on-premise active directory already that has users and groups created? Not a problem, as IAM can be integrated with an on-premise AD to provide access to your AWS account using a few simple steps.

- **Global reach**: Remember regions and availability zones from *Chapter 1, Introducing Amazon Web Services*? Well, IAM is one of the few AWS core services that spans globally. This means that users that are created using IAM can access and consume any AWS service from any geographic region! Neat, right?

- **Access mechanisms**: IAM can be accessed using a variety of different tools, the most common and frequently used being the AWS Management Console. Apart from this, IAM can also be accessed via the AWS CLI, via SDKs that support different platforms and programming languages such as Java, .NET, Python, Ruby, and so on, and programmatically via a secured HTTPS API as well.

Business use case scenario

Awesome! We have seen what IAM is along with its impressive features list, so now, let's put it to some good use! In *Chapter 1, Introducing Amazon Web Services*, we briefly discussed our use case scenario about hosting a website for an organization called All-About-Dogs. In this section, let's go ahead and define some users for this organization along with their potential roles:

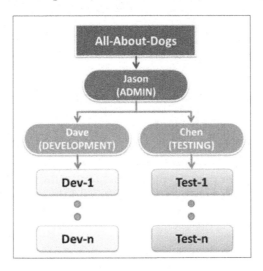

In this example, **Jason** is the manager of **All-About-Dogs**, and he is responsible for overseeing the entire operations of the organization. **Jason** goes ahead and hires **Dave** and **Chen** who will act as leads for the development and testing departments, respectively. **Dave** and **Chen** can then have multiple developers and testers within their teams as they see fit, a typical and simple hierarchy that most of us are familiar with and can relate to.

Getting started with the IAM Console

AWS IAM can be accessed using the AWS Management Console as well as a host of other CLIs, tools, and SDKs. In this section, you are going to learn how to use the AWS Management Console to create users and assign those users to individual groups and policies:

1. To begin with, sign in to the AWS Management Console using
    `https://console.aws.amazon.com/`.

2. Now, there are a lot of different ways to access the AWS IAM service; the easiest is to locate the service under the **Administration & Security** section as shown in the following screenshot. Selecting the **Identity & Access Management** option will launch the IAM console.

Welcome to your first AWS core service! Take some time to visually inspect each of the elements of the IAM dashboard. The dashboard can be basically split up into two sections, the navigation pane to the left, which contains all the individual links that will help you create your users and groups, and the main dashboard to the right where you can view your **IAM Resources** and various other security statuses:

The first thing that you will notice here under the **Security Status** field is an option to **Delete your root access keys**. Now why would you want to do something like that even before you start creating users? And what are root access keys?

Well, to begin with, in *Chapter 1*, *Introducing Amazon Web Services*, you signed in to AWS using your e-mail ID and password, right? Well, that is the root account that you just created. The root account, as the name suggests, has root-level access to all AWS services, including your billing account. So, as a good practice, AWS highly recommends that you do not use the root account unless you absolutely need to, and more importantly, you do not create and root keys as well. Root keys simply consist of an access ID and a secret key that can be used to programmatically access any AWS service. Each user that you create gets its own set of keys, out of which, the secret key has to be protected and kept under lock and key at all costs.

Coming back to the IAM console, let's take a quick look at some of the tasks that you can perform using it. The first thing you will notice is a big, clunky-looking URL that consists of some long numbers. Well, this is the URL that your new IAM users will be using once they are created to log in to the AWS Management Console.

The URL basically links to a sign-in page that is created automatically when you sign into the IAM service. But let's face it, it's not a simple URL and anyone would have a tough time remembering it as well. You can choose to customize the URL by providing an alias to it.

 The IAM URL contains the following format: `https://<AWS_Account_ID>.signin.aws.amazon.com/console/`.

Select the **Customize** option adjoining the IAM sign in link to get started. You should get a **Create Account Alias** dialog box. Provide a suitable alias name for your account and click on **Yes, Create** when done:

Voila! Your **IAM user's sign-in link** is now ready, but before you go ahead and use it, first you have to create some users and groups who will access it:

IAM users sign-in link:

https://all-about-dogs.signin.aws.amazon.com/console   Customize | Copy Link

Creating users and groups

With the basics out of the way, let's get to the main part of this chapter, that is, creating and working with users and groups.

Users, as the name suggests, are your everyday typical end users who will be interacting with the AWS products and services. Each user is provided with a unique password and a username so they can log in to the AWS Management Console. Along with the basic set of credentials, the users can also enhance their security by leveraging MFA. As discussed earlier, MFA provides a uniquely generated pin or code that is generated on a special hardware device called as a **hard token**. You can use this MFA pin or code along with your secure credentials to log in to the AWS Management Console.

Users are also provided with a set of access keys. These keys consist of an access key ID and a secret key, both of which can be used to log in to AWS programmatically. When the users are first created in IAM, they do not have a password or any access keys generated for them. This is your task as an AWS administrator, and you must make sure that each user has their own set of keys and passwords generated.

There are a lot of ways that you can start creating users. From the IAM dashboard, select the **Manage Users** option listed under the **Create individual IAM users** dialog box, as shown:

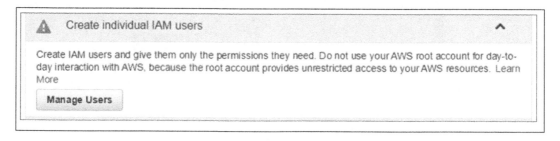

⚠ Create individual IAM users   ⌃

Create IAM users and give them only the permissions they need. Do not use your AWS root account for day-to-day interaction with AWS, because the root account provides unrestricted access to your AWS resources. Learn More

Manage Users

This will bring up the users console, using which we will create our very first IAM users. Select the **Create New Users** option to get started:

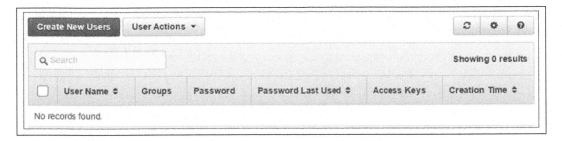

In the next page, type in the IAM usernames as required. You can enter up to five names at a time. You can optionally choose to create and generate access keys for each of the users that you create. Select the **Generate an access key for each user** option as shown and click on **Create** to proceed:

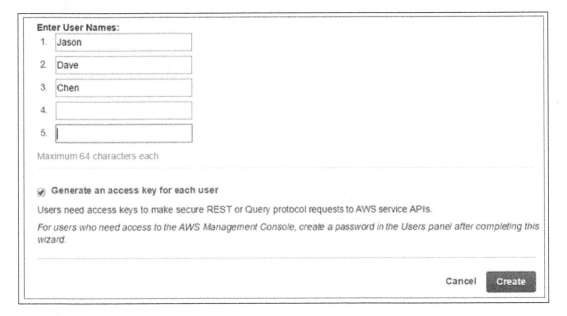

Select the **Download Credentials** option to save the user's access IDs and secret keys. This will download a CSV file on to your desktop, which has to be saved in a very secure location. It is very important that you save the keys, as this is the last time you will have access to it. Select **Close** after you have downloaded your credential keys successfully:

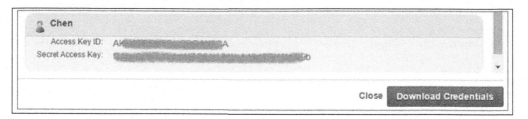

 Access keys are unique to each user and should not be shared with anyone under any circumstances. Save them in a secure place.

But wait! You are not done yet! You still need to assign your users their passwords. To do this, from the users console page, select the individual user's checkbox, click on the **User Actions** drop-down menu and select the **Manage Password** option as shown. You can use this drop-down menu to manage the user's access keys, signing certificates, MFA devices, and so on:

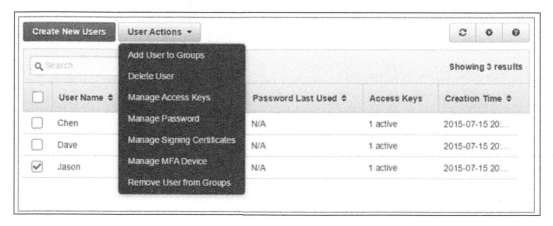

In the **Manage Password** page, you can either choose to **Assign an auto-generated password** for your users or provide a custom, temporary password, which the user can change at the first sign in attempt. In our case, we provided our user with a strong password that does not need to be changed at the first login attempt. Once the password is entered, click on **Apply** to save the changes:

Manage
Password

Users who will be using the AWS Management Console require a password. Select from the options below to manage the password for user Jason.

○ Assign an auto-generated password

⦿ Assign a custom password

    Password: ●●●●●●●●●●●●

    Confirm Password: ●●●●●●●●●●●●

☐ Require user to create a new password at next sign-in

                                                    Cancel   **Apply**

Follow the same process for the rest of your users as well. Make sure you provide them with strong passwords that contain at least one upper case letter, one special character, and some numerical values as well. You can additionally set password policies on your entire account by selecting the **Account Settings** option from the IAM console's navigation pane. Using the **Password Policy** page, select the security options that you wish to enable for your account's IAM user passwords. Remember to select **Apply password policy** to save and enforce the new password policy settings:

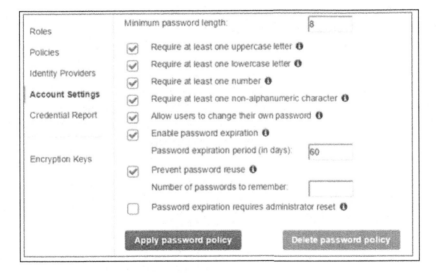

With your users created, the next logical entity to create is the group. A group is a collection of IAM users that has a particular set of permissions assigned to it. For example, a set of users who perform administrative tasks can be clubbed under a common group called as **administrators**, and so on and so forth. In this section, we will create an administrative group for our use case and later assign a user to it. So, let's get started!

First up, from the IAM console, select the **Groups** option from the navigation pane. This will bring up the groups console using which you can create and administer groups for your AWS account.

Select the **Create New Group** option to get started. Provide a suitable name for your administrative group; in this case, we provided the name **Admin-All-About-Dogs**. The **Group Name** can be anything, but it's advised to keep it meaningful. Click on **Next Step** to continue:

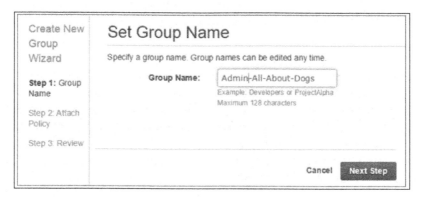

Next up, we assign permissions to the group using one or two policies. A policy is a document that lists one or more permissions. You can attach policies to virtually anything in AWS, from users and groups to individual AWS resources as well.

To attach a policy to a group, from the **Attach Policy** page, use the **Filter** menu and the search box to find suitable policies. In this case, we want this group to have full administrative privileges, and hence we are searching for an **Administrator Access policy**. In the list of policies, select the appropriate policy and click on **Next Step** to continue:

You can use and attach two policies per group.

In the **Review** page, review **Group Name** and the policies that are attached to the group. You can optionally choose to **Edit Group Name** or **Edit Polices** as per your requirements here. Once done, click on **Create Group** to proceed with the group's creation. Similarly, you can create groups for various other departments within your own organization, such as **Developers group**, **Testers group**, and so on:

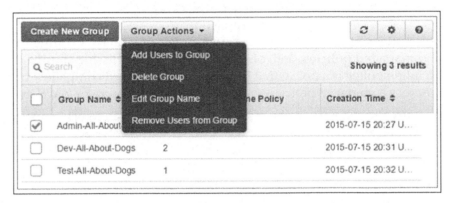

To add users to any particular group, simply select the group's checkbox and from the **Group Actions** drop-down menu select the **Add Users to Group** option. This will open up a separate page where you can select your previously created users. You can add one or more users to a group as you see fit. A particular user can also be a part of two or more groups at the same time; however, this is not a recommended practice and should be avoided unless absolutely required. Once the users are selected, click on the **Add Users** option to complete the process. With this stage completed, you have now successfully created and set up users and groups within your own organization. Now, wasn't that easy! Just remember to use the IAM users sign in link to sign in to the AWS Management Console from now on; the rest of the login process remains the same.

Understanding permissions and policies

To begin with, let's talk a bit about permissions first. We already used them during the creation of our users, but what actually are permissions and what are their uses?

Permissions provide you with access to and control of various AWS resources. They are also responsible for controlling actions that you can perform on the resources. By default, when you create an IAM user, the user starts as a blank slate, no keys, and no permissions at all. It is your responsibility to assign the users keys and the necessary permissions, which can range from simple novice tasks such as listing resources to creating, updating, and deleting resources, and so on.

Permissions can be classified into two main classes, each briefly explained here:

- **User-based permissions**: As the name implies, these permissions are attached to IAM users and allow them to perform some action over an AWS resource. User-based permissions can be applied to groups as well. User-based permissions branch out into two further categories called as **inline policies** and **managed policies**, both of which we will be discussing shortly. Basically, an inline policy is a policy that is created and managed completely by you, whereas a managed policy is created and managed more by AWS itself.

- **Resource-based permissions**: These are a special class of permissions that allow you to specify which user has what specific level of access to a particular AWS resource along with what actions they can perform on it. There are a handful of AWS services and resources that support such permissions, including S3 buckets, SNS topics, Amazon Glacier vaults, and so on. Unlike user-based permissions, these categories of permissions are only inline-based. This means that they are completely managed and created by you.

Not clear, eh? Not a problem. Let's walk through this simple example to get a better feel for it. In our use case, we have users created called **Jason**, **Dave**, and **Chen**. Each of these users can be specified a set of user permissions, for example, **Dave** can have the ability to list, read, and write on Amazon EC2 service, whereas **Chen** can only have read permissions on the EC2 instances. **Jason,** on the other hand, being a manager, can have all admin rights and can perform all actions on any of the AWS services.

Resource-based permissions, on the other hand, are allocated directly to resources, so in this case assume that an **S3 bucket** (a *bucket is a like a storage folder where you dump objects*) has been allocated permissions to allow both **Dave** and **Chen** read-write access, whereas **Jason** can read, write, and list objects stored in the bucket:

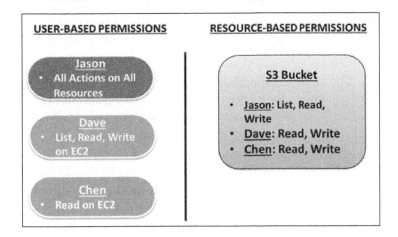

With permissions covered, let's look at policies in a bit more detail. We briefly used policies during the IAM group creation process, and there you learned that a policy is nothing but a collection of permissions put together in a JSON-formatted document. Policies can contain user-based or resource-based permissions. A single permission forms a statement in a policy, and a single policy can contain multiple statements.

Let's look at a simple policy for our reference:

```
{
"Version": "2012-10-17",
"Statement": [
{
"Effect": "Allow",
"Action": [
"ec2:DescribeInstances",
"ec2:DescribeImages"
    ],
"Resource": "arn:aws:iam::012345678910:user/Chen"
}
  ]
}
```

As you can see, this policy will basically allow the user **Chen** to only list the EC2 images and instances, in short, simple read-only access. Let's take a closer look at each of this policy's elements:

- `Version`: The `version` specifies the policy's language. As of date, the current version of the policy language is 2012-10-17. Although not required, it is a good practice to include the version field in your policy statements.

- `Statement`: The `statement` is the main starting point for your policy. Unlike the `version` field, the `statement` field is mandatory. The `statement` element is always enclosed within square brackets `[]` and can contain other individual statements within itself. Each individual statement should be enclosed by a set of curly brackets `{}` as shown.

- `Effect`: Another mandatory statement, the `Effect` element specifies whether the following `Action` statement should result in `Allow` or `Deny`. By default, the effect is always set to deny access to AWS resources. This ensures that you set explicit permissions for your IAM users when declaring policies.

- `Action`: The `Action` element describes what specific actions are required to be either allowed or denied. Each action statement consists of two main parts, a value that identifies the particular AWS service such as EC2, S3, IAM, and so on, followed by the action value, such as `DescribeInstances` and `DescribeImages`.

- `Resource`: The final element required for our policy is the `Resource` element. The `Resource` element is used to specify the object or service that the particular set of statements will cover. Resource names are specified by something called as an **Amazon Resource Name (ARN)**. ARNs are a crucial part of IAM and are used to uniquely identify AWS resources. In our reference policy, the ARN uniquely identifies the user **Chen** from our demo AWS account ID (`012345678910`) as the resource, which will obtain the necessary permissions based on the actions element.

 These are just the most commonly used set of elements that you can use to get started with your sets of policies. There are a lot more additional sets of elements that comprise a policy. Read more about them at `http://docs.aws.amazon.com/IAM/latest/UserGuide/AccessPolicyLanguage_ElementDescriptions.html`.

Now that we have a basic understanding of what a policy is and what it comprises, let's take a quick look at how you can create and assign them to your IAM users and groups using the AWS Management Console.

Creating and assigning policies

To create and assign policies, from the AWS Management Console, select the **Identity and Access Management** option as done before. Next up, select the **Policies** option from the IAM console's navigation plane. You should see the policy page as shown.

Using this page, you can filter and list existing policies (*both inline and manage policies*) using the **Filter** and **Search** options. You can even create, update, and delete existing policies; attach and detach policies from users and groups using this page. For starters, let's go ahead and create a simple policy for our IAM users. Select the **Create Policy** option as shown:

This will pop up the **Create Policy** wizard. Here, you will be provided with three options, briefly explained as follows:

- **Copy an AWS Managed Policy**: This option will list all the policies that are designed, created, and managed by AWS itself. This is by far the simplest way to get started with policies.

- **Policy Generator**: This is a neat tool that will help you build your very own customized policy. The tool includes drop-down options using which you can select various AWS services and their associated actions and effects. The tool even has built in policy validation that verifies whether your policy is syntactically correct or not before deploying it.

- **Create your Own Policy**: Using this feature, you can actually write your own policy or copy and paste an existing policy here. This feature too comes with a policy validator that verifies the syntax and validity of your custom policy before deployment.

For this scenario, let's go ahead and select the **Copy an AWS Managed Policy** option. In the **Set Permissions** page, you can use the **Filter** and **Search** bars to search for and select a policy of your choice. In this case, we are selecting **Administrator Access Policy** created by AWS itself. This policy will ensure that the IAM user attached to it is granted all administrative rights on all the AWS resources. Do note that this is a very crude and high-level permission and is not recommended for use in a production scenario.

In a production scenario, you would have to create individual administrator roles for each of the AWS service that you plan to use and then assign individual users to it as per your requirements. For now; click on the **Select** option adjoining the **AdministratorAccess** policy as shown:

This will bring you to the **Review Policy** page where you can edit and fine tune the policy as per your needs. Note that **Policy Document** has already been created for your convenience:

Policy Name

AdminAccess-All-About-Dogs

Description

Provides full access to AWS services and resources.

Policy Document

```
1 ▾ {
2        "Version": "2012-10-17",
3 ▾     "Statement": [
4 ▾         {
5               "Effect": "Allow",
6               "Action": "*",
7               "Resource": "*"
8           }
9       ]
10  }
```

☑ Use autoformatting for policy editing   Cancel   Validate Policy   Previous   Create Policy

In the **Review Policy** page, you can provide a suitable **Policy Name** and an optional **Description** for your new policy. You can even edit the **Policy Document** if you feel the need to, but in our case, we will leave it as it is. In case you end up editing the **Policy Document**, then make sure you select the **Validate Policy** option before you go ahead and deploy the policy.

 The * specified in the **Action and Resource** element is a wildcard and indicates any and all objects.

Once you have completed the changes, select the **Create Policy** option. With this step, your new custom policy is now ready to be attached to any group or user as you see fit.

To attach a particular policy to a set of users or groups, simply use the **Filter** and **Search** bar to find your newly created policy. Once displayed, select the policy you wish to apply by highlighting the checkbox adjoining it, select the **Policy Actions** drop-down list, and select the **Attach** option as shown:

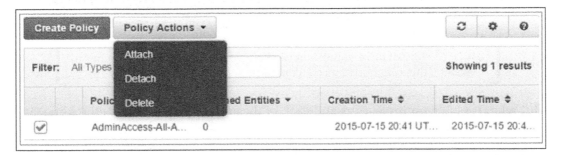

This will bring up an **Attach Policy** page. Here, you can select multiple users and groups at the same time and apply your selected policy to them all in a single go! In our case, we selected the user **Jason** and the **Admin-All-About-Dogs** group that we created in our earlier steps. Once you have selected the users and groups, complete the process by selecting the **Attach Policy** option.

Managing access and security using the AWS CLI

In the previous chapter, we briefly talked about the merits of working with a command line interface versus a GUI. We also got the AWS CLI installed and running on a simple CentOS box. In this section, we are going to go a bit further with that installation and actually configure the AWS CLI for use by an IAM user. Later on, we will see how to use the AWS CLI to perform some common IAM tasks as well. So without further ado, let's get started!

Configuring the AWS CLI is a very simple and straightforward process. All you need are the access ID and the secret keys from any one of your IAM users that we created during the earlier parts of this chapter. Next up, open up a terminal of your Linux box, which has the AWS CLI installed on it, and type in the following command:

```
# aws configure
```

Once entered, you will be prompted to enter the user's **Access Key ID** and the **Secret Access Key**, along with the default region name and the default output format to use. The default region name is a mandatory field and can be any of the regions from which your users will be operating, for example, us-east-1, us-west-2, and so on:

```
AWS Access Key ID [None]:TH1$is$0MUC#fuN
AWS Secret Access Key [None]:iH@vEN01De@W#@T1@mD01ng#ERe
Default region name [None]: us-west-2
Default output format [None]: table
```

The output format accepts any of these three values as the preferred method to display the output of the commands: table, text, or json.

> Any of these values can be changed at any time by rerunning the aws configure command.

But what if I have multiple users and each of these users need to access the same Linux box to run the commands? Do I need to share the keys with all the users? A valid question with a simple answer, NO! You never share your keys with anyone! As an alternative, you can set up named profiles for each of your users using their own set of keys using this simple command:

```
# aws configure --profile jason
```

Here, we are creating a named profile for our user named Jason. Similarly, you can create multiple named profiles of individual IMA users using this same syntax:

```
[root@YoYoNUX ~]#
[root@YoYoNUX ~]# aws configure --profile jason
AWS Access Key ID [None]: AK                     A
AWS Secret Access Key [None]: K                            7
Default region name [None]: us-west-2
Default output format [None]: table
[root@YoYoNUX ~]#
[root@YoYoNUX ~]#
```

AWS will store these credentials and configuration details in two separate files named ~/.aws/credentials and ~/.aws/config, respectively.

Okay, now that we have the basic configurations done, let's try out the CLI by executing some commands. To start off, let's try listing the users present in our account. Type in the following command:

```
# aws iam list-users --profile jason
```

You should get a list of IAM users displayed on your terminal. Notice the output format. Here, you may be viewing the output in a tabular format as our default output format is currently set to table. Also, note that we ran the CLI command using the named profile that we created a short while back. Awesome, isn't it?

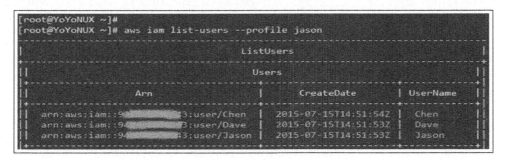

Let's try running a few more commands now! Create an IAM user, assign it to an existing group in our AWS account, and attach a policy to it! To begin with, create a new user using this simple command:

```
# aws iam create-user --user-name YoYo --profile jason
```

This command will only create a user for you. This user still does not have any passwords or access keys generated for it, so let's go ahead and create some! Type in the following command to create a password for your user:

```
# aws iam create-login-profile --user-name YoYo --password P@$$w0rD
--profile jason
```

Here, we passed two mandatory arguments with the commands `--user-name` and `–password`:

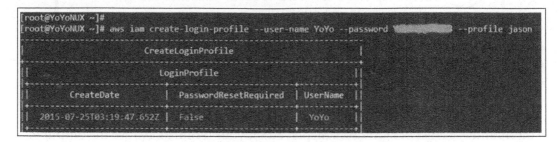

Besides these, you can additionally pass an optional argument called `--password-reset-required`. This field will ensure that the IAM user has to reset his/her password upon first login from the AWS Management Console. Only then will this new user be authorized to work with the CLI. In our case, we have not provided this argument, thus resulting in a fixed password which the user does not need to change.

Once the passwords are created, we go ahead and create the user's all important access key and Secret Key. To do so, type in the following command as shown:

```
# aws iam create-access-key --user-name YoYo --profile jason
```

The `create-access-key` command requires only one mandatory argument, which is the username itself. Once executed, it will display the user's access and Secret Keys respectively in the output. Make sure you save the Secret Key as this is the last time it will be shown to you for obvious security reasons. With this step, your new IAM user is all ready to be added to groups! Previously in this chapter we created a few groups for our own reference using the AWS Management Console. You can either attach your new users to existing groups or can even go ahead and create new groups as per your requirements. In this case, we will be creating a new group and attaching our user to it. Type in the following command to create a new group:

```
# aws iam create-group --group-name SuperUsersGroup --profile jason
```

The output should display the new group's ARN as well as the Group ID as shown:

```
+-------------------------------------------------------------+
|                       CreateGroup                           |
+-------------------------------------------------------------+
||                       Group                               ||
|+----------+------------------------------------------------+|
|| Arn      | arn:aws:iam::9██████████3:group/SuperUsersGroup||
|| CreateDate| 2015-07-25T12:51:28.653Z                      ||
|| GroupId  | A███████████████████                           ||
|| GroupName| SuperUsersGroup                                ||
|| Path     | /                                              ||
|+----------+------------------------------------------------+|
+-------------------------------------------------------------+
```

With the group created, it's now time to attach our new user to it. Simply type in the following command as shown:

```
# aws iam add-user-to-group --user-name YoYo --group-name SuperUsersGroup
--profile jason
```

This command accepts two mandatory arguments, which include the username as well as the group name to which the user has to be attached to. You should get no output from the execution of this command if it was run successfully.

With this step, we completed adding our new user to a new group. But wait, our task is not yet done. We still have to enforce some access permissions on this group; so let's quickly add a simple policy to it.

First up, create a simple JSON-based file on your Linux box. This JSON file will contain your new group's or user's set of permissions. For simplicity, I created a very basic policy that will grant its users complete access to all of AWS's products and resources. Run the following command to first create your policy:

```
# vi /tmp/MyPolicy.json
Add the following contents to your policy file as shown:
{
"Version": "2012-10-17",
"Statement": [
    {
"Effect": "Allow",
"Action": "*",
"Resource": "*"
    }
  ]
}
```

The commands will look as follows:

```
[root@YoYoNUX ~]# cat /tmp/MyPolicy.json
{
    "Version": "2012-10-17",
    "Statement": [
        {
            "Effect": "Allow",
            "Action": "*",
            "Resource": "*"
        }
    ]
}
```

Next, run the following command to attach this policy document to your newly created group or user:

```
# awsiam put-group-policy --user-name YoYo \
--policy-name Admin-Access-All-About-Dogs \
--policy-document file:///tmp/MyPolicy.json \
--profile jason
```

 You can replace the `--user-name` attribute with the `--group-name` attribute in case you want to assign the policy to a group.

With this step completed, you now should have a fully configured user and group created for your organization using the AWS CLI. Simple, wasn't it!

Planning your next steps

Working with users, groups, and policies is just the start. There are a lot more awesome features provided by AWS IAM that can help you with managing the access and security for your organization that we haven't covered in this chapter. Let's browse through some of these interesting features and services quickly.

For starters, let's talk about roles and identity providers. Roles are nothing but a group of permissions that grant users access to some particular AWS resources and services. But wait, doesn't a policy do the same thing? You're absolutely right! Both are, in a sense, a set of permissions, but the difference lies in where and how you apply them.

Policies are applied to users and groups that belong to a particular AWS account, whereas roles are applied to users who are generally not a part of your AWS account. In a sense, you use roles to delegate access to users, applications, and services that do not have access to your AWS resources. You can also use roles to create federated identities where a user from your organization's corporate directory gets access to your AWS resources on a temporary basis.

 To learn more about roles and how you can leverage them in your organization, use `http://docs.aws.amazon.com/IAM/latest/UserGuide/roles-toplevel.html`.

This temporary access to AWS resources can be provided using an identity provider as well. Ever used your Facebook or Google credentials to log in to a website? If yes, then this is a classic example of using an identity provider to provide external users access to some resources. In your case, your organization's active directory can be used as an identity provider to authenticate and grant your corporate users access to AWS resources. As of today, you can use either SAML 2.0 or OpenID Connect to establish trust between your AWS account and your external source of identity provider.

Besides these, AWS has also introduced a couple of new services as well that help with your account's easy administration and management. Here are a few of those services briefly explained:

- **AWSCloudTrail**: CloudTrail enables you, as an administrator, to log and record each and every API call that is made from within your account. These logs can contain information such as the API's request and response parameters, who made the API call, the time of the API call, and so on. These details are vital and can be used during security audits, compliance tracking, and so on. To know more about AWSCloudTrail, check `http://aws.amazon.com/cloudtrail/getting-started/`.

- **AWSConfig**: AWSConfig is a fully automated service that enables you to take a complete snapshot of all your AWS resource's configurations for compliance and auditing purposes. It can also be used as a change management tool to find out when your AWS resources were created, updated, and destroyed. To know more about AWSConfig, check `http://aws.amazon.com/config/details/`.

- **AWS Key Management Service**: As the name suggest, this new service enables you to manage your account's keys more effectively and efficiently. It also provides add-on functionality such as centralized key management, one click encryption of your data, automatic key rotations, and so on so forth. To know more about AWS Key Management Service, check `http://aws.amazon.com/kms/getting-started/`.

These are just some of the tools and services that you can leverage to make your AWS environment more efficient and secure. Feel free to have a look at each of these new services, and don't be afraid to take them out for a spin as well!

Recommendations and best practices

Here are a few key takeaways from this chapter:

- Get rid of the Root Account, use IAM wherever necessary. Hide away the Root key and avoid using it unless it's the end of the world!

- Create a separate IAM users for your organization, each with their own sets of access and Secret Keys. *DO NOT SHARE YOUR KEYS OR PASSWORDS!* Sharing such things is never a good idea and can cause serious implications and problems.

- Create separate administrators for each of the AWS services that you use.

- Use roles and groups to assign individual IAM users permissions. Always employ the least privilege approach wherein a particular group or role has the least amount of privileges assigned to it. Provide only the required level of access and permissions that the task demands.

- Leverage multi-factor authentication (MFA) wherever possible. Although passwords are good, they are still not the best option when it comes to authenticating users at times.

- Rotate your passwords and keys on a periodic basis. Create keys only if there is a requirement for it. If there are unused keys and/or users, then make sure you delete them on a regular basis.

- Maintain a logs and history of your AWS account and its services. Use AWSCloudTrail for security and compliance auditing.

- Use temporary credentials (IAM Roles) rather than sharing your account details with other users and applications.

- Leverage AWS Key Management Service to encrypt data and your keys wherever necessary.

Summary

Let's quickly recap all the things we covered so far in this chapter. First up, we took a look at security and clouds in general, followed by a walkthrough of the shared security model, followed by AWS. Later, we learned a bit about IAM and how you as an end user can leverage it to provide secure access to individual users. We also looked at the steps required to create users, groups, and policies using both the AWS Management Console as well as the AWS CLI. Toward the end of the chapter, we looked at a few important and newly introduced AWS administration and security services as well. Finally, we topped it all off with some essential recommendations and best practices!

The next chapter is even more amazing: we will dive into and explore the true power of AWS provided by one of its core service offerings—the Elastic Compute Cloud, or EC2. So stick around, we are just getting started!

3
Images and Instances

In the previous chapter, we learnt a lot about how AWS provides top of the line security and access management capabilities to its users in the form of IAM and various other tools.

In this chapter, we will explore one of the most popular and widely used AWS's core services, that is, **Elastic Compute Cloud** (**EC2**). This chapter will cover many important aspects about EC2, such as its use cases, its various terms and terminologies, and cost-effective pricing strategies to name a few. It will also show you how to get started with the service using both the AWS Management Console and the AWS CLI; so buckle up and get ready for an awesome time!

Introducing EC2!

Remember the never ending hassles of a long and tedious procurement process? All that time you spent waiting for a brand new server to show up at your doorstep so that you could get started on it? Something we all as sysadmins have gone through. Well, that all changed on August 25, 2006 when Amazon released the first beta version of one of its flagship service offerings called the Elastic Compute Cloud or EC2.

EC2 is a service that basically provides scalable compute capacity on an on-demand, pay-per-use basis to its end users. Let's break it up a bit to understand the terms a bit better. To start with, EC2 is all about server virtualization! And with server virtualization, we get a virtually unlimited capacity of virtual machines or, as AWS calls it, *instances*. Users can dynamically spin up these instances, as and when required, perform their activity on them, and then shut down the same while getting billed only for the resources they consume.

EC2 is also a highly scalable service, which means that you can scale up from just a couple of virtual servers to thousands in a matter of minutes, and vice versa—all achieved using a few simple clicks of a mouse button! This scalability accompanied by dynamicity creates an *elastic* platform that can be used for performing virtually any task you can think of! Hence, the term Elastic Compute Cloud! Now that's awesome!

But the buck doesn't just stop there! With virtually unlimited compute capacity, you also get added functionality that helps you to configure your virtual server's network, storage, as well as security. You can also integrate your EC2 environment with other AWS services such as IAM, S3, SNS, RDS, and so on. To provide your applications with add-on services and tools such as security, scalable storage and databases, notification services, and so on and so forth.

EC2 use cases

Let's have a quick look at some interesting and commonly employed use cases for AWS EC2:

- **Hosting environments**: EC2 can be used for hosting a variety of applications and software, websites, and even games on the cloud. The dynamic and scalable environment allows the compute capacity to grow along with the application's needs, thus ensuring better quality of service to end users at all times. Companies such as Netflix, Reddit, Ubisoft, and many more leverage EC2 as their application hosting environments.

- **Dev/Test environments**: With the help of EC2, organizations can now create and deploy large scale development and testing environments with utmost ease. The best part of this is that they can easily turn on and off the service as per their requirements as there is no need for any heavy upfront investments for hardware.

- **Backup and disaster recovery**: EC2 can be also leveraged as a medium for performing disaster recovery by providing active or passive environments that can be turned up quickly in case of an emergency, thus resulting in faster failover with minimal downtime to applications.

- **Marketing and advertisements**: EC2 can be used to host marketing and advertising environments on the fly due to its low costs and rapid provisioning capabilities.

- **High Performance Computing (HPC)**: EC2 provides specialized virtualized servers that provide high performance networking and compute power that can be used to perform CPU-intensive tasks such as Big Data analytics and processing. NASA's JPL and Pfizer are some of the companies that employ the use of HPC using EC2 instances.

Introducing images and instances

To understand images and instances a bit better, we first need to travel a little back in time; don't worry, a couple of years back is quite enough! This was the time when there was a boom in the implementation and utilization of the virtualization technology!

Almost all IT companies today run their workloads off virtualized platforms such as VMware vSphere or Citrix XenServer to even Microsoft's Hyper-V. AWS, too, got into the act but decided to use and modify a more off the shelf, open sourced Xen as its virtualization engine. And like any other virtualization technology, this platform was also used to spin up virtual machines using either some type of configuration files or some predefined templates. In AWS's vocabulary, these virtual machines came to be known as *instances* and their master templates came to be known as *images*.

By now you must have realized that instances and images are nothing new! They are just fancy nomenclature that differentiates AWS from the rest of the plain old virtualization technologies, right? Well, no. Apart from just the naming convention, there are a lot more differences to AWS images and instances as compared to your everyday virtual machines and templates. AWS has put in a lot of time and effort from time to time in designing and structuring these images and instances, such that they remain lightweighted, spin up more quickly, and can even be ported easily from one place to another. These factors make a lot of difference when it comes to designing scalable and fault tolerant application environments in the cloud.

We shall be learning a lot about these concepts and terminologies in the coming sections of this, as well as in the next chapter, but for now, let's start off by understanding more about these images!

Understanding images

As discussed earlier, images are nothing more than preconfigured templates that you can use to launch one or more instances from. In AWS, we call these images **Amazon Machine Images** (**AMIs**). Each AMI contains an operating system which can range from any modern Linux distro to even Windows Servers, plus some optional software application, such as a web server, or some application server installed on it.

It is important, however, to understand a couple of important things about AMIs. Just like any other template, AMIs are static in nature, which basically means that once they are created, their state remains unchanged. You can spin up or launch multiple instances using a single AMI and then perform any sort of modifications and alterations within the instance itself. There is also no restriction on the size of instances that you can launch based on your AMI. You can select anything from the smallest instance (also called as a *micro* instance) to the largest ones that are generally meant for high performance computing. Take a look at the following image of EC2 AMI:

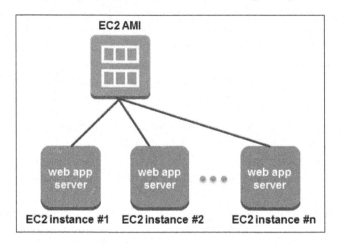

Secondly, an AMI can contain certain launch permissions as well. These permissions dictate whether the AMI can be launched by anyone (*public*) or by someone or some account which I specify (*explicit*) or I can even keep the AMI all to myself and not allow anyone to launch instances from it but me (*implicit*). Why have launch permissions? Well, there are cases where some AMIs can contain some form of propriety software or licensed application, which you do not want to share freely among the general public.

In that case, these permissions come in really handy! You can alternatively even create something called as a paid AMI. This feature allows you to share your AMI to the general public, however, with some support costs associated with it.

AMIs can be bought and sold using something called as the AWS Marketplace as well—a one stop shop for all your AMI needs! Here, AMIs are categorized according to their contents and you as an end user can choose and launch instances off any one of them. Categories include software infrastructure, development tools, business and collaboration tools, and much more! These AMIs are mostly created by third parties or commercial companies who wish to either sell or provide their products on the AWS platform.

[Click on and browse through the AWS Marketplace using
https://aws.amazon.com/marketplace.]

AMIs can be broadly classified into two main categories depending on the way they
store their root volume or hard drive:

- **EBS-backed AMI**: An EBS-backed AMI simply stores its entire root device
  on an **Elastic Block Store (EBS)** volume. EBS functions like a network shared
  drive and provides some really cool add on functionalities like snapshotting
  capabilities, data persistence, and so on. Even more, EBS volumes are not tied
  to any particular hardware as well. This enables them to be moved anywhere
  within a particular availability zone, kind of like a **Network Attached
  Storage (NAS)** drive. We shall be learning more about EBS-backed AMIs and
  instances in the coming chapter.

- **Instance store-backed AMI**: An instance store-backed AMI, on the other hand,
  stores its images on the AWS S3 service. Unlike its counterpart, instance store
  AMIs are not portable and do not provide data persistence capabilities as the
  root device data is directly stored on the instance's hard drive itself. During
  deployment, the entire AMI has to be loaded from an S3 bucket into the
  instance store, thus making this type of deployment a slightly slow process.

The following image depicts the deployments of both the instance store-backed and
EBS-backed AMIs. As you can see, the **root** and **data** volumes of the instance store-
backed AMI are stored locally on the **HOST SERVER** itself, whereas the second
instance uses EBS volumes to store its root device and data.

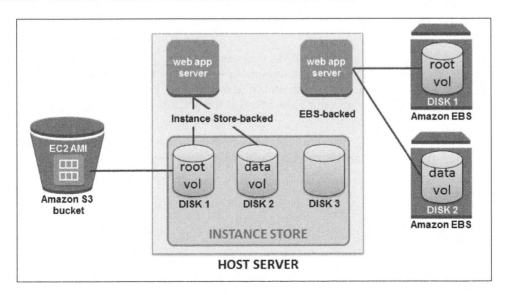

The following is a quick differentiator to help you understand some of the key differences between EB-backed and Instance store-backed AMIs:

	EBS backed	**Instance store backed**
Root device	Present on an EBS volume.	Present on the instance itself.
Disk size limit	Up to 16 TB supported.	Up to 10 GB supported.
Data persistence	Data is persistent even after the instance is terminated.	Data only persists during the lifecycle of the instance.
Boot time	Less than a minute. Only the parts of the AMI that are required for the boot process are retrieved for the instance to be made ready.	Up to 5 minutes. The entire AMI has to be retrieved from S3 before the instance is made ready.
Costs	You are charged for the running instance plus the EBS volume's usage.	You are charged for the running instance plus the storage costs incurred by S3.

Amazon Linux AMI

Amazon Linux AMI is a specially created, lightweight Linux-based image that is supported and maintained by AWS itself. The image is based off a **RedHat Enterprise Linux** (**RHEL**) distro, which basically means that you can execute almost any and all RHEL-based commands, such as yum and system-config, on it.

The image also comes pre-packaged with a lot of essential AWS tools and libraries that allow for easy integration of the AMI with other AWS services. All in all, everything from the yum repos to the AMIs security and patching is taken care of by AWS itself!

 The Amazon Linux AMI comes at no additional costs. You only have to pay for the running instances that are created from it. You can read more about the Amazon Linux AMI at `http://aws.amazon.com/amazon-linux-ami/`.

Later on, we will be using this Amazon Linux AMI itself and launching our very first, but not the last, instance into the cloud, so stick around!

Understanding instances

So far we have only being talking about images; so now let's shift the attention over to instances! As discussed briefly earlier, instances are nothing but virtual machines or virtual servers that are spawned off from a single image or AMI. Each instance comes with its own set of resources, namely CPU, memory, storage, and network, which are differentiated by something called as instance families or instance types. When you first launch an instance, you need to specify its instance type. This will determine the amount of resources that your instance will obtain throughout its lifecycle.

AWS currently supports five instance types or families, which are briefly explained as follows:

- **General purpose**: This group of instances is your average, day-to-day, balanced instances. Why balanced? Well, because they provide a good mix of CPU, memory, and disk space that most applications can suffice with while not compromising on performance. The general purpose group comprises the commonly used instance types such as t2.micro, t2.small, t2.medium, and the m3 and m4 series which comprises m4.large, m4.xlarge, and so on and so forth. On average, this family contains instance types that range from 1 VCPU and 1 GB RAM (t2.micro) all the way to 40 VCPUs and 160 GB RAM (m4.10xlarge).

- **Compute optimized**: As the name suggests, these are specialized group of instances that are commonly used for CPU-intensive applications. The group comprises two main instances types, that is, C3 and C4. On an average, this family contains instances that can range from 2 VCPUs and 2.75 GB RAM (c4.large) to 36 VCPUs and 60 GB RAM (c4.8xlarge).

- **Memory optimized**: Similar to the compute optimized, this family comprises instances that require or consume more RAM than CPU. Ideally, databases and analytical applications fall into this category. This group consists of a single instance type called R3 instances, and they can range anywhere from 2 VCPUs and 15.25 GB RAM (r3.large) to 32 VCPUs and 244 GB RAM (r3.8xlarge).

- **Storage optimized**: This family of instances comprises specialized instances that provide fast storage access and writes using SSD drives. These instances are also used for high I/O performance and high disk throughput applications. The group also comprises two main instance types, namely the I2 and D2 (no, this doesn't have anything to do with R2D2!). These instances can provide SSD enabled storage ranging from 800 GB (i2.large) all the way up to 48 TB (d2.8xlarge) — now that's impressive!

- **GPU instances**: Similar to the compute optimized family, the GPU instances are specially designed for handling high CPU-intensive tasks but by using specialized NVIDIA GPU cards. This instance family is generally used for applications that require video encoding, machine learning or 3D rendering, and so on. This group consists of a single instance type called G2, and it can range between 1 GPU (g2.2xlarge) and 4 GPU (g2.8xlarge).

 To know more about the various instance types and their use cases, refer to `http://aws.amazon.com/ec2/instance-types/`.

As of late, AWS EC2 supports close to 38 instance types, each with their own set of pros and cons and use cases. In such times, it actually becomes really difficult for an end user to decide which instance type is right for his/her application. The easiest and most common approach taken is to pick out the closet instance type that matches your application's set of requirements - for example, it would be ideal to install a simple MongoDB database on a memory optimized instance rather than a compute or GPU optimized instance. Not that compute optimized instances are a wrong choice or anything, but it makes more sense to go for memory in such cases rather than just brute CPU. From my perspective, I have always fancied the general purpose set of instances simply because most of my application needs seem to get balanced out correctly with it, but feel free to try out other instance types as well.

EC2 instance pricing options

Apart from the various instance types, EC2 also provides three convenient instance pricing options to choose from, namely on-demand, reserved, and spot instances. You can use either or all of these pricing options at the same time to suit your application's needs. Let's have a quick look at all three options to get a better understanding of them.

On-demand instances

Pretty much the most commonly used instance deployment method, the on-demand instances are created only when you require them, hence the term on-demand. On-demand instances are priced by the hour with no upfront payments or commitments required. This, in essence, is the true pay-as-you-go payment method that we always end up mentioning when talking about clouds. These are standard computational resources that are ready whenever you request them and can be shut down anytime during its tenure.

By default, you can have a max of 20 such on-demand instances launched within a single AWS account at a time. If you wish to have more such instances, then you simply have to raise a support request with AWS using the AWS **Management Console's Support** tab. A good use case for such instances can be an application running unpredictable workloads, such as a gaming website or social website. In this case, you can leverage the flexibility of on-demand instances accompanied with their low costs to only pay for the compute capacity you need and use and not a dime more!

 On-demand instance costs vary based on whether the underlying OS is a Linux or Windows, as well as in the regions that they are deployed in.

Consider this simple example: A t2.micro instance costs $0.013 per hour to run in the US East (N. Virginia) region. So, if I was to run this instance for an entire day, I would only have to pay $0.312! Now that's cloud power!

Reserved instances

Deploying instances using the on-demand model has but one slight drawback, which is that AWS does not guarantee the deployment of your instance. Why, you ask? Well to put it simply, using on-demand model, you can create and terminate instances on the go without having to make any commitments whatsoever. It is up to AWS to match this dynamic requirement and make sure that adequate capacity is present in its datacenters at all times. However, in very few and rare cases, this does not happen, and that's when AWS will fail to power on your on-demand instance.

In such cases, you are better off by using something called as reserved instances, where AWS actually guarantees your instances with resource capacity reservations and significantly lower costs as compared to the on-demand model. You can choose between three payment options when you purchase reserved instances: all upfront, partial upfront, and no upfront. As the name suggests, you can choose to pay some upfront costs or the full payment itself for reserving your instances for a minimum period of a year and maximum up to three years.

Consider our earlier example of the t2.micro instance costing $0.0013 per hour. The following table summarizes the upfront costs you will need to pay for a period of one year for a single t2.micro instance using the reserved instance pricing model:

Payment method	Upfront cost	Monthly cost	Hourly cost	Savings over on-demand
No upfront	$0	$6.57	$0.009	31%
Partial upfront	$51	$2.19	$0.0088	32%
All upfront	$75	$0	$0.0086	34%

Reserved instances are the best option when the application loads are steady and consistent. In such cases, where you don't have to worry about unpredictable workloads and spikes, you can reserve a bunch of instances in EC2 and end up saving on additional costs.

Spot instances

Spot instances allow you to bid for unused EC2 compute capacity. These instances were specially created to address a simple problem of excess EC2 capacity in AWS. How does it all work? Well, it's just like any other bidding system. AWS sets the hourly price for a particular spot instance that can change as the demand for the spot instances either grows or shrinks. You as an end user have to place a bid on these spot instances, and when your bid exceeds that of the current spot price, your instances are then made to run! It is important to also note that these instances will stop the moment someone else out bids you, so host your application accordingly. Ideally, applications that are non-critical in nature and do not require large processing times, such as image resizing operations, are ideally run on spot instances.

Let's look at our trusty t2.micro instance example here as well. The on-demand cost for a t2.micro instance is $0.013 per hour; however, I place a bid of $0.0003 per hour to run my application. So, if the current bid cost for the t2.micro instance falls below my bid, then EC2 will spin up the requested t2.micro instances for me until either I choose to terminate them or someone else out bids me on the same — simple, isn't it?

Spot instances compliment the reserved and on-demand instances; hence, ideally, you should use a mixture of spot instances working on-demand or reserved instances just to be sure that your application has some compute capacity on standby in case it needs it.

Working with instances

Okay, so we have seen the basics of images and instances along with various instance types and some interesting instance pricing strategies as well. Now comes the fun part! Actually deploying your very own instance on the cloud!

In this section, we will be using the AWS Management Console and launching our very first t2.micro instance on the AWS cloud. Along the way, we shall also look at some instance lifecycle operations such as start, stop, reboot, and terminate along with steps, using which you can configure your instances as well. So, what are we waiting for? Let's get busy!

To begin with, I have already logged in to my AWS Management Console using the IAM credentials that we created in our previous chapter. If you are still using your root credentials to access your AWS account, then you might want to revisit *Chapter 2, Security and Access Management*, and get that sorted out! Remember, using root credentials to access your account is a strict no no!

 Although you can use any web browser to access your AWS Management Console, I would highly recommend using Firefox as your choice of browser for this section.

Once you have logged into the **AWS Management Console**, finding the EC2 option isn't that hard. Select the **EC2** option from under the **Compute** category, as shown in the following screenshot:

This will bring up the EC2 dashboard on your browser. Feel free to have a look around the dashboard and familiarize yourself with it. To the left, you have the **Navigation** pane that will help you navigate to various sections and services provided by EC2, such as **Instances**, **Images**, **Network and Security**, **Load Balancers**, and even **Auto Scaling**. The centre dashboard provides a real-time view of your EC2 resources, which includes important details such as how many instances are currently running in your environment, how many volumes, key pairs, snapshots, or elastic IPs have been created, so on and so forth.

The dashboard also displays the current health of the overall region as well as its subsequent availability zones. In our case, we are operating from the US West (Oregon) region that contains additional AZs called as us-west-2a, us-west-2b, and us-west-2c. These names and values will vary based on your preferred region of operation.

Next up, we launch our very first instance from this same dashboard by selecting the **Launch Instance** option, as shown in the following screenshot:

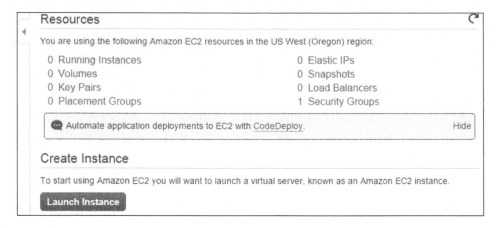

On selecting the **Launch Instance** option, you will be directed to a wizard driven page that will help you create and customize your very first instance. This wizard divides the entire instance creation operation into seven individual stages, each stage having its own set of configurable items. Let's go through these stages one at a time.

Stage 1 – choose AMI

Naturally, our first instance has to spawn from an AMI, so that's the first step! Here, AWS provides us with a whole lot of options to choose from, which includes a **Quick Start** guide, which lists out the most frequently used and popular AMIs, and includes the famous Amazon Linux AMI as well, as shown in the following screenshot:

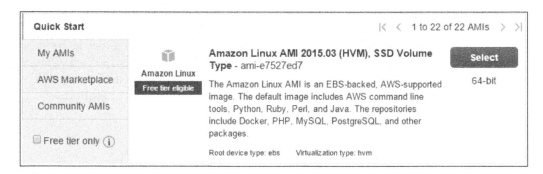

There are also a host of other operating systems provided here as well which includes Ubuntu, SUSE Linux, Red Hat, and Windows Servers.

Each of these AMIs has a uniquely referenced AMI ID, which looks something like this: **ami-e75272d7**. We can use this AMI ID to spin up instances using the AWS CLI, something which we will perform in the coming sections of this chapter. They also contain additional information such as whether the root device of the AMI is based on an EBS volume or not, whether the particular AMI is eligible under the Free tier or not, and so on and so forth.

Besides the **Quick Start** guide, you can also spin up your instances using the **AWS Marketplace** and the **Community AMIs** section as well. Both these options contain an exhaustive list of customized AMIs that have been created by either third-party companies or by developers and can be used for a variety of purposes. But for this exercise, we are going to go ahead and select **Amazon Linux AMI** itself from the **Quick Start** menu.

Stage 2 – choose an instance type

With the AMI selected, the next step is to select the particular instance type or size as per your requirements. You can use the **Filter by** option to group and view instances according to their families and generations as well. In this case, we are going ahead with the general purpose **t2.micro** instance type, which is covered under the free tier eligibility and will provide us with 1 VCPU and 1 GB of RAM to work with! The following screenshot shows the configurations of the instance:

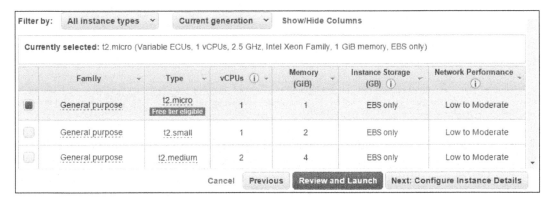

Ideally, now you can launch your instance right away, but this will not allow you to perform any additional configurations on your instance, which just isn't nice! So, go ahead and click on the **Next: Configure instance Details** button to move on to the third stage.

Stage 3 – configure instance details

Now here it gets a little tricky for first timers. This page will basically allow you to configure a few important aspects about your instance, including its network settings, monitoring, and lots more. Let's have a look at each of these options in detail:

- **Number of instances**: You can specify how many instances the wizard should launch using this field. By default, the value is always set to one single instance.

- **Purchasing option**: Remember the spot instances we talked about earlier? Well here you can basically request for spot instance pricing. For now, let's leave this option all together:

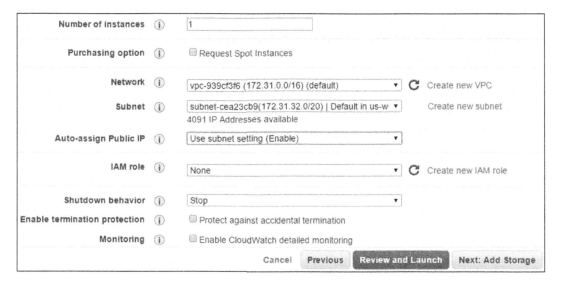

- **Network**: Select the default **Virtual Private Cloud** (**VPC**) network that is displayed in the dropdown list. You can even go ahead and create a new VPC network for your instance, but we will leave all that for later chapters where we will actually set up a VPC environment.

  In our case, the VPC has a default network of 172.31.0.0/16, which means we can assign up to 65,536 IP addresses using it.

- **Subnet**: Next up, select the **Subnet** in which you wish to deploy your new instance. You can either choose to have AWS select and deploy your instance in a particular subnet from an available list or you can select a particular choice of subnet on your own. By default, each subnet's Netmask defaults to /20, which means you can have up to 4,096 IP addresses assigned in it.

- **Auto-assign Public IP**: Each instance that you launch will be assigned a Public IP. The Public IP allows your instance to communicate with the outside world, a.k.a. the Internet! For now, select the use **Subnet setting (Enable)** option as shown.

- **IAM role**: You can additionally select a particular IAM role to be associated with your instance. In this case, we do not have any roles particularly created.

- **Shutdown behaviour**: This option allows you to select whether the instance should stop or be terminated when issued a shutdown command. In this case, we have opted for the instance to stop when it is issued a shutdown command.

- **Enable termination protection**: Select this option in case you wish to protect your instance against accidental deletions.

- **Monitoring**: By default, AWS will monitor few basic parameters about your instance for free, but if you wish to have an in-depth insight into your instance's performance, then select the **Enable CloudWatch detailed monitoring** option.

- **Tenancy**: AWS also offers you to power on your instances on a single-tenant, dedicated hardware in case your application's compliance requirements are too strict. For such cases, select the **Dedicated** option from the **Tenancy** dropdown list, else leave it to the default **Shared** option. Do note, however, that there is a slight increase in the overall cost of an instance if it is made to run on a dedicated hardware.

Once you have selected your values, move on to the fourth stage of the instance deployment process by selecting the **Next: Add Storage** option.

Stage 4 – add storage

Using this page, you can add additional EBS volumes to your instances. To add new volumes, simply click on the **Add New Volume** button. This will provide you with options to provide the size of the new volume along with its mount points. In our case, there is an 8 GB volume already attached to our instance. This is the t2.micro instance's root volume, as shown in the following screenshot:

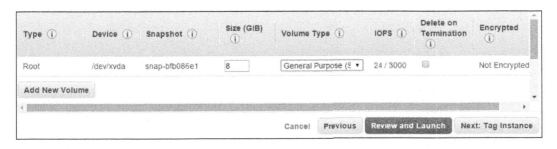

Try and keep the volume's size under 30 GB to avail the free tier eligibility.

You can optionally increase the size of the volume and enable add-on features such as **Delete on Termination** as per your requirement. Once done, proceed to the next stage of the instance deployment process by selecting the **Next: Tag instance** option.

Stage 5 – tag instances

The tag instances page will allow you to specify tags for your EC2 instance. Tags are nothing more than normal key-value pairs of text that allow you to manage your AWS resources a lot easily. You can start, stop, and terminate a group of instances or any other AWS resources using tags. Each AWS resource can have a maximum of 10 tags assigned to it. For example, in our case, we have provided a tag for our instance as **ServerType:WebServer**. Here, **ServerType** is the key and **WebServer** its corresponding value. You can have other group of instances in your environment tagged as **ServerType:DatabaseServer** or **ServerType:AppServer** based on their application. The important thing to keep in mind here is that AWS will not assign a tag to any of your resources automatically. These are optional attributes that you assign to your resources in order to facilitate in easier management:

Once your tags are set, click on the **Next: Configure Security Group** option to proceed.

Stage 6 – configure security groups

Security groups are an essential tool used to safeguard access to your instances from the outside world. Security groups are nothing but a set of firewall rules that allow specific traffic to reach your instance. By default, the security groups allow for all outbound traffic to pass while blocking all inbound traffic. By default, AWS will auto-create a security group for you when you first start using the EC2 service. This security group is called as *default* and contains only a single rule that allows all inbound traffic on port 22.

In the **Configure Security Groups** page, you can either choose to **Create a new security group** or **Select an existing security group**. Let's go ahead and create one for starters. Select the **Create a new security group** option and fill out a suitable **Security group name** and **Description**. By default, AWS would have already enabled inbound SSH access by enabling port 22:

You can add additional rules to your security group based on your requirements as well. For example, in our instance's case, we want the users to receive all inbound HTTP traffic as well. So, select the **Add Rule** option to add a firewall rule. This will populate an additional rule line, as shown in the preceding screenshot. Next, from the **Type** dropdown, select **HTTP** and leave the rest of the fields to their default values. With our security group created and populated, we can now go ahead with the final step in the instance launch stage.

Stage 7 – review instance launch

Yup! Finally, we are here! The last step toward launching your very first instance! Here, you will be provided with a complete summary of your instance's configuration details, including the AMI details, instance type selected, instance details, and so on. If all the details are correct, then simply go ahead and click on the **Launch** option. Since this is your first instance launch, you will be provided with an additional popup page that will basically help you create a key pair.

A key pair is basically a combination of a public and a private key, which is used to encrypt and decrypt your instance's login info. AWS generates the key pair for you which you need to download and save locally to your workstation. Remember that once a particular key pair is created and associated with an instance, you will need to use that key pair itself to access the instance. You will not be able to download this key pair again; hence, save it in a secure location. Take a look at the following screenshot to get an idea of selecting the key pair:

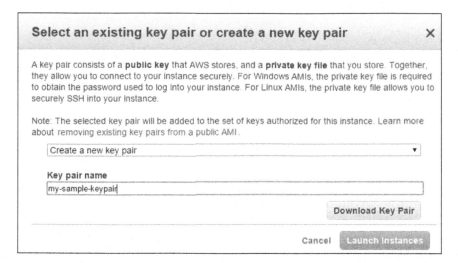

In EC2, the Linux instances have no login passwords by default; hence, we use key pairs to log in using SSH. In case of a Windows instance, we use a key pair to obtain the administrator password and then log in using an RDP connection.

Select the **Create a new key pair** option from the dropdown list and provide a suitable name for your key pair as well. Click on the **Download Key Pair** option to download the `.PEM` file. Once completed, select the **Launch Instance** option. The instance will take a couple of minutes to get started. Meanwhile, make a note of the new instance's ID (in this case, **i-53fc559a**) and feel free to view the instance's launch logs as well:

Phew! With this step completed, your instance is now ready for use! Your instance will show up in the EC2 dashboard, as shown in the following screenshot:

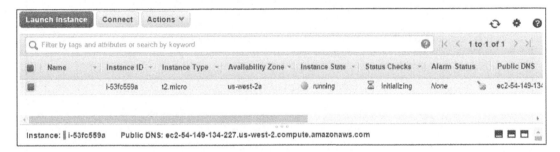

The dashboard contains and provides a lot of information about your instance. You can view your instance's ID, instance type, power state, and a whole lot more info from the dashboard. You can also obtain your instance's health information using the **Status Checks** tab and the **Monitoring** tab. Additionally, you can perform power operations on your instance such as start, stop, reboot, and terminate using the **Actions** tab located in the preceding instance table.

Before we proceed to the next section, make a note of your instance's **Public DNS** and the **Public IP**. We will be using these values to connect to the instances from our local workstations.

Connecting to your instance

Once your instance has launched successfully, you can connect to it using three different methods that are briefly explained as follows:

- **Using your web browser**: AWS provides a convenient Java-based web browser plugin called as MindTerm, which you can use to connect to your instances. Follow the next steps to do so:

    1. From the EC2 dashboard, select the instance which you want to connect to and then click on the **Connect** option.

    2. In the **Connect To Your Instance** dialog box, select the option **A Java SSH Client directly from my browser (Java required)** option. AWS will autofill the **Public IP** field with your instance's public IP address.

3. You will be required, however, to enter the **User name** and the **Private key path,** as shown in the following screenshot:

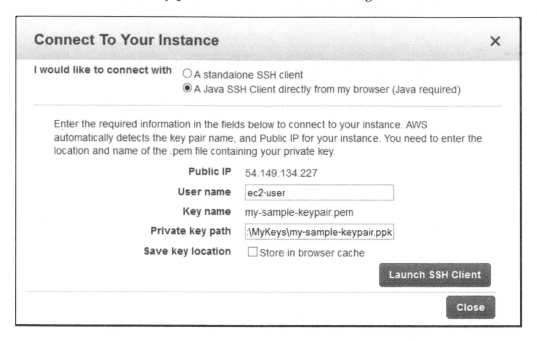

4. The **User Name** for an Amazon Linux AMIs is **ec2-user** by default. You can optionally choose to store the location of your private key in the browser's cache; however, it is not at all required. Once all the required fields are filled in, select the **Launch SSH Client** option.

 For most RHEL-based AMIs, the user name is either root or the ec2-user, and for Ubuntu-based AMIs, the user name is generally Ubuntu itself.

5. Since this is going to be your first SSH attempt using the MindTerm plugin, you will be prompted to accept an end user license agreement.

6. Select the **Accept** option to continue with the process. You will be prompted to accept few additional prompts along the way, which include the setting up of your home directory and known hosts directory on your local PC.

7. Confirm all these settings and you should now see the MindTerm console displaying your instance's terminal, as shown in the following screenshot:

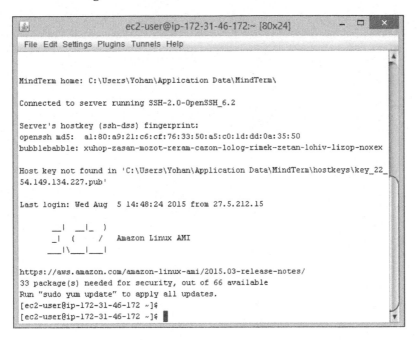

- **Using Putty**: The second option is by far the most commonly used and one of my favorites as well! Putty, or PuTTY, is basically an SSH and telnet client that can be used to connect to your remote Linux instances. But before you get working on Putty, you will need a tool called **PuttyGen** to help you create your private key (*.ppk).

You can download Putty, PuttyGen, and various other SSH and FTP tools from http://www.chiark.greenend.org.uk/~sgtatham/putty/download.html.

After creating your private key, follow the next steps to use Putty and PuttyGen:

1. First up, download and install the latest copy of Putty and PuttyGen on your local desktops.

2. Next, launch PuttyGen from the start menu. You should see the PuttyGen dialog as shown in the following screenshot.

3. Click on the **Load** option to load your PEM file. Remember, this is the same file that we downloaded during stage 7 of the instance launch phase.

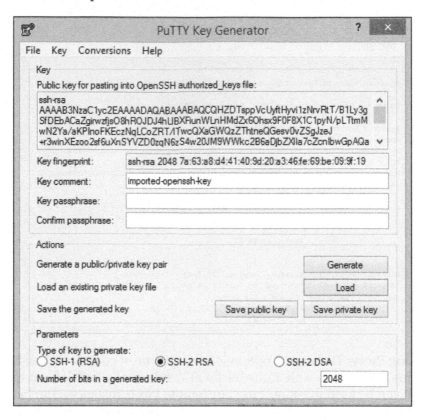

4. Once loaded, go ahead and save this key by selecting the **Save private key** option.

PuttyGen will probably prompt you with a warning message stating that you are saving this key without a passphrase and would you like to continue.

5. Select **Yes** to continue with the process. Provide a meaningful **name** and **save** the new file (*.PPK) at a secure and accessible location. You can now use this PPK file to connect to your instance using Putty.

Now comes the fun part! Launch a Putty session from the **Start** menu. You should see the Putty dialog box as shown in the following screenshot. Here, provide your instance's Public DNS or **Public IP in the Host Name (or IP address)** field as shown. Also make sure that the **Port** value is set to **22** and the **Connection type** is selected as **SSH**.

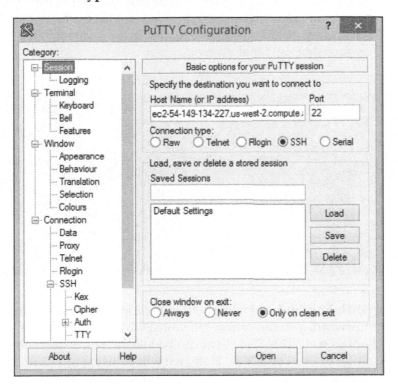

6. Next, using Putty's **Navigation | Category** pane, expand the **SSH** option and then select **Auth,** as shown in the following screenshot. All you need to do here is browse and upload the recently saved PPK file in the **Private key file for authentication** field. Once uploaded, click on **Open** to establish a connection to your instance.

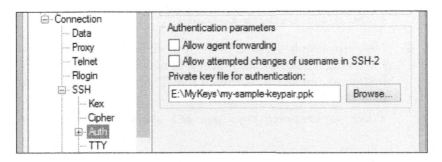

7. You will be prompted by a security warning since this is the first time you are trying to connect your instance. The security dialog box simply asks whether you trust the instance that you are connecting to or not. Click on the **Yes** tab when prompted.

8. In the Putty terminal window, provide the user name for your Amazon Linux instance (`ec2-user`) and hit the *Enter* key. Voila! Your first instance is now ready for use, as shown in the following screenshot. Isn't that awesome!

- **Using SSH**: The third and final method is probably the most simple and straightforward. You can connect to your EC2 instances using a simple SSH client as well. This SSH client can be installed on a standalone Linux workstation or even on a Mac. Here, we will be using our CentOS 6.5 machine that has the AWS CLI installed and configured in it and following the next steps, we will be able to look into our EC2 dashboard:

    1. First up, transfer your private key (`*.PEM`) file over to the Linux server using and SCP tool. In my case, I always use WinSCP to achieve this. It's a simple tool and pretty straightforward to use. Once the key is transferred, run the following command to change the key's permissions:

    ```
    # chmod 400 <Private_Key>.pem
    ```

    2. Next up, simply connect to the remote EC2 instance by using the following SSH command. You will need to provide your EC2 instance's public DNS or its public IP address, which can be found listed on the EC2 dashboard:

    ```
    # ssh -I <Private_Key>.pem ec2-user@<EC2_Instance_PublicDNS>
    ```

And following is the output of the preceding command:

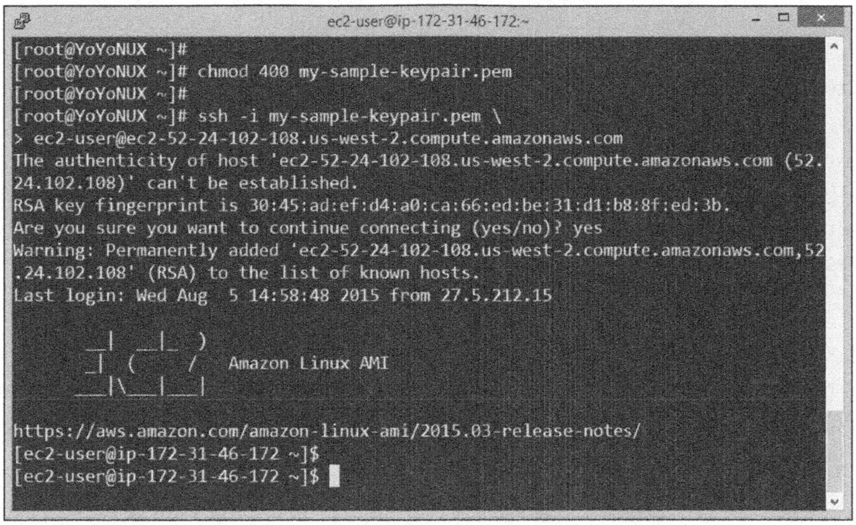

Configuring your instances

Once your instances are launched, you can configure virtually anything in it, from packages, to users, to some specialized software or application, anything and everything goes!

Let's begin by running some simple commands first. Go ahead and type the following command to check your instance's disk size:

```
# df -h
```

Here is the output showing the configuration of the instance:

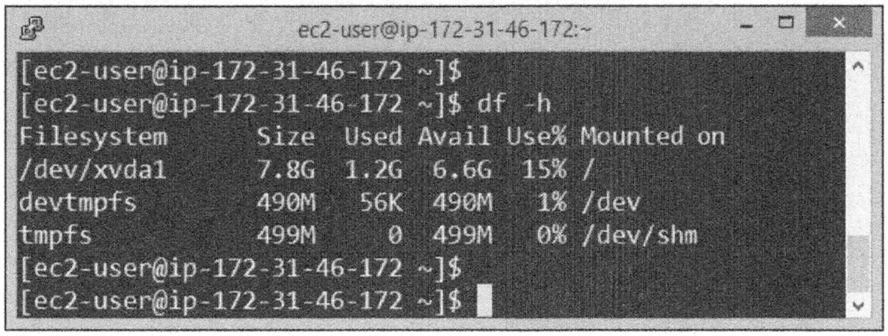

You should see an 8 GB disk mounted on the root (/) partition, as shown in the preceding screenshot. Not bad, eh! Let's try something else, like updating the operating system. AWS Linux AMIs are regularly patched and provided with necessary package updates, so it is a good idea to patch them from time to time. Run the following command to update the Amazon Linux OS:

```
# sudo yum update -y
```

Why sudo? Well, as discussed earlier, you are not provided with root privileges when you log in to your instance. You can change that by simple changing the current user to root after you login; however, we are going to stick with the ec2-user itself for now.

What else can we do over here? Well, let's go ahead and install some specific software for our instance. Since this instance is going to act as a web server, we will need to install and configure a basic Apache HTTP web server package on it.

Type in the following set of commands that will help you install the Apache HTTP web server on your instance:

```
# sudo yum install httpd
```

Once the necessary packages are installed, simply start the Apache HTTP server using the following simple commands:

```
# sudo service httpd start
# sudo chkconfig httpd on
```

You can see the server running after running the preceding commands, as shown in the following screenshot:

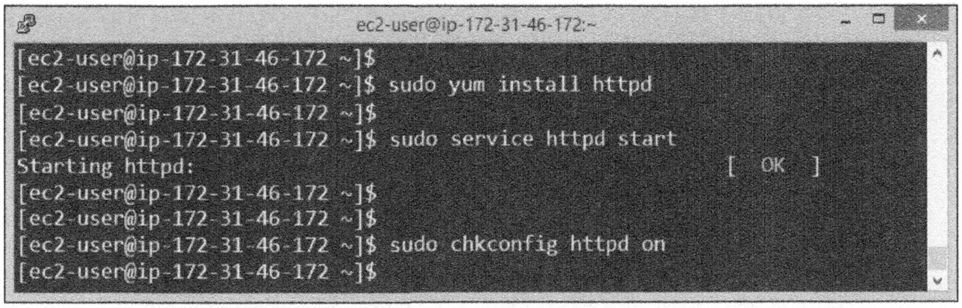

You can verify whether your instance is actually running a web server or not by launching a web browser on your workstation and typing either in the instance's public IP or public DNS. You should see the Amazon Linux AMI test page, as shown in the following screenshot:

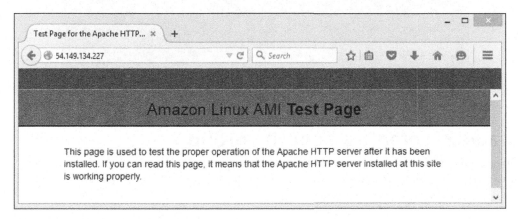

There you have it! A fully functional and ready-to-use web server using just a few simple steps! Now wasn't that easy!

Launching instances using the AWS CLI

So far, we have seen how to launch and manage instances in EC2 using the EC2 dashboard. In this section, we are going to see how to leverage the AWS CLI to launch your instance in the cloud! For this exercise, I'll be using my trusty old CentOS 6.5 machine, which has been configured from *Chapter 2*, *Security and Access Management*, to work with the AWS CLI. So, without further ado, let's get busy!

Stage 1 – create a key pair

First up, let's create a new key pair for our instance. Note that you can use existing key pairs to connect to new instances; however, we will still go ahead and create a new one for this exercise. Type in the following command in your terminal:

```
# aws ec2 create-key-pair --key-name <Key_Pair_Name> \
> --output text > <Key_Pair_Name>.pem
```

Once the key pair has been created, remember to change its permissions using the following command:

```
# chmod 400 <Key_Pair_Name>.pem
```

And you can see the created key:

```
[root@YoYoNUX ~]#
[root@YoYoNUX ~]# aws ec2 create-key-pair --key-name DumboKey \
> --output text > DumboKey.pem \
> --profile jason
[root@YoYoNUX ~]#
[root@YoYoNUX ~]# chmod 400 DumboKey.pem
[root@YoYoNUX ~]#
[root@YoYoNUX ~]#
```

Stage 2 – create a security group

Once again, you can very well reuse an existing security group from EC2 for your new instances, but we will go ahead and create one here. Type in the following command to create a new security group:

```
# aws ec2 create-security-group --group-name <SG_Name> \
> --description "<SG_Description>"
```

For creating security groups, you are only required to provide a security group name and an optional description field along with it. Make sure that you provide a simple yet meaningful name here:

```
[root@YoYoNUX ~]#
[root@YoYoNUX ~]# aws ec2 create-security-group --group-name DumboSG \
> --description "This is yet another simple security group" \
> --profile jason
---------------------------------
|     CreateSecurityGroup       |
+----------+--------------------+
|  GroupId |   sg-6431ef00      |
+----------+--------------------+
[root@YoYoNUX ~]#
[root@YoYoNUX ~]#
```

Once executed, you will be provided with the new security group's ID as the output. Make a note of this ID as it will be required in the next few steps.

Stage 3 – add rules to your security group

With your new security group created, the next thing to do is to add a few firewall rules to it. We will be discussing a lot more on this topic in the next chapter, so to keep things simple, let's add one rule to allow inbound SSH traffic to our instance. Type in the following command to add the new rule:

```
# aws ec2 authorize-security-group-ingress --group-name <SG_Name> \
> --protocol tcp --port 22 --cidr 0.0.0.0/0
```

To add a firewall rule, you will be required to provide the security group's name to which the rule has to be applied. You will also need to provide the protocol, port number, and network CIDR values as per your requirements:

```
[root@YoYoNUX ~]#
[root@YoYoNUX ~]# aws ec2 authorize-security-group-ingress --group-name DumboSG \
> --protocol tcp --port 22 --cidr 0.0.0.0/0 \
> --profile jason
[root@YoYoNUX ~]#
[root@YoYoNUX ~]#
```

Stage 4 – launch the instance

With the key pair and security group created and populated, the final thing to do is to launch your new instance. For this step, you will need a particular AMI ID along with a few other key essentials such as your security group name, the key pair, and the instance launch type, along with the number of instances you actually wish to launch.

Type in the following command to launch your instance:

```
# aws ec2 run-instances --image-id ami-e7527ed7 \
> --count 1 --instance-type t2.micro \
> --security-groups <SG_Name> \
> --key-name <Key_Pair_Name>
```

And here is the output of the preceding commands:

```
[root@YoYoNUX ~]#
[root@YoYoNUX ~]# aws ec2 run-instances --image-id ami-e7527ed7 \
> --count 1 --instance-type t2.micro \
> --security-groups DumboSG \
> --key-name DumboKey \
> --profile jason
[root@YoYoNUX ~]#
```

 In this case, we are using the same Amazon Linux AMI (**ami-e7527ed7**) that we used during the launch of our first instance using the EC2 dashboard.

The instance will take a good two or three minutes to spin up, so be patient! Make a note of the instance's ID from the output of the ec2 run-instance command. We will be using this instance ID to find out the instance's public IP address using the EC2 describe-instance command as shown:

```
# aws ec2 describe-instances --instance-ids <Instance_ID>
```

Make a note of the instance's public DNS or the public IP address. Next, use the key pair created and connect to your instance using any of the methods discussed earlier.

Cleaning up!

Spinning up instances is one thing; you should also know how to stop and terminate them! To perform any power operations on your instance from the EC2 dashboard, all you need to do is select the particular instance and click on the **Actions** tab as shown. Next, from the **Instance State** submenu, select whether you want to **Stop**, **Reboot,** or **Terminate** your instance, as shown in the following screenshot:

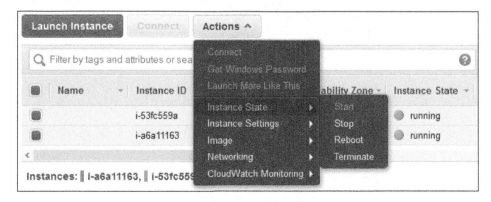

It is important to remember that you only have instance stopping capabilities when working with EBS-backed instances. Each time an EBS-backed instance is stopped, the hourly instance billing stops too; however, you are still charged for the EBS volume that your instance is using. Similarly, if your EBS-backed instance is terminated or destroyed, then by default the EBS root volume attached to it is also destroyed, unless specified otherwise, during the instance launch phase.

Planning your next steps

So far, all we have worked with are Linux instances, so the next step that I recommend is that you go ahead and deploy your very first Windows server instance as well. Just a few pointers worth remembering are to make sure you enable the firewall rule for RDP protocol (TCP Port 3389) in the security group and to generate the administrator password using the key pair that you create. For more in-depth steps, check out this simple tutorial at http://docs.aws.amazon.com/AWSEC2/latest/WindowsGuide/EC2Win_GetStarted.html.

The second thing worth trying out are spot instances. Now, you may be wondering that spot instances seem kind of hard to grasp, but in reality they are a lot easier and cost efficient to work with. Try and spin up a simple t2.micro Linux instance using spot pricing and compare the difference with a traditional on-demand instance. To know more about spot instances, check out http://aws.amazon.com/ec2/purchasing-options/spot-instances/.

Another really cool thing worth the time and effort is the AWS Management Portal for vCenter! Yes! You heard it right! You can actually manage your AWS resources using your standard VMware vCenter Server! All you need to do is install a simple plugin and, voila, your entire AWS infrastructure can be managed using the familiar vCenter dashboard. But the fun doesn't just stop there. You can also export your on premise virtual machines hosted on the vSphere platform over to AWS using a tool called as VM Import/ Export. Once installed within your VMware vSphere environment, you can easily migrate any Linux and Windows Server based virtual machine to your AWS account using a few simple steps! Now that's really amazing! To know more about the AWS Management Portal for vCenter, refer to http://aws.amazon.com/ec2/vcenter-portal/.

 Both the AWS Management portal for vCenter as well as the VM Import/ Export tool are absolutely free of cost! You only have to pay for the AWS resources that you consume and not a penny more!

And last but not least, have some fun with configuring your instances! Don't stop just at a simple Web Server; go ahead and set up a full fledge WordPress application on your instances or launch multiple instances and set up JBoss Clustering among them and so on. The more you configure and use the instances, the more you will get acquainted with the terms and terminologies and find out how easy it is working with AWS! Just remember to clean up your work after it is done.

Recommendations and best practices

Here are a few key takeaways from this chapter:

- First and foremost, create and use separate IAM users for working with EC2. *DO NOT USE* your standard root account credentials!

- Use IAM roles if you need to delegate access to your EC2 account to other people for some temporary period of time. Do not share your user passwords and keys with anyone.

- Use a standard and frequently deployed set of AMIs as they are tried and tested by AWS thoroughly.

- Make sure that you understand the difference between instance store-backed and EBS-backed AMIs. Use the instance store with caution and remember that you are responsible for your data, so take adequate backups of it.

- Don't create too many firewall rules on a single security group. Make sure that you apply the least permissive rules for your security groups.

- Stop your instances when not in use. This will help you save up on costs as well.

- Use tags to identify your EC2 instances. Tagging your resources is a good practice and should be followed at all times.

- Save your key pairs in a safe and accessible location. Use passphrases as an added layer of security if you deem it necessary.

- Monitor your instances at all times. We will be looking at instance monitoring in depth in the coming chapters; however, you don't have to wait until then! Use the EC2 Status and Health Check tabs whenever required.

Summary

So, let's wrap up what we have learnt so far! First up, we looked at what exactly the AWS EC2 service is and how we can leverage it to perform our daily tasks. Next, we understood a bit about images and instances by looking at the various instance types and pricing options provided. Finally, we also managed to launch a couple of instances in EC2 using both the EC2 dashboard as well as the AWS CLI. We topped it all off with some interesting next steps and a bunch of recommendations and best practices!

In the next chapter, we will continue with the EC2 service and explore some of the advanced network, security, and storage options that come along with it, so stay tuned!

4
Security, Storage, Networking, and Lots More!

In the previous chapter, you learned a lot about EC2 and its images and instances. We were able to launch our first instance in AWS, connect to it, and even configure it as per our requirements.

In this chapter, we will be continuing where we left off and will cover some of the remaining EC2 concepts, such as security groups, networking, and a bit about volumes as well. We will also be looking at a few easy steps using which you can create and publish your very own AMIs. So stick around, we are just getting started!

An overview of security groups

We talked briefly about security groups in the previous chapter, but in this section, we will be looking at them in a bit more in detail. Security Groups are simple, yet powerful ways using which you can secure your entire EC2 environment. You can use Security Groups to restrict and filter out both the ingress and egress traffic of an instance using a set of firewall rules. Each rule can allow traffic based on a particular protocol—TCP or UDP, based on a particular port—such as 22 for SSH, or even based on individual source and destination IP addresses. This provides you with a lot of control and flexibility in terms of designing a secure environment for your instances to run from.

Let's look at how you can edit an existing Security Group using the EC2 dashboard.

From the EC2 dashboard, select the **Security Groups** option located under the **Network & Security** section as shown here:

This will display a list of currently created and in use Security Groups present in your EC2 environment. Each Security Group is provided with a unique identifier called the **Group ID** and a **Group Name**. You will also notice the presence of the **default Security Group**, as shown in the following screenshot. This default Security Group is created by AWS when you first start and sign up for the EC2 service. If you do not specify a Security Group during the instance launch phase, then by default, AWS assigns this default Security Group to it.

The default Security Group has no ingress (inbound) traffic rules set; there is only one egress (outbound) rule, which allows your instances to connect to the outside world using any port and any protocol. You can add, delete, and modify any rules from this group; however, you cannot delete the default Security Group. As a good practice, avoid using the default Security Group. Instead, create separate and customized Security Groups based on your application's needs and always keep the rules as minimalistic as possible. Here is an option of creating a new Security Group:

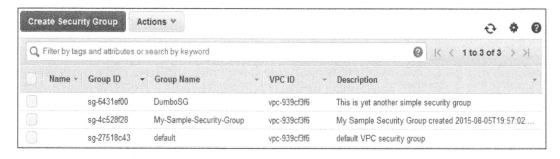

Let's go ahead and see how you can edit Security Groups and modify an already configured firewall rule.

 You can modify the firewall rules of your Security Groups any time, even when your instance is running.

From the dashboard, select a particular **Security Group** you wish to modify. Next, from the **Actions** drop-down list, select the option **Edit inbound rules**, as shown:

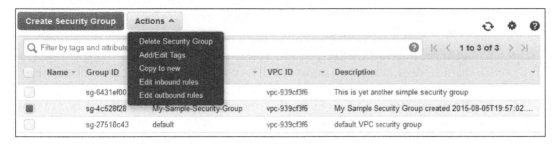

As discussed earlier, each firewall rule comprises four fields. The first field is the **Type** field, which specifies the type of application for which you need to allow access. By default, AWS already has provided a list of common application types to choose from, which includes **SSH, RDP, HTTP, HTTPS, POP3, IMAP, MySQL, SMTP,** and so on so forth. You can additionally create custom TCP/ UDP application types using this same drop-down list as well. For now, we will use the **SSH** and **HTTP** types, as shown here:

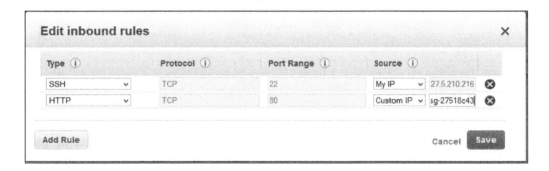

An important thing to note here is that selecting these preconfigured application types will autofill the next two fields as well. Thus, if you wish to specify a different port for say SSH or HTTP, then you are better off selecting **Custom TCP Rule** from the application type as discussed earlier. Next up is the **Source** field where you can basically specify any of these three options:

- **Anywhere**: Using this option as the source, your particular application port will be accessible from any and all networks out there (0.0.0.0/0). This is not a recommended configuration for any production environment and should be avoided at all times.

- **My IP**: As the name suggest, AWS will try and autofill the IP address of your local computer here. The only thing that you need to be aware of here is that your computer's IP address should not be based on a DHCP network as you may not be able to connect to your application if your local computer's IP address keeps on changing.

- **Custom IP**: Perhaps the most preferable out of the three options, the Custom IP option allows you to specify your own custom source IP address or IP range as per your requirements. For example, allow the particular application to access only via traffic coming from the network 203.20.31.0/24 CIDR. You can even add other Security Group IDs here as a reference.

Additionally, you can even add new rules to an existing Security Group by selecting the **Add Rule** button, and delete existing rules by selecting the **Delete Rule icon** (X). Just remember to save your Security Group settings by selecting the **Save** option before you close the pop-up box. Feel free to take a look at a Security Group's outbound rules as well. All you have to do is select a particular **Security Group** from the EC2 dashboard, and from the **Actions** tab, select the **Edit outbound rules** option. You should see the default **allow all access** outbound rule, as shown here:

You can even create new Security Groups using the **Create Security Group** option provided on the EC2 dashboard. Selecting this option will provide you with a simple interface using which you can create and populate a Security Group with both inbound and outbound rules.

Provide a suitable **Security group name** and **Description** for your new Security Group. Ideally, as a good practice, always name your Security Groups using some meaningful conventions that can help you identify their purpose. Next up, select the default VPC subnet from the **VPC** drop-down list. You can create up to 100 Security Groups in a VPC, with each Security Group having up to fifty firewall rules.

Fill in your inbound and outbound rules, and click on **Create** once done:

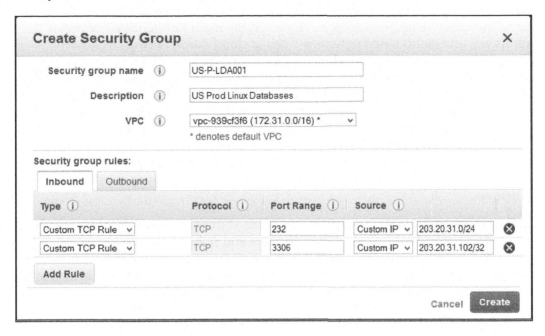

You can then assign this new Security Group to your instances either during the launch phase or by selecting an existing instance from the EC2 dashboard and changing its Security Group under the **Change Security Groups** option.

Feel free to create more such Security Groups in your EC2 account. Make sure you follow the least privilege approach and allow traffic only for the required set of ports and application services and nothing more.

Understanding EC2 networking

Before we understand how EC2 networking actually works, it is essential to understand the difference between networks provided by your traditional data centres and public clouds such as AWS. A traditional data centre network generally comprises a number of physical switches and routers that are connected to physical hardware and are responsible for transmitting and forwarding data or packets from one place to another.

The same also applies in the case of cloud computing; however, in place of the hardware, you now have virtual devices such as virtual servers, virtual network cards, virtual switches, and routers. However, the main differentiator between traditional and cloud based networks is that a cloud-based network is heavily filtered. Most public cloud providers, including AWS itself, allow only unicast datagrams over their networks, restricting all broadcast datagrams. Why, you ask? Well, mostly for security purposes and to avoid DDoS attacks, besides other reasons as well. This is an important point to remember, however, as often your applications may require broadcast capabilities over a network to discover some services and in such cases these applications may not necessarily fit on a public cloud. There are ways to get past this limitation; however, that is a different topic altogether. For now, let's take a look at how our EC2 instances are provided with their networks and IP addresses.

To begin with, each instance that you launch in your EC2 environment is provided with two unique IP addresses, called a private and public IP address, respectively. This is the default behavior of an instance and is not under your control by default, unless you are working with a VPC, which we will be discussing in the next chapter. When you first launch an instance, AWS will provide it with a unique private IP address using its own internal DHCP service. You can use this private IP address to communicate with the instances present in the same network; however being a private IP address, you cannot use this network for any communication with the outside (*Internet*) world. Along with the private IP address, you also get an internal DNS hostname for your instance. The internal or private DNS resembles something like this string, **ip-172-31-46-172.us-west-2.compute.internal**, and as you can see, it tells us a lot about our instance as well. For example, this particular private DNS hostname resolves a private IP of **172-31-46-172** and also this particular instance is currently deployed in the us-west-2 region. Neat, right! Let's take a look at the following screenshot, which shows example of a private and public IP address:

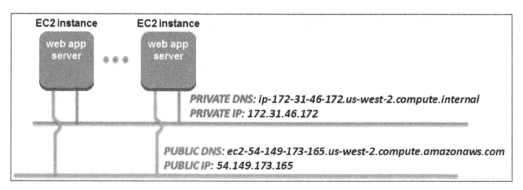

The same applies to the public IP address as well with the exception that this particular IP address is reachable from the Internet and can be used to communicate with the outside world. AWS maps the public IP address of an instance to its corresponding private IP address using simple NAT and, just like its counterpart, provides it with a public DNS value as well. The public DNS resembles something like this string, **ec2-54-149-173-165.us-west-2.compute.amazonaws.com**, and as you can see, this also provides us with similar information about the instance's public IP address as well as where the instance has been launched from.

Keeping these basics in mind, there are also a few additional pieces of information that you need to know about your instance's networking. You can control your instance's IP address to a big extent depending on whether they are launched from a standard EC2 environment or in a VPC.

In standard EC2 environment or as AWS calls it, **EC2-Classic**, you really don't have much control over your instance's networking. Each instance is provided with a single unique private as well as a public IP address and DNS, respectively. These values are released to the general IP pool when your instances are either stopped or terminated. You cannot reuse these IP addresses and DNS values once they are released to the general pool.

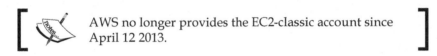

AWS no longer provides the EC2-classic account since April 12 2013.

On the other hand, a VPC provides much control and flexibility when it comes to your instance's IP addressing. Using a VPC, you can define and run instances from specially created subnets, which can either be isolated (*private subnets*) or connected to the Internet (*public subnets*) depending on your requirements. You can additionally provide your instances with more than one private and public IP address as well using a VPC, something we will be looking at with great detail in the coming chapter. Instances in a VPC, however, do not release their private IP addresses back to the general pool when they are stopped.

Determining your instances IP addresses

AWS provides a few easy ways to determine your instance's IP addresses. The simplest by far is using the **Description** tab from the EC2 dashboard as shown here:

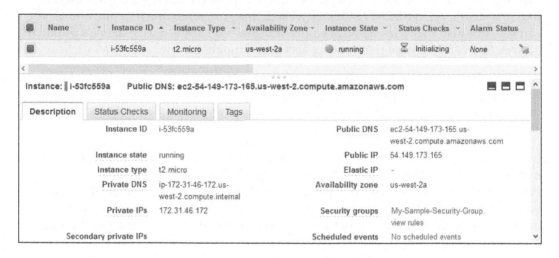

Select any particular running instance from the EC2 dashboard and view the instance's **Private DNS**, **Private IPs**, **Public DNS**, and **Public IP**. Since my instances are deployed in a VPC by default, you should see an additional row called **Secondary private IPs** as well. These are the additional private IPs that you can allocate to your instance as per your needs. If you don't see these additional rows, then don't worry! You are probably running your instances from an EC2-Classic account and that's fine for now.

Another way of listing your instance's network information is by using something called **instance metadata**. Instance metadata is simply data about your instance. Information such as your instance's AMI ID, instance's hostname, block device mapping, network details, and a lot more can be obtained by querying against the instance's metadata.

 To know more about the various instance metadata categories and how to use them, go to http://docs. aws.amazon.com/AWSEC2/latest/UserGuide/ec2-instance-metadata.html.

To determine your instance's IP addresses using instance metadata, simply connect to your running instance and run the following command:

```
# curl http://169.254.169.254/latest/meta-data/local-ipv4
```

You should receive your instance's private IP address, as shown in the following screenshot. In case you are wondering what's up with the `169.254.169.254` IP address, we'll try to keep it simple; it is a special-use IP address (also called a link-local address) used by EC2 to distribute metadata to your instances.

```
ec2-user@ip-172-31-46-172:~
[ec2-user@ip-172-31-46-172 ~]$
[ec2-user@ip-172-31-46-172 ~]$ curl http://169.254.169.254/latest/meta-data/local-ipv4
172.31.46.172[ec2-user@ip-172-31-46-172 ~]$
[ec2-user@ip-172-31-46-172 ~]$
```

Similarly, you can list your instance's public IP address by typing in the following command in your instance:

```
# curl http://169.254.169.254/latest/meta-data/public-ipv4
```

You should receive your instance's Public IP address, as shown here:

```
ec2-user@ip-172-31-46-172:~
[ec2-user@ip-172-31-46-172 ~]$
[ec2-user@ip-172-31-46-172 ~]$ curl http://169.254.169.254/latest/meta-data/public-ipv4
52.27.19.173[ec2-user@ip-172-31-46-172 ~]$
[ec2-user@ip-172-31-46-172 ~]$
```

> Running a Windows instance? You can still query its instance metadata by substituting `curl` with `wget` and running the command in your Windows command prompt.

Feel free to dig around with instance metadata and list down your instance's hostname, instance ID, security groups, and much more.

Working with Elastic IP addresses

Okay, so each of your instances receives a public and private IP address and in standard normal circumstances these IP addresses do not persist with the instance when it is powered off. But what if you want to assign a static IP address to your instance? A static IP address that remains associated with your instance even if it is powered off? In that case, you will need to use something called an **Elastic IP Address (EIP)**.

EIPs are nothing but a bunch of static public IP addresses that AWS allocates to your account, not to your instances. Each AWS account can be associated with up to five EIPs; however, you can always request AWS to provide additional ones as per your requirements and needs by filling out a simple request form. Your EIPs will remain associated with your AWS account until you choose to release them explicitly.

The really cool part of an EIP is that it can be reassigned to a different running instance dynamically as and when needed. For example, let's consider our initial use case, hosting a customer's website on AWS. As with all websites, this design calls for a web server and a database server to begin with. Assume that we created and allocated an EIP to the web server instance, as shown in the image here. This EIP can then be mapped to a proper website name, such as `all-about-dogs.com`, using any DNS service, such as AWS Route 53 and so on.

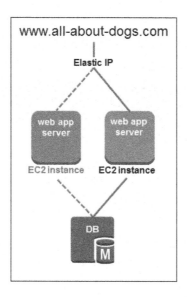

Now, if the web server instance undergoes any upgrades or maintenance activities, you can simply create a new, similar web server instance and point your EIP to it. Once the scheduled maintenance activity is over, simply swap the EIP back to the previous web server instance. Simple, isn't it! When you add an EIP to your instance, AWS automatically releases that instance's public IP address to the general IP pool. On disassociating the EIP from your instance, AWS will once again provide your instance with a new public IP address from the general IP pool. All this happens really quickly, just a matter of minutes!

How is an EIP charged? Well, for the first EIP that you attach to a running instance, you don't have to pay anything. However, you will need to shell out a minimum of $0.005 per additional EIP for each instance on a per hourly basis.

AWS imposes a small hourly charge (approx. $0.005) on EIPs if they are attached to instances in a stopped state or not associated with running instances. This is just to make sure that the EIPs are used efficiently and not wasted.

Let's look at few simple steps using which you can create, associate, and disassociate EIPs using the AWS Management Console!

Create an Elastic IP address

To create an Elastic IP address using the AWS Management dashboard, first login to the dashboard using your IAM credentials and select the EC2 service option as EIPs are a part of the EC2 services. Next, from the navigation pane, select the **Elastic IPs** option. This will bring up the **Elastic IP management dashboard** as shown here. Since this is going to be our first EIP, simply go ahead and select the **Allocate New Address** option. In the confirmation dialog box, select **Yes, Allocate** to complete the process.

Your new Elastic IP is now ready to use! Remember, once again, that these Elastic IP addresses are associated with your account and bear additional costs with them, so use them wisely.

Allocating Elastic IP addresses

Once your EIP has been created, you can go ahead and allocate it to any running instance from your current EC2 scope. Scope here can mean either EC2-Classic or a VPC environment, depending on where your instances are currently deployed. In my case, the instances are all running out of a VPC, so this particular EIP can be associated with any instance currently running within my VPC. How do you tell the scope of an EIP? Well, that's simple! Select the particular EIP and view its details on the EIP management dashboard. You should see a column called **Scope** stating whether you can deploy this EIP in a **VPC** or an **EC2-Classic** environment.

To allocate the EIP, select the **EIP**, and from the **Actions** tab, select the option **Associate Address**, as shown:

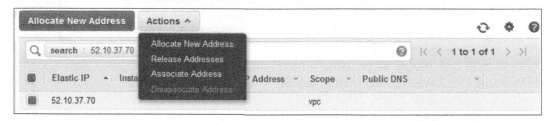

You should see the **Allocate New Address** pop-up dialog box as shown. There are two ways in which you can allocate your EIPs to your instances, either by providing their **Instance ID** or by providing the instance's **Network Interface** information. Provide the **Instance's ID** for now and leave the **Network Interface** option blank. Optionally, you can even select the **Reassociation** checkbox if you wish to re-allocate an EIP from one attached instance to a new instance.

You will receive a warning message informing you that associating an EIP to your instance will release the current public IP attached to it. Accept the warning and select the **Associate** tab to complete the EIP allocation process:

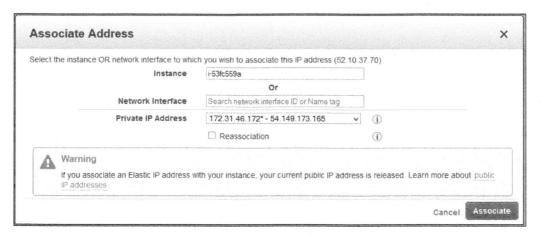

Verify whether the EIP was successfully attached to your instance or not by viewing the status on the Elastic IP management dashboard.

Disassociating and releasing an Elastic IP address

Disassociating an EIP from an instance is an equally important task and can be performed quite easily using the EIP management dashboard. Select the particular EIP from the dashboard and from the **Actions** tab. Then select the **Dissociate Address** option. This will pop up a confirmation box detailing the EIP and its associated instance ID information, as shown here. Select **Yes, Disassociate** to complete the process:

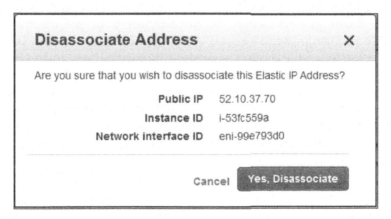

On disassociation, AWS will automatically allocate a free and available public IP address to the instance from its general IP pool. There is no guarantee that your instance will receive the same public IP address as the instance had before the EIP was added as these public IPs are always circulated and assigned on a random basis.

To release the EIP back to the pool, select the **EIP** from the dashboard. From the **Actions** tab, select the **Release Addresses** option. You will be provided with a confirmation box describing the current EIP address. Select **Yes, Release** to complete the process, as shown:

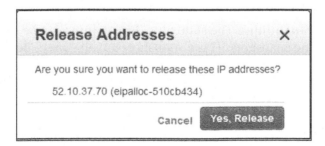

Understanding EBS volumes

We briefly touched base on EBS volumes back in the previous chapter where we were comparing EBS-backed and instance store-backed images. In this section, you are going to learn a bit more about EBS volumes, their features, benefits, different types, along with steps on how to create, attach, and delete them as well. So, what are we waiting for? Let's get started!

First up, let's understand EBS volumes a bit better. EBS volumes are nothing more than block-level storage devices that you can attach to your EC2 instances. They are highly durable and can provide a host of additional functionalities to your instances, such as data persistence, encryption, snapshotting capabilities, and so on. Majority of the time, these EBS volumes are used for storing data for a variety of applications and databases, however you can use it just as a normal hard drive as well. The best part of EBS volumes is that they can persist independently from your instances. So powering down an instance or even terminating it will not affect the state of your EBS volumes. Your data will stay on it unless and until you explicitly delete it.

Let's look at some of the key features and benefits that EBS volumes have to offer:

- **High availability**: Unlike your instance store-backed drives, EBS volumes are automatically replicated by AWS within the availability zone in which they are created. You can create an EBS volume and attach it to any instance present in the same availability zone; however, one EBS volume cannot be attached to multiple instances at the same time. A single instance, however, can have multiple EBS volumes attached to it at any given time.

- **Encryption capabilities**: EBS volumes provide an add-on feature using which you can encrypt your volumes using standard encryption algorithms, such as AES-256, and keys as well. These keys are autogenerated the first time you employ encryption on a volume using the AWS **Key Management Service (KMS)**. You can additionally even use IAM to provide fine-grained access control and permissions to your EBS volumes.

- **Snapshot capabilities**: The state of an EBS volume can be saved using point-in-time snapshots. These snapshots are all stored incrementally on your Amazon S3 account and can be used for a variety of purposes, such as creating new volumes based on an existing one, resizing volumes, backup and data recovery, and so on.

 EBS volumes cannot be copied from one AWS region to another. In such cases, you can take a snapshot of the volume and copy the snapshot over to a different region using the steps mentioned at http://docs.aws.amazon.com/AWSEC2/latest/UserGuide/ebs-copy-snapshot.html.

EBS volume types

There are three different types of EBS volumes available today, each with their own sets of performance characteristics and associated costs. Let's briefly look into each one of them and their potential uses:

- **General purpose volumes (SSD)**: These are by far the most commonly used EBS volume types as they provide a good balance between cost and overall performance. By default, this volume provides a standard 3 IOPS per GB of storage, so a 10 GB general purpose volume will get approximately 30 IOPS and so on so forth, with a max value of 10,000 IOPS. You can create general purpose volumes that can range in size from 1 GB to a maximum of 16 TB. Such volumes can be used for a variety of purposes, such as instance root volumes, data disks for dev and test environments, database storage, and so on.

- **Provisioned IOPS volumes (SSD)**: These are a specialized set of SSDs that can consistently provide a minimum of 100 IOPS burstable up to 20,000 IOPS. You can create Provisioned IOPS Volumes that range in size from a minimum of 4 GB all the way up to 16 TB. Such volumes are ideally suited for applications that are IO intensive, such as databases, parallel computing workloads such as Hadoop, and so on.

- **Magnetic volumes**: Very similar to traditional tape drives and magnetic disks, these volumes are a good match for workloads where data is accessed infrequently, such as log storage, data backup and recovery, and so on. On an average, these volumes provide up to a 100 IOPS with an ability to burst up to 1,000 IOPS. You can create Magnetic volumes that range in size from a minimum of 1 GB all the way up to 1 TB.

Getting started with EBS Volumes

Now that we have a fair idea of what an EBS Volume is, let's look at some simple ways that you can create, attach, and manage these volumes.

To view and access your account's EBS Volumes using **AWS Management Console**, simply select the **Volumes** option from the EC2 dashboard's navigation pane, as shown here:

ELASTIC BLOCK STORE

Volumes

Snapshots

This will bring up the **Volume Management** dashboard as shown here. In my case, I already have a volume present here that is shown as in use. This is our first instance's root device volume that we launched in *Chapter 3, Images and Instances*. Each EBS-backed instance's volume will appear here in the **Volume Management** dashboard. You can use this same dashboard to perform a host of activities on your volumes, such as create, attach, detach, and monitor performance, to name a few.

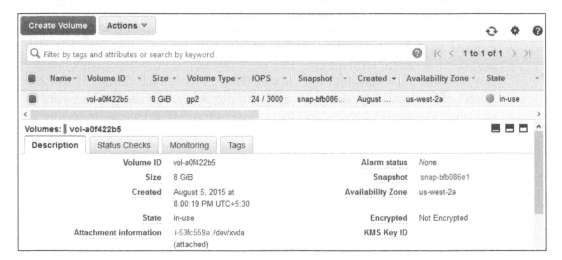

You can view any particular EBS Volume's details by simply selecting it and viewing its related information in the **Description** tab, as shown. Here, you can view the volume's **ID**, **Size**, **Created date**, the volume's current **State** as well as its **Attachment information,** which displays the volume's mount point on a particular instance. Additionally, you can also view the volume's health and status by selecting the **Monitoring** and **Status Checks** tab, respectively. For now, let's go ahead and create a new volume using the volume management dashboard.

Creating EBS volumes

From the **Volume Management** dashboard, select the **Create Volume** option. This will pop up the **Create Volume** dialog box as shown here:

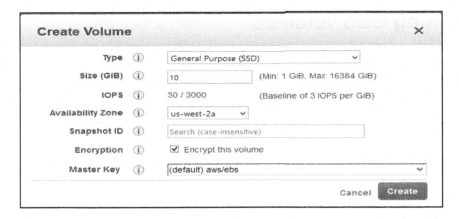

Fill in the details as required in the **Create Volume** dialog box. For this tutorial, I went ahead and created a simple 10-GB general purpose volume:

- **Type**: From the **Type** drop-down list, select either **General Purpose (SSD)**, **Provisioned IOPS (SSD)**, or **Magnetic** as per your requirements.

- **Size (GiB)**: Provide the size of your volume in GB. Here, I provided 10 GB.

- **IOPS**: This field will only be editable if you have selected Provisioned IOPS (SSD) as the volume's type. Enter the max **IOPS value** as per your requirements.

- **Availability Zone**: Select the appropriate **availability zone** in which you wish to create the volume. Remember, an EBS volume can span availability zones, but not regions.

- **Snapshot ID**: This is an optional field. You can choose to populate your EBS volume based on a third party's **snapshot ID**. In this case, we have left this field blank.

- **Encryption**: As mentioned earlier, you can choose whether or not you wish to encrypt your EBS Volume. Select **Encrypt this volume checkbox** if you wish to do so.

- **Master Key**: On selecting the **Encryption** option, AWS will automatically create a default key pair for the AWS's KMS. You can make a note of the KMS Key ID as well as the KMS Key ARN as these values will be required during the volume's decryption process as well.

Once your configuration settings are filled in, select **Create** to complete the volume's creation process. The new volume will take a few minutes to be available for use. Once the volume is created, you can now go ahead and attach this volume to your running instance.

Attaching EBS volumes

Once the EBS volume is created, make sure it is in the **available** state before you go ahead and attach it to an instance. You can attach multiple volumes to a single instance at a time, with each volume having a unique device name. Some of these device names are reserved, for example, `/dev/sda1` is reserved for the root device volume. You can find the complete list of potential and recommended device names at `http://docs.aws.amazon.com/AWSEC2/latest/UserGuide/device_naming.html`.

The following screenshot shows the option of attaching a volume:

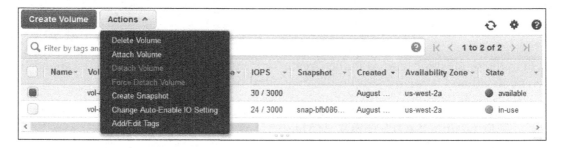

To attach a volume, select the **volume** from the **Volume Management** dashboard. Then select the **Actions** tab and click on the **Attach Volume** option. This will pop up the **Attach Volume** dialog box, as shown:

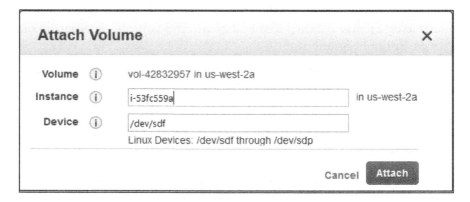

Type in your **instance's ID** in the **Instance** field and provide a suitable name in the **Device** field as shown. In this case, I provided the recommended device name of /**dev/sdf** to this volume. Click on **Attach** once done. The volume attachment process takes a few minutes to complete. Once done, you are now ready to make the volume accessible from your instance.

Accessing volumes from an instance

Once the volume is attached to an instance, you can basically format it and use it like any other block device. In this case, I'll be using the same Amazon Linux instance that we created back in *Chapter 3, Images and Instances*. You can attach and mount volumes to Windows-based instances as well.

To get started, first up connect to your running instance using putty or any other SSH client of your choice. Next, type in the following command to check the current disk partitioning of your instance:

```
# sudo df -h
```

You should see a /dev/xvda1 like filesystem mounted on the root (/) partition along with few other temp filesystems, as shown here. This is more or less the standard disk partitioning scheme that your instances will have.

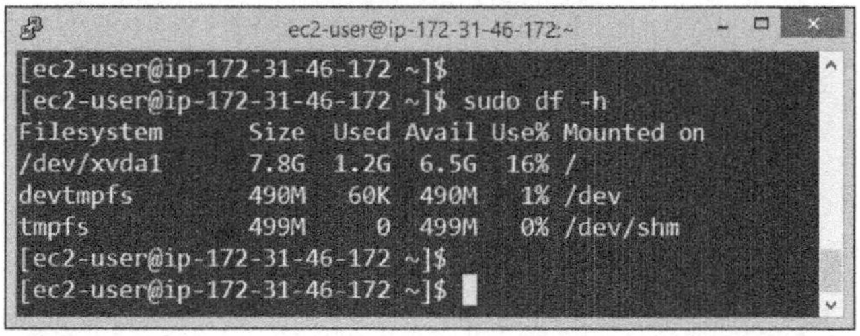

Next, run the following command to list out partitions on your current instance. You should see a default /dev/xvda partition along with its partition table and an unformatted disk partition with the name /dev/xvdf as shown in the following screenshot. The /dev/xvdf command is the newly added EBS volume that we will need to format in the upcoming steps:

```
# sudo fdisk -l
```

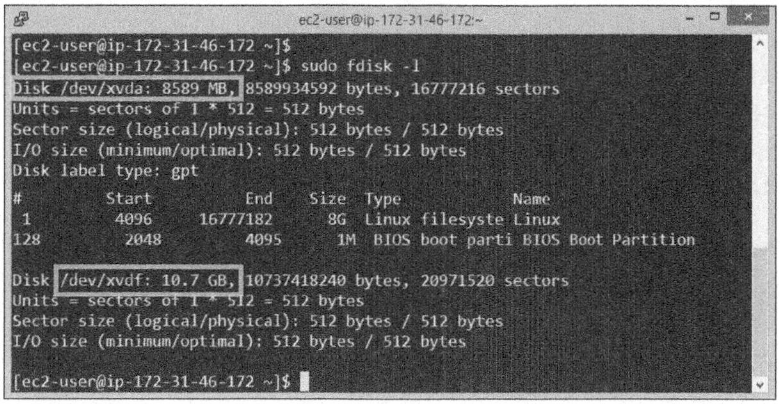

Once you have verified the name of your newly added disk, you can go ahead and format with a filesystem of your choice. In this case, I have gone ahead and used the `ext4` filesystem for my new volume:

```
# sudo mkfs -t ext4 /dev/xvdf
```

Now that your volume is formatted, you can create a new directory on your Linux instance and mount the volume to it using your standard Linux commands:

```
# sudo mkdir /my-new-dir
# sudo mount /dev/xvdf /my-new-dir
```

Here is the screenshot of creating new directory using the preceding commands:

Here's a useful tip! Once you have mounted your new volume, you can optionally edit the Linux instance's `fstab` file and add the volume's mount information there. This will make sure that the volume is mounted and available even if the instance is rebooted. Make sure you take a backup copy of the `fstab` file before you edit it, just as a precautionary measure.

Detaching EBS volumes

Detaching EBS volumes is a fairly simple and straightforward process. You will first need to unmount the volume from your instance and then simply detach it using **Volume Management dashboard**.

Run the following command to unmount the EBS volume from the instance:

```
# sudo umount /dev/sdf
```

Make sure you are unmounting the correct volume from the instance. *Do not* try and unmount the `/dev/sda` or any other root partitions.

Once the volume is successfully unmounted from the instance, detach the volume by selecting the **Detach Volume** option from the **Actions** tab, as shown here:

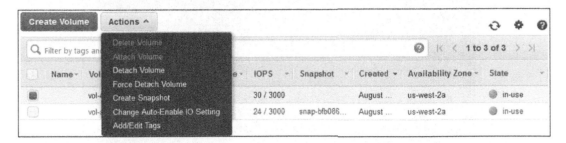

Managing EBS volumes using the AWS CLI

You can create, attach, and manage EBS volumes using the AWS CLI as well. Let's go ahead and create a new EBS volume using the AWS CLI. Type in the following command:

```
# aws ec2 create-volume \
--size 5 --region us-west-2 --availability-zone us-west-2a \
--volume-type gp2
```

 The `--volume-type` attribute accepts any one of these three values:

- **gp2**: General Purpose instances (SSD)
- **io1**: Provisioned IOPS volumes (SSD)
- **standard**: Magnetic volumes

The following code will create a 5 GB General Purpose volume in the `us-west-2a` availability zone.

The new volume will take a couple of minutes to be created. You should see a similar output as the following screenshot. Make a note of the new volume's `Volume ID` before proceeding to the next steps.

```
root@YoYoNUX:~                                          _ □ ×
[root@YoYoNUX ~]# aws ec2 create-volume \
> --size 5 --region us-west-2 --availability-zone us-west-2a \
> --volume-type gp2 \
> --profile jason
+---------------------------------------------------------------+
|                          CreateVolume                         |
+---------------------------------+-----------------------------+
|  AvailabilityZone  |  us-west-2a                              |
|  CreateTime        |  2015-08-19T14:02:46.117Z               |
|  Encrypted         |  False                                   |
|  Iops              |  15                                      |
|  Size              |  5                                       |
|  SnapshotId        |                                          |
|  State             |  creating                                |
|  VolumeId          |  vol-40993355                            |
|  VolumeType        |  gp2                                     |
+---------------------------------+-----------------------------+
[root@YoYoNUX ~]#
```

Now that the new volume is created, we can go ahead and attach it to our instance. Type in the following command:

```
# aws ec2 attach-volume \
--volume-id vol-40993355 \
--instance-id i-53fc559a \
--device /dev/sdg
```

The following command will attach the volume with the volume ID `vol-40993355` to our instance (`i-53fc559a`), and the device name will be `/dev/sdg`. Once again, you can supply any meaningful device name here, but make sure that it abides by AWS's naming conventions and best practices as mentioned in `http://docs.aws.amazon.com/AWSEC2/latest/UserGuide/device_naming.html`.

Once the volume is attached to your instance, the next steps are pretty easy and straightforward. First format the new volume with a suitable filesystem of your choice. Next up, create a new directory inside your instance and mount the newly formatted volume on it. Voila! Your volume is now ready for use.

You can detach and delete the volume as well using the AWS CLI. First up, we will need to unmount the volume from the instance. To do so, type in the following command in your instance:

```
# unmount /dev/sdg
```

Make sure you are unmounting the correct volume and not the root partition. Once the volume is unmounted, simply detach it from the instance using the following AWS CLI code:

```
# aws ec2 detach-volume \
--volume-id vol-40993355
```

The output of the preceding command is as follows:

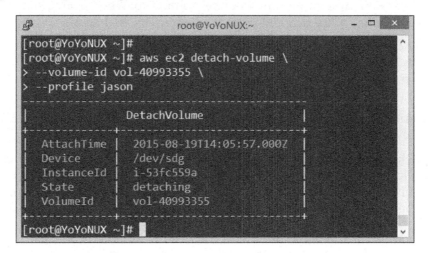

Finally, go ahead and delete the volume using the following AWS CLI code:

```
# aws ec2 delete-volume \
--volume-id vol-40993355
```

Remember that you cannot delete volumes if they are attached or in use by an instance, so make sure that you follow the detachment process before deleting it.

Backing up volumes using EBS snapshots

We do know for a fact that AWS automatically replicates EBS volumes so that your data is preserved even in case the complete drive fails. But this replication is limited only to the availability zone in which the drive or EBS volume was created, which means if that particular availability zone was to go down for some reason, then there is no way for you to back up your data. Fortunately for us, AWS provides a very simple yet highly efficient method of backing EBS volumes, called as EBS snapshots.

An EBS snapshot in simple terms is a state of your volume at a particular point in time. You can take a snapshot of a volume anytime you want. Each snapshot that you take is stored incrementally in Amazon S3, but, you will not be able to see these snapshots in your S3 buckets; they are kind of hidden away and stored separately.

You can achieve a wide variety of tasks using snapshots. A few are listed as follows:

- **Create new volumes based on existing ones**: Snapshots are a great and easy way to spin up new volumes. A new volume spawned from a snapshot is an exact replica of the original volume, down to the last detail.

- **Expand existing volumes**: Snapshots can also be used to expand an existing EBS Volume's size as well. It is a multistep process, which involves you taking a snapshot of your existing EBS volume and creating a larger new volume from the snapshot.

- **Share your volumes**: Snapshots can be shared within your own account (*private*) as well publicly.

- **Backup and disaster recovery**: Snapshots are a handy tool when it comes to backing up your volumes. You can create multiple replicates of an existing volume within an AZ, across AZs that belong to a particular region, as well as across regions, using something called an EBS Snapshot copy mechanism.

To create a snapshot of your volumes, all you need to do is select the particular **volume** from the **Volume Management dashboard**. Click on the **Actions** tab and select the **Create Snapshot** option, as shown here:

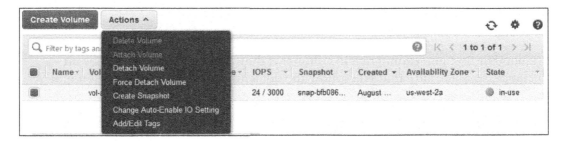

 It is really a good practice to stop your instance before taking a snapshot if you are taking a snapshot of its root volume. This ensures a consistent and complete snapshot of your volume at all times.

You should see the **Create Snapshot** dialog box as shown in the following screenshot. Provide a suitable **Name** and **Description** for your new snapshot. An important thing to note here is that this particular snapshot is not supporting encryption, but why? Well, that's simple! Because the original volume was not encrypted, neither will the snapshot be encrypted. Snapshots of encrypted volumes are automatically encrypted. Even new volumes created from an encrypted snapshot are encrypted automatically. Once you have finished providing the details, click on **Create** to complete the snapshot process:

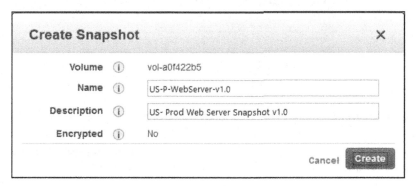

You will be shown a confirmation box, which will display this particular snapshot's ID. Make a note of this ID for future reference.

The new snapshot will take a good 3–4 minutes to go from **Pending** to **Completed**. You can check the status of your snapshot by viewing the **Status** as well as the **Progress** fields in the **Description** tab, as shown here:

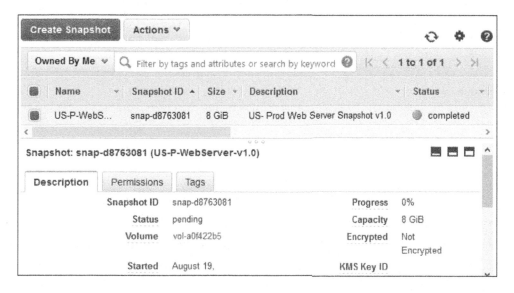

Once the snapshot process is completed, you can use this particular snapshot and **Create Volume, Copy** this snapshot from one region to another, and **Modify Snapshot Permissions** to private or public as you see fit. These options are all present in the **Actions** tab of your **Snapshot Management dashboard**:

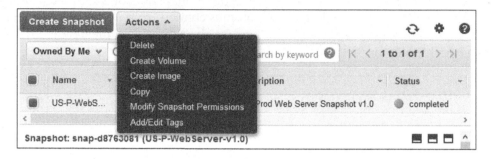

But for now, let's go ahead and use this snapshot to create our very first AMI. Yes, you can use snapshots to create AMIs as well. From the **Actions** tab, select the **Create Image** option. You should see the **Create Image from EBS Snapshot** wizard as shown here. Fill in the required details and click on **Create** to create your very first AMI:

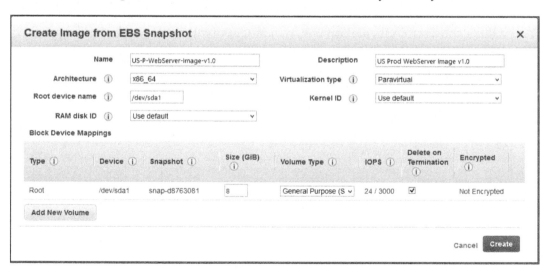

The details contain the following options:

- **Name**: Provide a suitable and meaningful name for your AMI.
- **Description**: Provide a suitable description for your new AMI.
- **Architecture**: You can either choose between **i386** (32 bit) or **x86_64** (64 bit).

- **Root device name**: Enter a suitable name for your root device volume. Ideally, a root device volume should be labelled as **/dev/sda1** as per EC2's device naming best practices.

- **Virtualization type**: You can choose whether the instances launched from this particular AMI will support **Paravirtualization** (PV) or **Hardware Virtual Machine** (HVM) virtualization.

 You can read more about the various Virtualization types supported by EC2 at http://docs.aws. amazon.com/AWSEC2/latest/UserGuide/ virtualization_types.html.

- **RAM disk ID, Kernel ID**: You can select and provide your AMI with its own RAM disk ID (ARI) and Kernel ID (AKI); however, in this case I have opted to keep the default ones.

- **Block Device Mappings**: You can use this dialog to either expand your root volume's size or add additional volumes to it. You can change the **Volume Type** from **General Purpose (SSD)** to **Provisioned IOPS (SSD)** or **Magnetic** as per your AMI's requirements. For now, I have left these to their default values.

Click on **Create** to complete the AMI creation process. The new AMI will take a few minutes to spin up. In the meantime, you can make a note of the new AMI ID from the **Create Image from EBS Snapshot** confirmation box, as shown:

You can view your newly created AMI under the AMIs option from the EC2 dashboard's navigation pane:

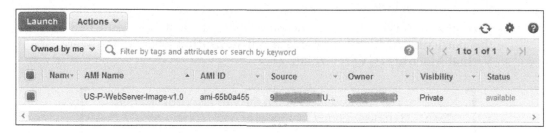

So, here we have it! You very own AMI, created and ready to use.

An important point to note here is that you will not be able to delete this particular EBS Snapshot now as it is in use by your AMI. You will have to deregister your AMI first from the AMI Management dashboard and then try and delete the snapshot.

Planning your next steps

There are still a few important pieces that I would really recommend you try after you have created your AMI. First up, try and launch a new instance from it. Once the instance is launched, go ahead and check whether your instance has the correct root partition name and size as allocated or not. Next up, try and copy your AMI to a different region. You can refer to http://docs.aws.amazon.com/AWSEC2/latest/UserGuide/CopyingAMIs.html for the required steps. Copying an AMI from one region to another is just a simple way to build scalable and highly available applications. You can try the same with your EBS volume as well. Go ahead and take a snapshot of any volume of your choice and copy it over to some other AWS region and attach it to a running instance.

Besides these steps, there is some additional EBS Volume related information that I would really recommend you guys read. First up is something called **EBS-optimized instances**. These are specially created instances that provided dedicated throughput and IOPS for performance-intensive applications. This is an add-on feature provided by AWS and is charged separately on an hourly basis. To know more about EBS-Optimized Instances, go to http://docs.aws.amazon.com/AWSEC2/latest/UserGuide/EBSOptimized.html.

Secondly, I would recommend reading the EBS Performance tips that are provided by AWS. These tips will help you analyze and benchmark your volumes for I/O performance-intensive applications, configure RAID on your Linux instances, and help you learn how to prewarm your EBS Volumes. These are all additional tips and practices that you can choose to leverage in case you are working with production environments and high-performance-intensive applications.

Another very interesting thing worth mentioning is public datasets. These are basically really large repositories of publically available datasets such as the US census data, transportation statistics, human genomic data, and so on. The whole idea here is that AWS hosts these and provides these datasets for use completely free of charge, so you don't spend hours of your time locating and downloading them. Simply create a volume from any one of these public datasets which are in the form of public snapshots and start analyzing them. Awesome, isn't it! You can read more about public datasets at `http://aws.amazon.com/public-data-sets/`.

Recommendations and best practices

Here are a few handy recommendations and best practices to keep in mind when working with volumes:

- Create and use IAM policies and allow only a particular set of users from accessing your EBS volumes.

- Create and take periodic snapshots of your volumes. Always remember to provide suitable names and descriptions for your snapshots so that they can be easily identified and re-used.

- Always take snapshots during the nonbusiness hours of your application.

- Clean up unused or older snapshots to save on unnecessary costs.

- Encrypt your EBS volumes if you have some sensitive data stored on them.

- Select and use the correct type of EBS volume as per your application's needs. Use performance-optimized volumes for your high-performance applications and magnetic volumes for applications that do not need a lot of data read and write.

Summary

We learned plenty of things in this chapter, so let's take a quick recap of the things covered so far. First up, we learned how to edit and create Security Groups. Next, we saw how our instances are provided with their networking, and we also saw how to attach an Elastic IP address to our instance. Finally, we dived into the world of EBS volumes and created, attached, detached, and deleted volumes using both the AWS Management Console and the AWS CLI. Toward the end, we even created our very first AMI and finally finished off with a set of key recommendations and best practices.

5
Building Your Own Private Clouds Using Amazon VPC

So, in the previous chapter, we covered a lot of different things! We started off with some introductions and working examples of security groups and later on continued with understanding how EC2 networking really works, with a brief look at Elastic IP addresses. To top this off, we also learnt a lot about EBS volumes and their types and how we can create, attach, and manage them.

This chapter, however, is going to be a lot different and interesting as in this chapter, we will explore and learn about an awesome service provided by AWS called **Virtual Private Cloud** (**VPC**)! We will learn about the different VPC concepts and terminologies, deployment strategies, and a whole lot more, so stick around; we are just getting started!

An overview of Amazon VPC

So far we have learnt a lot about EC2, its features, and uses, and how we can deploy scalable and fault tolerant applications using it, but EC2 does come with its own sets of minor drawbacks. For starters, you do not control the IP addressing of your instances, apart from adding an Elastic IP address to your instance. By design, each of your instances will get a single private and public IP address, which is routable on the Internet—again, something you cannot control. Also, EC2 security groups have the capability to add rules for inbound traffic only; there is no support for providing any outbound traffic rules. So, although EC2 is good for hosting your applications, it is still not that secure. The answer to all your problems is Amazon VPC!

Amazon VPC is a logically isolated part of the AWS cloud that enables you to build and use your own logical subnets and networks. In a simpler sense, you get to build your own network topology and spin up instances within it. But what actually separates VPC from your classic EC2 environment is the ability to isolate and secure your environment. Using VPCs, you can choose which instances are accessible over the Internet and which are not. You can create a bunch of different subnets within a single VPC, each with their own security policies and routing rules. VPCs also provided an added layer of protection by enforcing something called as **Network Access Control Lists (ACLs)** besides your standard use of security groups. This ensures that you have total control over what traffic is routed in and out of your subnets and the VPC as well.

VPCs also provide an added functionality using which you can connect and extend your on-premise datacenters to the AWS cloud. This is achieved using an IPsec VPN tunnel that connects from your on premise datacenter's gateway device to the VPC's **Virtual Private Gateway,** as shown in the following image:

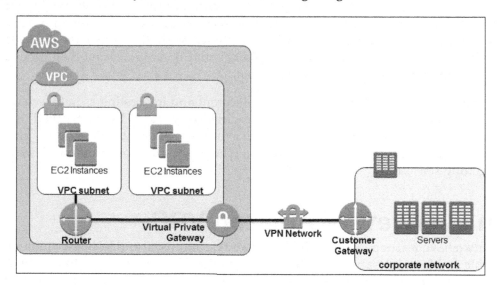

An important point to note here is that a VPC is still a part of the AWS Cloud. It is not physically separate hosting provided by AWS, it simply is a logically isolated part of the EC2 infrastructure. This isolation is done at the network layer and is very similar to a traditional datacenter's network isolation; it's just that we as end users are shielded from the complexities of it.

 To know more about VPN and virtual private gateways, refer to http://docs.aws.amazon.com/AmazonVPC/latest/ UserGuide/VPC_VPN.html.

With this brief overview in mind, let's look at some of VPC's key concepts and terminologies to get a better understanding of how things work.

VPC concepts and terminologies

By now you must have understood that VPC is nothing more than a network service provided by AWS using which you can create logically isolated environments for your EC2 instances. And just like any other network service, VPC too works on some key concepts, explained as follows.

Subnets

Perhaps the most important part of the VPC, the subnets are nothing more than a range of valid IP addresses that you specify. VPC provides you with two different subnet creation options: a publically or Internet routed subnet called as a **public subnet** and an isolated subnet called as a **private subnet**. You can launch your instances in either of these subnets depending on whether you wish your instances to be routed on the Internet or not.

How does it all work? Pretty simple! When you first create a VPC, you provide it with a set of IP addresses in the form of a CIDR, for example, `10.0.0.0/16`. The `/16` here indicates that this particular VPC can support up to 65,536 IP addresses ($2^{(32-16)}$ = 65,536, IP address range 10.0.0.0 - 10.0.255.255)! Now that's a lot! Once the VPC's CIDR block is created, you can go ahead and carve out individual subnets from it. For example, a subnet with the CIDR block `10.0.1.0/24` for hosting your web servers and another CIDR block `10.0.5.0/24` for your database servers and so on and so forth.

The idea here is that from the 65,536 IP address block, we carved out two subnets, each supporting 256 IPs (`/24` CIDR includes 256 IP addresses in it). Now you can specify the subnet for the web servers to be public, as they will need to be routed to the Internet and the subnet for the database servers to be private as they need to be isolated from the outside world.

 To know more about CIDRs and how they work, refer to `https://en.wikipedia.org/wiki/Classless_Inter-Domain_Routing`.

There is one additional thing worth mentioning here. By default, AWS will create a VPC for you in your particular region the first time you sign up for the service. This is called as the default VPC. The default VPC comes preconfigured with the following set of configurations:

- The default VPC is always created with a CIDR block of /16, which means it supports 65,536 IP addresses in it.

- A default subnet is created in each AZ of your selected region. Instances launched in these default subnets have both a public and a private IP address by default as well.

- An Internet Gateway is provided to the default VPC for instances to have Internet connectivity.

- A few necessary route tables, security groups, and ACLs are also created by default that enable the instance traffic to pass through to the Internet. Refer to the following figure:

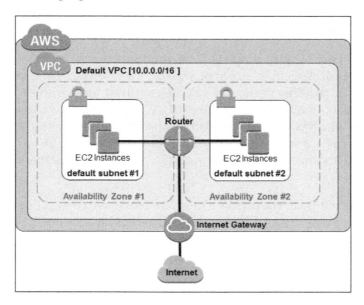

You can use this default VPC just as any other VPC by creating additional subnets in it, provisioning route tables, security groups, and so on. In fact, the instances that we launched back in *Chapter 3*, *Images and Instances*, were based out of the default VPC!

> Any other VPC that you create besides the default VPC is called as the non-default VPC. Each non-default VPC in turn contains non-default subnets, and so on and so forth.

Security groups and network ACLs

We have talked a lot about security groups in the past two chapters already. We do know that security groups are nothing but simple firewall rules that you can configure to safeguard your instances. You can create a maximum of 100 security groups for a single VPC, with each Security Group containing up to 50 firewall rules in them. Also, it is very important to remember that a Security Group does not permit inbound traffic by default. You have to explicitly set inbound traffic rules to allow traffic to flow to your instance. However, all outbound traffic from the instance is allowed by default.

Network ACLs are something new. These provide an added security measure over security groups as they are instance specific, whereas Network ACLs are subnet specific. Unlike your security groups, however, you can both allow and restrict inbound and outbound traffic using ACL rules. Speaking of ACL rules, they are very much similar to your Security Group rules, however, with one small exception. Each ACL rule is evaluated by AWS based on a number. The number can be anything from 100 all the way up to 32,766. The ACL rules are evaluated in sequence starting from the smallest number and going all the way up to the maximum value. The following is a small example of how ACL rules look:

Inbound ACL rules				
Rule No.	Source IP	Protocol	Port	Allow/Deny
100	0.0.0.0/0	All	All	ALLOW
*	0.0.0.0/0	All	All	DENY
Outbound ACL rules				
Rule No.	Dest IP	Protocol	Port	Allow/Deny
100	0.0.0.0/0	all	all	ALLOW
*	0.0.0.0/0	all	all	DENY

These are the ACL rules created by AWS for your default VPC; as a result, this particular ACL is called as the default Network ACL as well. What do these rules mean? For starters, the rule number 100 for both the inbound and outbound ACL specifies the traffic to flow from any protocol running on any port in and out of the subnet. The * is also considered as a rule number and is a must in all ACLs. It basically means that you drop any packets that do not match the ACL's rules. We will be checking out ACLs and security groups in action later on in this chapter when we create our very own VPC for the first time.

Routing tables

Route tables are pretty straightforward and easy to implement in a VPC. They are nothing but simple rules or routes that are used to direct network traffic from a subnet. Each subnet in a VPC has to be associated with a single route table at any given time; however, you can attach multiple subnets to a single route table as well.

Remember the default VPC and the default subnets? Well, a similar default route table is also created when you first start using your VPC. This default route table is called as the **main route table** and it generally contains only one route information that enables traffic to flow within the VPC itself. Subnets that are not assigned to any route tables are automatically allocated to the main route table. You can edit and add multiple routes in the main route table as you see fit; however, you cannot modify the local route rule. The following an example of a main route table viewed from the VPC Management dashboard:

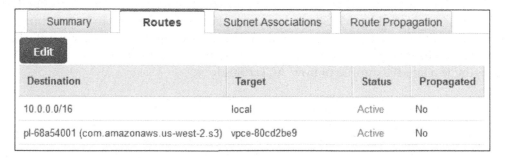

As you can see, there are a couple of entries made in this table. The first is the local route rule that allows traffic to flow within this particular subnet (**10.0.0.0/16**). The second route is something called as a route for VPC endpoints. This is a private connection made between your VPC and some other AWS service; in this case, the service is S3. Let's look VPC endpoints a little closely.

VPC endpoints

VPC endpoints basically allow you to securely connect your VPC with other AWS services. These are virtual devices that are highly available and fault tolerant by design. They are scaled and managed by AWS itself, so you don't have to worry about the intricacies of maintaining them. All you need to do is create a VPC endpoint connection between your VPC and an AWS service of your choice, and voila! Your instances can now communicate securely with other AWS services. The instances in the VPC communicate with other services using their private IP addresses itself, so there's no need to route the traffic over the Internet.

AWS currently only supports VPC endpoint connections for Amazon S3. More services are planned to be added shortly.

When an endpoint is created, you first need to select either of your VPC's route tables. The traffic between your VPC instances and the AWS service will be routed using this particular route table. Similar to any other route information, a VPC endpoint route also contains a **Destination** field and a **Target** field. The **Destination** filed contains the AWS service's prefix list ID, which is generally represented by the following ID: pl-xxxxxxxx. The **Target** field contains the endpoint ID, which is represented in the following format: vpce-xxxxxxxx.

In the following route table example, the prefix list ID (**pl-68a54001**) represents the S3 service whereas the target **vpce-80cd2be9** represents the endpoint ID:

VPC Endpoint Route	
Destination	**Target**
10.0.0.0/16	Local
pl-68a54001	vpce-80cd2be9

Endpoints also provided an additional feature using which you can control and govern access to the remote AWS service. This is achieved using something called as **endpoint policies**.

Endpoint policies are nothing more than simple IAM-based resource policies that are provided to you when an endpoint is first created. AWS creates a simple policy document that allows full access to the AWS service by default. The following is a sample endpoint policy that is created by AWS for the S3 service:

```
{
  "Statement": [
                  {
"Action": "*",
"Effect": "Allow",
"Resource": "*",
"Principal": "*"
}
  ]
}
```

To know more about the endpoint policies and features, refer to http://docs.aws.amazon.com/AmazonVPC/latest/UserGuide/vpc-endpoints.html.

Internet Gateways

Internet Gateways, as the name suggest, are primarily used to provide Internet connectivity to your VPC instances. All you have to do is create and attach an Internet Gateway device to your VPC and add a route entry in your public subnet's route table to point to the Internet Gateway! That's it! The default VPC comes with an Internet gateway already deployed in it. So, any instance that you launch from the default subnet obtains Internet connectivity automatically. This does not apply for non-default VPCs, however, as an instance launched in a non-default subnet does not receive a public IP address by default. You would have to either assign one to the instance during the launch phase or modify your non-default subnet's public IP address attributes.

Once you have created and attached an Internet Gateway to your VPC, you will also have to make sure that the public subnet's route table has an entry for this gateway.

Plus, you will also have to create the correct set of security groups and network ACL rules to allow your subnet's traffic to flow through the Internet. The following is an example of a VPC's route table showing the route for a subnet's traffic to the Internet Gateway (**igw-8c3066e9**):

Destination	Target	Status	Propagated
10.0.0.0/16	local	Active	No
pl-68a54001 (com.amazonaws.us-west-2.s3)	vpce-80cd2be9	Active	No
0.0.0.0/0	igw-8ce066e9	Active	No

Besides the Internet connectivity, Internet Gateways also perform NAT on the instance's private IPs. The instances in a subnet are only aware of their private IP addresses that they use to communicate internally. The Internet Gateway maps the instance's private IP with an associated public or Elastic IP and then routes traffic outside the subnet to the Internet. Conversely, the Internet Gateway also maps inbound traffic from the Internet to a public or Elastic IP and then translates it to the instance's private IP address. This is how your instances receive Internet from within a VPC, which brings us to yet another interesting topic called as NAT instances.

NAT instances

So, we have just learnt that the Internet Gateway NATs the IP addresses of instances placed out in the public subnet so that they can communicate with the Internet, but what about instances in the private subnets? How do they communicate with the Internet without having direct Internet connectivity via the gateway?

That's where a NAT instance comes into play. A NAT Instance is a special instance created inside your public subnet that NATs outbound traffic from instances based in your private subnet to the Internet. It is important to note here that the NAT instance will only forward the outbound traffic and not allow any traffic from the Internet to reach the private subnets, similar to a one way street.

You can create a NAT Instance out of any AMI you wish; however, AWS provides few standard Linux-based AMIs that are well suited for such purposes. These special AMIs are listed out in the community AMIs page and all you need to do is filter out the `amzn-ami-vpc-nat` AMI from the list and spin up an instance from it.

The following example depicts the traffic flow from a private subnet (**10.0.1.0/24**) to the NAT instance inside a public subnet (**10.0.0.0/24**) via a route table:

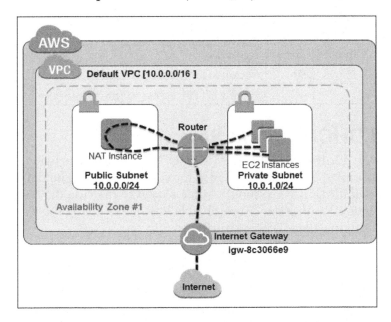

In the preceding example, outbound traffic from the public subnet's route table is routed to the Internet Gateway (**igw-8c3066e9**) while the outbound traffic from the private subnet's route table is routed to the NAT instance. Along with the route tables, it is also essential that you correctly populate the Security Group for your NAT instance. The following is a simple NAT instance Security Group example for your reference:

NAT instance - inbound security Rules			
Source	**Protocol**	**Port**	**Remarks**
10.0.1.0/24	TCP	80	Permit inbound HTTP traffic from private subnet
10.0.1.0/24	TCP	443	Permit inbound HTTPS traffic from private subnet
<HOSTIP>*	TCP	22	Permit SSH login to NAT instance from remote N/W

 The * replace the <HOSTIP> field with the IP address of your local desktop machine.

The following are the outbound security rules:

NAT Instance - outbound security rules			
Source	**Protocol**	**Port**	**Remarks**
0.0.0.0/0	TCP	80	Permit HTTP access to Internet for the NAT instance
0.0.0.0/0	TCP	443	Permit HTTPS access to Internet for the NAT instance

DNS and DHCP Option Sets

VPCs provide an additional feature called as DHCP Option Sets using which you can set and customize the DNS and DHCP for your instances. The default VPC comes with a default DHCP Options Set that is used to provide the instances with a dynamic private IP address and a resolvable hostname. Using the DHCP Options Set, you can configure the following attributes for your VPC:

- **Domain Name Servers (DNS)**: You can list down up to four DNS servers here of your own choice or even provide the Amazon DNS server details. The Amazon DNS server is provided in your VPC and runs on a reserved IP address. For example, if your VPC has the subnet of 10.0.0.0/16, then the Amazon DNS Server will probably run on the IP 10.0.0.2. You can additionally provide the Amazon DNS Server's IP address, 169.254.169.253, or the value AmazonProvidedDNS as required. Values entered here are automatically added to your Linux instances /etc/resolv. conf file for name resolution.

Domain name: You can either provide your own domain name value or choose to use the default AWS domain name values using this option. The default AWS domain names can be provided only if you have selected **AmazonProvidedDNS** as your DNS server. For example, instances launched in the US West region with the Amazon DNS server value will get a resolvable private DNS hostname as `us-west-2.compute.internal`.

- **NTP servers**: You can list up to four NTP server IP addresses using the DHCP Options Set wizard. Note, however, that this will only accept IP address values and not FQDNs such as `pool.ntp.org`.

- **NetBIOS name server**: You can list down up to four NetBIOS name servers as well; however, this field is optional.

- **NetBIOS node type**: You can specify the NetBIOS node value, which can either be 1, 2, 4, or 8. AWS recommends that you specify 2 as broadcast, and multicasts are not currently supported.

You can create and attach only one DHCP option set with a VPC at a time. AWS uses the default DHCP option if you do not specify one explicitly for your VPC. Instances either running or newly launched will automatically pick up these DNS and DHCP settings, so there is no need for you to restart or relaunch your existing instances.

VPC limits and costs

Okay, so far we have understood a lot about how the VPC works and what its components are, but what is the cost of all this? Very simple, it's nothing! VPC is a completely free of cost service provided by AWS; however, you do have to pay for the EC2 resources that you use, for example, the instances, the Elastic IP addresses, EBS volumes, and so on. Also, if you are using your VPC to connect to your on premise datacenter using the VPN option, then you need to pay for the data transfers over the VPN connection as well as for the VPN connection itself. AWS charges $0.05 per VPN connection hour.

Besides this, VPCs also have a few limits set on them by default. For example, you can have a maximum of five VPCs per region. Each VPC can have a max of one Internet gateway as well as one virtual private gateway. Also, each VPC has a limit of hosting a maximum of up to 200 subnets per VPC. You can increase these limit by simply requesting AWS to do so. To view the complete list of VC limits, refer to `http://docs.aws.amazon.com/AmazonVPC/latest/UserGuide/VPC_Appendix_Limits.html`.

Working with VPCs

Enough talk! It's time to get into some action! In this section, we are going to look at how AWS facilitates the easy deployment of VPCs using something called as the VPC wizard as well as how to create your very first, fully fledged and operational VPC! So, what are we waiting for? Let's get started!

VPC deployment scenarios

VPC provides a simple, easy-to-use wizard that can spin up a fully functional VPC within a couple of minutes. All you need to do is select a particular deployment scenario out of the four scenarios provided and configure a few basic parameters such as subnet information, availability zones in which you want to launch your subnets, and so on, and the rest is all taken care of by AWS itself.

Let's have a quick look at the four VPC deployment scenarios:

- **VPC with a single public subnet**: This is by far the simplest of the four deployment scenarios. Using this scenario, VPC will provision a single public subnet with a default Internet Gateway attached to it. The subnet will also have a few simple and basic route tables, security groups, and network ACLs created. This type of deployment is ideal for small-scaled web applications or simple websites that don't require any separate application or subnet tiers.

- **VPC with public and private subnets (NAT)**: Perhaps the most commonly used deployment scenario, this option will provide you with a public subnet and a private subnet as well. The public subnet will be connected to an Internet gateway and allow instances launched within it to have Internet connectivity, whereas the private subnet will not have any access to the outside world. This scenario will also provision a single NAT instance inside the public subnet using which your private subnet instances can connect with the outside world but not vice versa. Besides this, the wizard will also create and assign a route table to both the public and private subnets, each with the necessary routing information prefilled in them. This type of deployment is ideal for large-scale web applications and websites that leverage a mix of public facing (web servers) and non-public facing (database servers).

VPC with public and private subnets and hardware VPN access: This deployment scenario is very much similar to the VPC with public and private subnets, however, with one component added additionally, which is the Virtual Private Gateway. This Virtual Private Gateway connects to your on premise network's gateway using a standard VPN connection. This type of deployment is well suited for organizations that wish to extend their on premise datacenters and networks in to the public clouds while allowing their instances to communicate with the Internet.

- **VPC with a private subnet only and hardware VPN access**: Unlike the previous deployment scenario, this scenario only provides you with a private subnet that can connect to your on premise datacenters using standard VPN connections. There is no Internet Gateway provided and thus your instances remain isolated from the Internet. This deployment scenario is ideal for cases where you wish to extend your on premise datacenters into the public cloud but do not wish your instances to have any communication with the outside world.

With this understanding, let's go ahead and deploy our very first, fully functional VPC using the VPC wizard!

Getting started with the VPC wizard

Before we go ahead and deploy our VPC, let's first have a quick look at our use case. We need to create a secure website hosting environment for our friends at All-About-Dogs.com, complete with the following requirements:

- Create a VPC (US-WEST-PROD-1 - 192.168.0.0/16) with separate secure environments for hosting the web servers and database servers.
- Only the web servers environment (US-WEST-PROD-WEB - 192.168.1.0/24) should have direct Internet access.
- The database servers environment (US-WEST-PROD-DB - 192.168.5.0/24) should be isolated from any direct access from the outside world.
- The database servers can have restricted Internet access only through a jump server (*NAT Instance*). The jump server needs to be a part of the web server environment.
- The web servers environment should full have access to Amazon S3.

The following is what the proposed environment should look like:

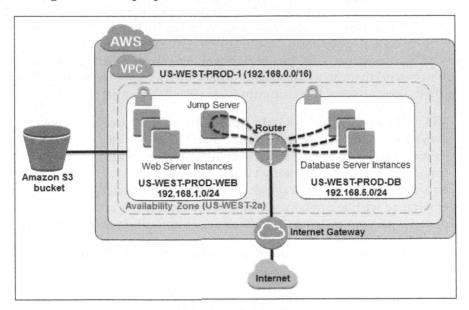

To get started with VPC, we first have to log in to the AWS Account using your IAM credentials. Next, from the **AWS Management Console**, select the **VPC** option from under the **Networking** group, as shown in the following screenshot:

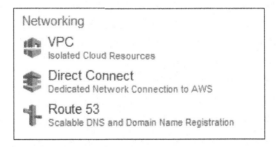

This will bring up the **VPC Dashboard** using which you can create, manage, and delete VPCs as per your requirements. The VPC dashboard lists the currently deployed VPCs, Subnets, Network ACLs, and much more under the **Resources** section.

You can additionally view and monitor the health of your VPC service by viewing the status provided by the **Service Health** dashboard, as shown in the following screenshot. In my case, I'm operating my VPC out of the US West (Oregon) region.

The **VPC Dashboard** also lists any existing VPN connections that you might have set up earlier. You can view the **VPN Connections, Customer Gateways** information as well as the **Current Status** of the VPN connection by using this dashboard. Remember that a VPN connection has a cost associated with it when it is provisioned and in the available state. You can additionally use this dashboard and even launch your instances directly into a VPC using the **Launch EC2 Instances** option. These instances will most probably be launched in your default VPC in case you haven't already created another one.

With all this said and done, let's go ahead and create our VPC using the VPC Wizard. Select the **Start VPC Wizard** option. The wizard is a simple two-step process that will guide you with the required configuration settings for your VPC. You will be prompted to select any one out of the four VPC scenarios, so with our use case in mind, go ahead and select the **VPC with Public and Private Subnets** option. Do note that this will create a /16 network with two /24 subnets by default, one public subnet and the other a private subnet. You can always create more subnets as required once the VPC is created.

Also worth mentioning here is that this VPC scenario will create and launch a NAT instance as well in the public subnet. This instance will be powered on automatically once your VPC is created, so be aware about its existence and power it down unless you want to get charged for it.

 This NAT instance launched by the wizard does not support the t2.micro instance type (*Free Tier eligibility*) during launch; however, you can always change this once your instance is launched from the EC2 Management dashboard.

The second step of the wizard is where you get to configure your VPC network and subnets. Fill in the following details as required:

- **IP CIDR block**: Provide the IP CIDR block address for your VPC's network. Ideally, provide a /16 subnet that will provide you with a good 65,531 IP addresses to use.

- **VPC name**: Provide a suitable name for your VPC. In this case, I have standardized and used the following naming convention: `<REGION>-<DEV/ PROD Environment>-<UNIQUE_ID>`; so in our case, this translates to `US-WEST-PROD-1`.

- **Public subnet**: Now, since we are going with a public and private subnet combination scenario, we have to fill in our public subnet details here. Provide a suitable subnet block for your instances to use. In this case, I have provided a **/24** subnet which provides a good 251 usable IP addresses:

```
Step 2: VPC with Public and Private Subnets

        IP CIDR block:*  [ 192.168.0.0/16    ]   (65531 IP addresses available)
          VPC name:  [ US-WEST-PROD-1   ]

       Public subnet:*  [ 192.168.1.0/24    ]   (251 IP addresses available)
    Availability Zone:*  [ us-west-2a   v ]
   Public subnet name:  [ US-WEST-PROD-WEB ]

       Private subnet:*  [ 192.168.5.0/24    ]   (251 IP addresses available)
    Availability Zone:*  [ us-west-2a   v ]
  Private subnet name:  [ US-WEST-PROD-DB  ]
                        You can add more subnets after AWS creates the VPC.
```

- **Availability Zone**: Here's the fun part! You can deploy your subnets in any availability zone available in that particular region. Now, US-WEST (Oregon) has three AZs and you can use any of those there. In my case, I have gone ahead and selected **us-west-2a** as the default option.

- **Public subnet name**: Provide a suitable public subnet reference name. Here, too, I have gone ahead and used the standard naming convention, so this particular subnet gets called as **US-WEST-PROD-WEB**, signifying the web server instances that will get deployed here.

- **Private subnet, Availability zone, Private subnet name**: Go ahead and fill out the private subnet's details using the similar IP addressing and naming conventions. Remember that although you can set up your private subnet in a different AZ, as compared to the public subnet, ideally doing that is not recommended. If you really want to set up a failover-like scenario, then create a separate public and private subnet environment in a different AZ altogether, for example, us-west-2c. So, even in case us-west-2a suffers an outage, which by the way can happen, your failover subnets will still be functioning out of the **us-west-2c** AZ. Refer to the following screenshot:

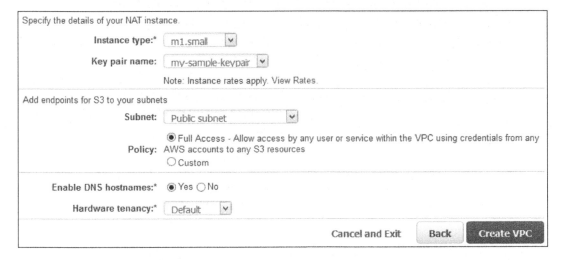

Next up, we specify the details of our NAT instance:

- **Instance type**: Select your NAT instance type from the available dropdown menu. In my case, I have gone ahead and selected the **t2.micro** instance type as that is the smallest type available. Do remember that selecting any other option will incur additional costs as only the t2.micro instance type is covered under the free tier eligibility.

- **Key pair name**: Select an already existing key pair from the dropdown list. Make sure you have this particular key pair stored safely on your local computer, as without it you will not be able to SSH into the NAT instance. You can alternatively create a new key pair here as well using the same EC2 Management Console.

Moving on, we now add the S3 endpoints to our particular subnet. You can add the endpoint to either your private or public subnets, or both of them, depending on your requirements.

- **Subnet**: As per our VPC's requirements, the S3 endpoint is only made available to the public subnet, so go ahead and select the **Public subnet** option from the dropdown list.

- **Policy**: You can either choose to allow any user or service within the newly created VPC to access your S3 or specify a custom IAM access policy as you see fit. In our case, let's go ahead and select **Full Access** for now.

- **Enable DNS hostnames**: Enabling this option will provide your instances with the ability to resolve their DNS hostnames on the Internet. Select the **Yes** option and continue.

- **Hardware tenancy**: Although a VPC runs off a completely isolated network environment, the underlying server hardware is still shared by default. You can change this tenancy option by selecting either the **default** or **dedicated** option from the dropdown list provided.

Pricing for a dedicated instance is slightly different than your traditional EC2 instances. Check out the complete pricing details for a dedicated EC2 instance at `http://aws.amazon.com/ec2/purchasing-options/dedicated-instances/`.

Once all the required information is filled out, go ahead and click on the **Create VPC** option. The VPC creation takes a few seconds to complete. You can even view your new VPC's default routes, security groups, and Network ACLs being created. Toward the end you will notice your NAT instance powering on, and after a few seconds of deployment your VPC is now ready for use!

Here's a handy tip for all first timers! As soon as your NAT instance is created, you can go ahead and change its default instance type to t1.micro from the **EC2 Management Dashboard**.

To do so, first open up the **EC2 Management Dashboard** in a new tab on your browser. You should see an instance in the running state, as shown in the following screenshot. First up, stop your instance using the **Actions** tab. Select the **Instance State** option and click on **Stop**. Wait for the instance state to change to **Stop** before you proceed any further. Next, select the instance, and from the **Actions** tab, select **Instance Settings** and then **Change Instance Type**.

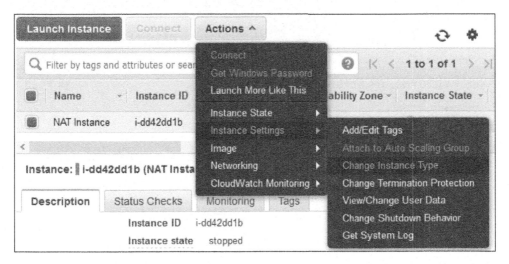

From the **Change Instance Type** dialog box, select the **t1.micro** option and click on **Apply**. Voila! Your NAT instance is now officially a part of your free tier as well! Simple, isn't it!

Let's have a quick look at what actually happens behind the scenes when you create a VPC using the VPC Wizard. First up, let's look at the VPC itself.

Viewing VPCs

Once the VPC is created and ready, you can view it from the **VPC Management Dashboard** as well. Simply select the **Your VPCs** option from the **Navigation pane** provided on the left-hand side of the dashboard.

You should see your newly created VPC, as shown in the following screenshot. You can use the search bar to filter out results as well. Select the particular VPC to view its details.

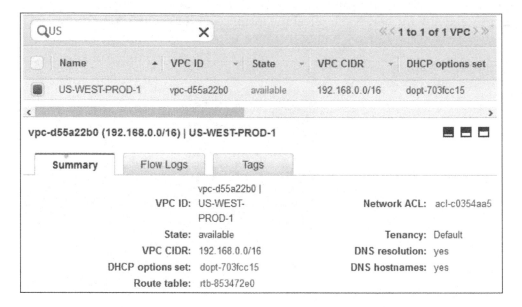

Use the **Summary** tab to view the description of your selected VPC. Here, you can view the VPC's default **DHCP options set** as well as the **Tenancy** and **DNS hostnames** and **DNS resolution** options. You can optionally change these values by selecting the particular VPC and from the **Actions** tab, selecting either **Edit DHCP Options Set** or **Edit DNS Hostnames**.

 You can view your default VPC using the **VPC Management Dashboard** as well. Simply check the default VPC column against your listed VPCs. If the value in that column is **Yes**, then that particular VPC is your account's default VPC!

You can create additional VPCs as well using the **Create VPC** option; however, as a good practice, always keep things simple and minimal. Don't go over creating VPCs. Rather use and create as many subnets as you require. Speaking of subnets, let's have a look at newly created VPC's two subnets!

Listing out subnets

You can view, add, and modify existing subnets using the **VPC Management Dashboard** as well. Simply select the **Subnets** option from the **Navigation Pane**. This will list out all the subnets present in your account, so use the search bar to filter out the new ones that we just created. Type in the name of the subnet in the Search bar until the particular subnet gets listed out, as shown in the following screenshot:

You can view additional information associated with your subnet by simply selecting it and viewing the **Summary** tab. The **Summary** tab will list out the particular subnet's associated **Route table**, **Network ACL**, **CIDR**, and **State** as well. Besides these values, you can also configure your subnet's ability to auto assign public IPs to its instances. By default, this feature is disabled in your subnet, but you can always enable it as per your requirements. To do so, simply select your **Public Subnet**, and from the **Subnet Actions** tab, select the option, as shown in the following screenshot:

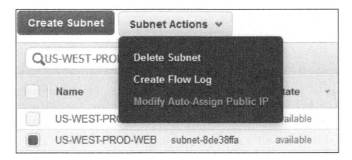

In the **Modify Auto-Assign Public IP** dialog box, simply select the **Enable auto-assign public IP** option and click on **Save** to complete the change setting. Do note that you can always override this behavior for each individual instance at its launch time.

Besides the **Summary** tab, the **Subnet Dashboard** option also provides additional tabs such as **Route Table**, **Network ACL,** and so on. You can use these tabs to view the subnet's associated route table as well the network ACL; however, you cannot add or modify the individual rules from here. To add or modify rules, you need to go to the **Network ACL** option or the **Route Tables** option from the **navigation pane**. Let's have a quick look at the route tables created for our VPC.

Working with route tables

As discussed earlier in this chapter, VPCs come with a default route table (*Main Route Table*) associated with a subnet. So, since we have two subnets created in this VPC, we get two route tables as well, out of which one is the main route table. How do you tell whether a route table is the main one? Quite simple, actually! Just look for the **Main Column** in the **Route Table Dashboard,** as shown in the following screenshot. If the value in that column is **Yes**, then that particular route table is your VPC's main route table. Now, here's a catch! If you do not explicitly associate a route table with a subnet, then the subnet ends up using the main route table. In our case, both the route tables created do not have any subnets associated with them by default, so let's first get that done.

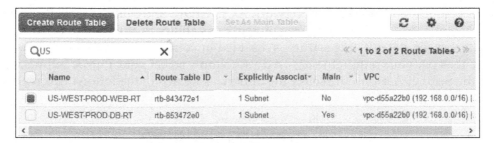

To associate a route table with a subnet explicitly, first you need to select the particular route table from the dashboard. In this case, I have selected the public subnet's router (**US-WEST-PROD-WEB-RT**). Next, from the **Subnet Associations** tab, click on the **Edit** button, as shown in the following screenshot. From here, you can select either of the two subnets that are listed down; however, since this is a public subnet's route table, let's go ahead and select the listed public subnet (**US-WEST-PROD-WEB**) as shown. Click on **Save** to save the configuration changes.

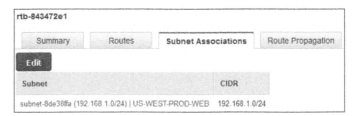

With this step completed, your subnet is now explicitly attached with a particular route table. But what about the individual route rules? How do we list and modify them? That's simple as well. Simply select the **Routes** tab to list your route table's existing rule set. Here, you should see at least three route rules, as shown in the following screenshot. The first rule is created by VPC for each and every route table, and it basically allows communication within the VPC itself. You cannot delete this rule, so don't even try it!

The next rule is basically a VPC endpoint route rule. Remember the S3 endpoint that we configured earlier with the public subnet? Well this rule will basically allow communication to occur between the instances belonging to this subnet and Amazon S3, and the best part is that this rule is auto-populated when you create a VPC endpoint!

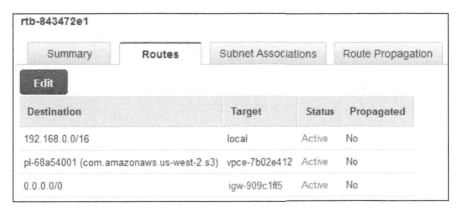

The final rule in the list basically allows for the instances to communicate over the Internet using the Internet Gateway as the target. You can optionally choose to edit these rules by selecting the **Edit** option. Once you have made your required changes, be sure to **Save** the configuration changes before you proceed with the next steps. Don't forget to associate the private subnet (**US-PROD-WEST-DB**) with the remaining route table (**US-WEST-PROD-DB-RT**) as well.

Listing Internet Gateways

As discussed earlier in this chapter, Internet Gateways are scalable and redundant virtual devices that provide Internet connectivity for your instances present in the VPC. You can list currently available Internet Gateways within your VPC by selecting the **Internet Gateways** option from the VPC's **navigation pane**.

The VPC wizard will create and attach one Internet Gateway to your VPC automatically; however, you can create and attach an Internet Gateway to a VPC at any time using the Internet Gateway. Simply click on the **Create Internet Gateway** option and provide the **VPC** to which this Internet Gateway has to be attached, that's it! You can list down available Internet Gateways and filter the results using the search bar provided as well. To view your Internet Gateway's details, simply select the particular Internet Gateway and click on the **Summary** tab. You should see your **Internet Gateway's ID**, **State** (**attached** or **detached**), as well as the **Attachment state** (**available** or **not available**), as shown in the following screenshot:

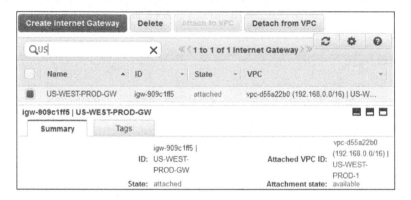

Also remember that to really use the Internet Gateway, your public subnet's route table must contain a route rule that directs all Internet-bound traffic from the subnet to the Internet Gateway.

 The Internet-bound route rule is auto-populated by the VPC Wizard when we first configured the VPC and can be viewed in the Public Subnet's route table.

Working with security groups and Network ACLs

The VPC is all about providing your applications a much more secure environment than what your traditional EC2 service can offer. This security is provided in two layers in the form of security groups and Network ACLs. The security groups can be used to set rules that can control both inbound and outbound traffic flow from the instance and hence work more at the instance level. The Network ACLs on the other hand operate at the subnet level, either allowing or disallowing certain type of traffic to flow in and out of your subnet. Important thing to remember here is that the Network ACLs are actually optional and can be avoided altogether if your security requirements are at a minimal. However, I would strongly recommend that you use both the security groups and Network ACLs for your VPC environments. As the saying goes - *better safe, than sorry!*

Coming back to your newly created VPC, the VPC wizard creates and populates a **default Security Group** and a **default Network ACL** option for you to use in an as-is condition. The default Security Group has a single inbound and outbound rule, as explained in the following:

Default inbound security rule			
Source	Protocol	Port Range	Remarks
Security_Group_ID	All	All	Permits inbound traffic from instances belonging to the same security group

Default Outbound Security Rule			
Destination	Protocol	Port Range	Remarks
0.0.0.0/0	All	All	Permits all outbound traffic from the instances

You can add, edit, and modify the rules in the default Security Group; however, you cannot delete it. As a good practice, it is always recommended that you do not use this default Security Group but rather create your own. So, let's go ahead and create three security groups: one for the web servers in the public subnet, one for the database servers in the private subnet, and one for the specially created NAT Instance.

To create a new Security Group using the VPC Dashboard, select the **Security Groups** option from the **navigation pane**. Next, from the **Security Groups dashboard**, select **Create Security Group**, as shown in the following screenshot:

Using the **Create Security Group** wizard, fill in the required information as described in the following:

- **Name tag**: A unique tag name for your Security Group.
- **Group name**: A suitable name for your Security Group. In this case, I have provided it as **US-WEST-PROD-WEB-SG**.
- **Description**: An optional description for your security group.

- **VPC**: Select the newly created VPC from the dropdown list, as shown in the following screenshot. Click on **Yes, Create** once done.

Once your Security Group has been created, select it from the **Security Groups dashboard** and click on the **Inbound Rules** tab. Click on the **Edit** option to add the following rule sets:

Web server inbound security rule			
Source	**Protocol**	**Port Range**	**Remarks**
0.0.0.0/0	TCP	22	Permit inbound SSH access to web server instance
0.0.0.0/0	TCP	80	Permit inbound HTTP access to web server instance
0.0.0.0/0	TCP	443	Permit inbound HTTPS access to web server instance

Similarly, click on the **Outbound Rules** tab and fill out the Security Group's outbound rules as described in the following:

Web server outbound security rule			
Destination	**Protocol**	**Port Range**	**Remarks**
DB_SECURITY_GROUP	TCP	1433	Permits outbound Microsoft SQL Server traffic to the database servers
DB_SECURITY_GROUP	TCP	3306	Permits outbound MySQL traffic to the database servers

Replace DB_SECURITY_GROUP with the Security Group ID of your database server's Security Group. Remember to save the rules by selecting the **Save** option, as shown in the following screenshot:

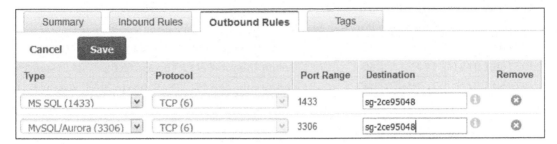

Similarly, let's go ahead and create a Security Group for our database servers as well. Populate the inbound rules as described in the following:

Database server inbound security rule			
Source	Protocol	Port Range	Remarks
WEB_SECURITY_GROUP	TCP	1433	Permits Web Server instances to access the Microsoft SQL Server
WEB_SECURITY_GROUP	TCP	3306	Permits Web Server instances to access the MySQL Server

Replace WEB_SECURITY_GROUP with the Security Group ID of your web server's Security Group ID and save the rules before you continue with the outbound rules additions:

Database server outbound security rule			
Source	Protocol	Port Range	Remarks
0.0.0.0/0	TCP	80	Permit outbound HTTP access to database server instance
0.0.0.0/0	TCP	443	Permit outbound HTTPS access to database server instance

Note that here we are permitting only the outbound Internet access to the database servers so that they can receive important patches and updates from the net. In reality, the Internet bound traffic from these servers will be routed through the NAT instance, which will forward the traffic to the Internet via your Internet Gateway.

Finally, go ahead and create the NAT instance's Security Group. Populate the inbound security rules as mentioned in the following:

NAT instance inbound security rule			
Source	Protocol	Port Range	Remarks
0.0.0.0/0	TCP	22	Permits inbound SSH access to the NAT Instance
192.168.1.0/24	TCP	80	Permit inbound HTTP access to the NAT instance
192.168.1.0/24	TCP	443	Permit inbound HTTPS access to NAT instance

NAT instance outbound security rule			
Source	Protocol	Port Range	Remarks
0.0.0.0/0	TCP	80	Permit outbound HTTP access to NAT instance
0.0.0.0/0	TCP	443	Permit outbound HTTPS access to NAT instance

With the security groups created, you are now ready to launch your instances into the VPC. Let's have a quick look at the steps required to do so!

Launching instances in your VPC

Once your VPC is ready and the security groups and Network ACLs have been modified as per requirement, you are now ready to launch instances within your VPC. You can either launch instances directly from the **VPC Management Dashboard** or from the **EC2 Management Console** as well. In this case, let's go ahead and use the EC2 Management Console.

Creating the web servers

From the **EC2 Management Console**, select the **Launch Instance** option. This will bring up the **Instance Wizard**, using which you can create and launch your web server instances. In my case, I'm using the AMI (**US-P-WebServer-Image-v1.0**) that we created earlier in *Chapter 4, Security, Storage, Networking, and Lots More!* Click on **My AMIs** and you should see the custom-created AMI listed there, as shown in the following screenshot. Select the AMI and continue with the instance creation process.

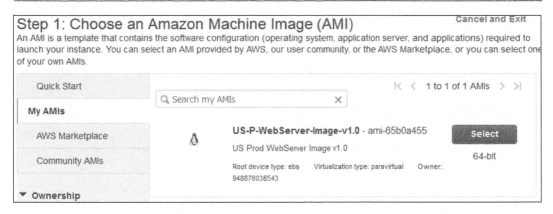

From the next page, select any instance type for the new web server instances. In my case, I went ahead and used the default **t1.micro** instance type.

Next, from the **Configure Instance Details** page, select the newly created VPC (**US-WEST-PROD-1**) from the **Network** dropdown list and provide the web server's public subnet (**US-WEST-PROD-WEB**), as shown in the following screenshot. You can optionally choose to change the **Auto-assign Public IP** setting; however, in this case, make sure that this setting is set to **Enable** otherwise your web server instances will not receive their public IPs.

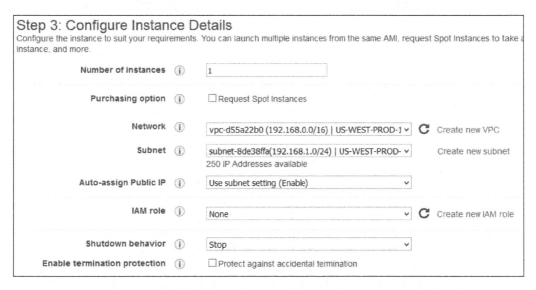

Add the required **Storage**, **Tag** the instance, and provide it with the web server **Security Group** that we created a while back. Once you have completed the formalities, review your instance's settings and finally launch it in your VPC!

Once the instance starts, verify whether it received both the private and the public IP or not. Log in to your web server instance and check whether it can reach the Internet or not by simply pinging to one of Google's DNS servers like 8.8.8.8. If all goes well, then your web server instances are all ready for production use!

Creating the database servers

The same process applies for the database servers as well. Simply remember to select the correct subnet (**US-WEST-PROD-DB**) for the database servers, as shown in the following screenshot:

Network ⓘ	vpc-d55a22b0 (192.168.0.0/16) | US-WEST-PROD-1 ⌄ C	Create new VPC
Subnet ⓘ	subnet-8ee38ff9(192.168.5.0/24) | US-WEST-PROD- ⌄	Create new subnet
	251 IP Addresses available	
Auto-assign Public IP ⓘ	Use subnet setting (Disable) ⌄	

Also note the **Auto-assign Public IP** setting for the database server's private subnet. By default, this should be disabled for the private subnet as we don't want our database instances to communicate with the Internet directly. All Internet-bound traffic from the database servers will pass via the NAT instance only. But how do you test whether your database servers are working correctly? By design, you cannot SSH into the database servers directly from your local desktops as the private subnet is isolated from the Internet. So, an alternative would be to set up something called as a **Bastion Host**. A Bastion Host is a special instance that acts as a proxy using which you can SSH into your database instances. This Bastion Host will be deployed in your public subnet and will basically only route SSH traffic from your local network over to the database server instances. But remember, this feature comes with its own set of security risks! Running a weak or poorly configured Bastion Host can prove to be harmful in production environments, so use them with care!

Planning next steps

Well we have covered a lot in this chapter, but there are a few things still that you can try out on your own with regards to VPCs. First up, is cleaning up a VPC! Creating a VPC is easy enough and so is its deletion. You can delete an unused VPC from the **VPC Management dashboard** by simply selecting the **VPC**, clicking on the **Actions** tab, and selecting the **Delete VPC** option. This will bring up the **Delete VPC** dialog as shown in the following screenshot:

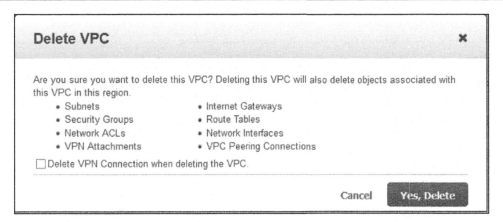

As you can see, the delete VPC option will delete all aspects of your VPC, including subnets, Network ACLs, Internet Gateways, and so on. You can optionally even delete any VPN connections as well by selecting the **Delete VPN Connections when deleting the VPC** checkbox. Remember that once you delete a VPC, you can't recover it back, so make sure that you don't have any active instances running on it before you go ahead and delete it. Also remember to clean up on the instances as well, especially the NAT Instance and the Bastion Host if you have created them.

The second thing that I would recommend trying out is called as **VPC peering**. VPC peering is nothing more than network connections between two different VPCs. Instances in one VPC communicate with instances present in another VPC using their private IP addresses alone, so there is no need to route the traffic over the Internet as well. You can connect your VPC with a different VPC that is either owned by you or by someone else's **Bastion Host**. All it needs is a request to be generated from the source VPC and sent to the destination VPC, along with a few route rules that will allow the traffic to flow from one point to the other. The following is the image describing the VPC peering:

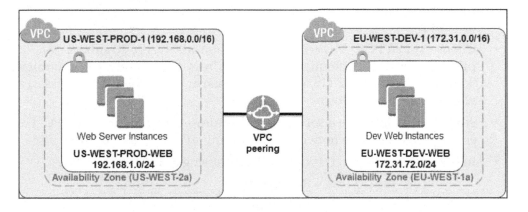

You can read more about VPC peering at `http://docs.aws.amazon.com/AmazonVPC/latest/UserGuide/vpc-peering.html`.

The third thing that really is worth testing out is the hardware VPN connectivity with your VPC. I know you are probably thinking that since it's a hardware VPN connectivity, it means that I need some special hardware equipment like a router and so on. Well that's not quite true! You can set up an easy VPN connection using software as well, for example, OpenVPN. OpenVPN basically allows you to create a secure network connection from your local network to Amazon VPC using a VPN connection.

All you need to do is deploy an OpenVPN server in your VPC and configure that to accept incoming traffic from your private network. Then, install an OpenVPN client on your remote desktop and try connecting to the OpenVPN server placed in the VPC. If all goes well, you should have access to your VPC instances from your local desktop! Do note that you will have to open up additional security rules and network ACLs to allow this type of traffic to flow through your VPC subnet.

Last but not least, I would also recommend for you to have a look at VPC's Flow Logs. This is a simple logging feature provided in VPC to capture traffic information and store it using Amazon CloudWatch Logs. Flow Logs can help you analyze your network traffic flow for bottlenecks, observe certain traffic trends, as well as monitor traffic that reaches your instances. You can read more about Flow Logs at `http://docs.aws.amazon.com/AmazonVPC/latest/UserGuide/flow-logs.html`.

Best practices and recommendations

The following are some key best practices and recommendations to keep in mind when using VPCs:

- Plan and design your VPC before actually implementing one. Determine the right choice of subnet that your application will need and build your VPC around it.

- Choose your VPC's network block allocation wisely. A /16 subnet can provide you with a potential 65,534 IP addresses that rarely will get utilized. So ideally, go for a /18 (16,382 IP addresses) or a /20 (4094 IP addresses) as your VPC network choice.

- Always plan and have a set of spare IP address capacity for your VPC. For example, consider the network block for my VPC as 192.168.0.0/18.

- In this case, we design the subnet IP addressing as follows:
  ○ `192.168.32.0/19` Public Subnet
  ○ `192.168.64.0/19` Public Subnet spares

- ° `192.168.128.0/20` Private Subnet
- ° `192.168.192.0/20` Private Subnet spares

- Remember that you cannot edit a network block's size once it is created for a VPC. The only way to change the network block is by deleting this VPC and creating a new one in its place.

- Use different security groups to secure and manage traffic flows from your instances. For example, a separate Security Group for web servers and a different one for your database servers. Avoid using the default security groups at all times.

- Leverage multiple AZs to distribute your subnets across geographies. For example, the US-WEST region has three AZs, namely us-west-2a, us-west-2b, and us-west-2c. So an ideal situation would have you divide your VPC's network block and create subnets in each of these AZs evenly. The more AZs, the better the fault tolerance for your VPC.

- Leverage IAM to secure your VPC at the user level as well. Create dedicated users with restricted access to your VPC and its resources.

- Create and stick with a standard naming convention so that your VPC's resources can be easily identified and tagged. For example, in our scenarios, we named the VPC as US-WEST-PROD-1, which clearly identifies this particular VPC to be hosted in the US-WEST region and to be a PRODUCTION environment.

Summary

So it's been a pretty long and intense chapter so far with lots to learn and try out! Let's have a quick recap of the things covered!

Well we started off with a brief overview of VPCs and its components and terminologies such as subnets, route tables, Network ACLs, Internet Gateways, and much more. Next we had an in-depth look at some of the VPC deployment scenarios and even went ahead and created our first VPC using the VPC wizard. Toward the end, we looked at some key considerations to keep in mind when dealing with security groups and NAT instances and finally topped it all off with some handy best practices and recommendations!

6
Monitoring Your AWS Infrastructure

In the previous chapter, we covered a whole lot about Amazon VPC: its features, components, and architecture. We also looked at how you can create and deploy your own fully functional VPC using just a few simple steps!

In this chapter, we will focus primarily on how to monitor your cloud infrastructure, especially your EC2 instances using AWS's monitoring service called as **Amazon CloudWatch**. CloudWatch is a cheap and easy-to-use centralized monitoring service that provides a variety of features such as alerts, logging, notifications, custom metrics, and much more! So, what are we waiting for? Let's get started right away!

An overview of Amazon CloudWatch

Before we move on to Amazon CloudWatch, it is important to understand the difference in a traditional monitoring solution and a monitoring solution based on the clouds. Unlike your traditional environments, infrastructure in the cloud can scale up and down dynamically in a matter of minutes. Most traditional server monitoring tools cannot match up to this elastic requirement in real time and thus often end up either providing the wrong information or triggering a delayed response. There is also the problem of sheer numbers! A standalone monitoring tool can find it difficult to handle the monitoring of thousands of virtual machines at a single go. Plus, you as sysadmins also need to manage the monitoring tool, which adds an extra overhead as well. That's where a cloud-based monitoring solution is so different. A standard cloud-based monitoring tool provides the following feature sets:

- Ease of use and management: Most of the cloud-based monitoring tools come with easy integration and management facilities, using which you can start monitoring your cloud infrastructure in minutes.

- Dynamically track instances as they are created, add them to the monitoring inventory, and remove them from the inventory when they are deleted.

- Trigger real-time events and notifications based on preset alarms.

- Monitor the instance's operating system, networking, CPU, and disk utilizations, as well as its applications which can be web servers, databases, application servers, and so on.

- Perform/trigger actions based on certain thresholds getting crossed.

These are just some of the key features that are provided by Amazon CloudWatch as well, and you don't have to install or configure it. It's available as a ready-to-use service and you only pay for the amount of service that you use! Awesome, isn't it! Let's have a quick look at Amazon Cloud Watch's overall architecture as well as some of its key components and concepts.

Concepts and terminologies

Before we go ahead and start using CloudWatch, it is essential to understand some of its key concepts and terminologies.

Metrics

Metrics form the core of Amazon CloudWatch's functionality. Essentially, these are nothing more than certain values to be monitored. Each metric has some data points associated with it which tend to change as time progresses. For example, the CPU usage of any one of your instances is a metric and the values of the CPU usage over a period of time are its associated data points! Each data point has an associated timestamp provided with it along with a unit of measure.

There are a ton of metrics that AWS provides that can be used in as-is scenarios; however, you can additionally create custom metrics as well, as per your requirements. An important point to remember here is that a metric is region specific, which means that a metric is only going to be available in the region in which it was created. A metric is uniquely identified by a name, a namespace, or a set of dimension.

Namespaces

Namespaces are a standard string of characters that you define when you first create a metric. These namespaces act as containers for your metrics and help in keeping them isolated from one another. There is no default namespace provided as such, so you will have to create one for each element that gets added to CloudWatch. By default, all AWS namespaces follow the following naming convention: `AWS/<SERVICE_NAME>` where `<SERVICE_NAME>` can be EC2, RDS, S3, and so on. For a full list of AWS namespaces, refer to `http://docs.aws.amazon.com/AmazonCloudWatch/latest/DeveloperGuide/aws-namespaces.html`.

Dimensions

Dimensions are simple key-value pairs that help you identify your metrics. These come in real handy when you need to filter out certain result sets which a CloudWatch query returns. You can assign up to 10 dimensions to a single metric. For example, consider the following combination of dimensions:

- Server=WEB, Domain=US-WEST
- Server=DB, Domain=US-WEST
- Server=NAT, Domain=US-WEST

You can easily retrieve statistics based on these dimension combinations; however, it is important to note that you will not be able to retrieve any statistics for the combinations that you did not create. For example, just querying **Server=NAT** or **Domain=US-WEST** or even **Server=NAT, Domain=Null** will not give you any results as the corresponding metrics were never created.

Time stamps and periods

Time stamps are assigned to each of your metric's data points. These are simple date and time values that are generally provided using the UTC or GMT time zones. The time stamp **2015-09-12T20:45:30Z** translates to the September 9, 2015 at 8:45:30 PM as per the UTC time zone. If no time stamp value is provided, then CloudWatch will automatically assign that data point one based on its time of arrival or generation.

Periods are the length of time associated with a particular statistic. To put it in simple words, a period is the time between a start time and the end time. You can specify a period as short as 60 seconds and all the way up to 86,400 seconds, which accounts for a complete day. Periods play a crucial role in the creation of alarms. An alarm is generally meant to be triggered when a certain threshold value is crossed, right? Now in many cases, you will receive false alarms even if these threshold values are crossed for a few seconds. That's just going to flood your mailbox with unwanted notifications! So ideally, we specify the alarms with a threshold and a time period, say 20 seconds. So, if the threshold is breached for more than 20 seconds, only then will CloudWatch raise the alarm. This way you have a more granular control over when your alarms get triggered.

Units and statistics

Units help you get conceptual meaning of your metric data. Specifically, these are very similar to units of measure, for example, the metric *NetworkIn* that is used to track the number of bytes an instance receives will have a measuring unit of bytes (for example, 300 Bytes). Similarly, the metric *CPUUtilization* which is used to track your instance's CPU utilization will have a measuring unit of Percent (for example, 20% CPU utilization) and so on so forth. Here are some of the units that you will commonly come across when working with CloudWatch:

- Count
- Bytes, Kilobytes, Megabytes, Gigabytes, Terabytes
- Bytes/Second, Kilobytes/Second, Megabytes/Second, Gigabytes/Second, Terabytes/Second
- Percent
- Milliseconds, Microseconds, Seconds

 If you do not specify a unit for a metric, then CloudWatch will auto-assign it with the None unit.

Statistics are metric data that has been aggregated over a period of time. There are five statistics provided by CloudWatch, as described in the following:

Statistic Name	Statistic Description
Minimum	This specifies the lowest data value observed during a specific period of time. This statistic is useful in determining the lowest points of activity for your application.

Statistic Name	Statistic Description
Maximum	This specifies the highest data value observed during a specific period of time. This statistic is useful in determining the highest points of activity for your application.
Sum	This statistic adds each of the metric data points together for the supplied period of time and is helpful in determining the total volume of a metric.
Average	The average is indicated by Sum divided by the sample count. The average statistic comes in handy when you want to scale your resources especially your EC2 instances.
SampleCount	This statistic provides the actual number of data points present in the sample during the supplied period of time. It is useful in cases of statistical calculations.

For a better understanding, the following is simple example depicting a few raw metric data points collected over a period of time and their statistics:

Raw Metric Data Points	Sum	Minimum	Maximum	Average	SampleCount
120,130,50,160,185	645	50	185	129	5
15,25,100,210,15,235	600	15	235	100	6

Alarms

An alarm basically watches over a particular metric for a stipulated period of time and performs some actions based on its trigger. These actions can be anything from sending a notification to the concerned user using the **Simple Notification Service (SNS)** or something a bit more complicated such as triggering and auto-scaling an event. However, do remember that you can create and associate alarms to any AWS resource provided that they reside in the same region.

Tying it all together, the following is what a CloudWatch alarm basically looks like:

- Namespace=AWS/EC2
- Metric name=CPUUtilization (Percent)
- Period=5minutes
- Statistics: Average
- Threshold: 70
- Dimensions (Name=Web Server, Value="i-dd42dd1b")
- Alarm action: <EMAIL_ID>

So, we get to know a lot about this alarm just by looking at it. First off, we can tell that this alarm is going to monitor the CPU utilization of one of our specified instances using its instance ID. Secondly, we can also tell that the alarm will monitor the average CPU utilization of the instance. If the CPU utilization breaches the threshold value of 70 percent for a period of 5 minutes, then the alarm will automatically trigger an e-mail notification based on the e-mail ID that you specify. Simple, isn't it! The following is what the preceding example looks like schematically:

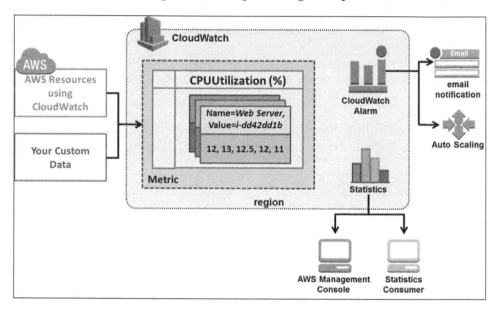

We will be learning a lot more about alarms later on in this chapter and will even go ahead and create a few for our environment, but for now, let us have a quick look at CloudWatch's limits and associated costs.

CloudWatch limits and costs

CloudWatch, by default, monitors all of your instances, volumes, and **Elastic Load Balancers** (**ELB**) at a regular five-minute interval for absolutely no charge at all. This is CloudWatch's default behavior; however, you can always change the interval to as low as a minute if you need it. Changing the interval to a minute will cost you approximately $3.50 per instance per month. Besides this, CloudWatch also provides 10 metrics, 10 alarms, a thousand e-mail notifications using SNS, and up to a million API requests each month for no charge at all! Additional metrics and alarms are charged approximately $0.50 and $0.10, respectively, on a monthly basis. CloudWatch also provides you with free 5 GB of incoming data and 5 GB of data archiving.

From a limits point of view, here are a few important limits that you need to keep in mind when working with CloudWatch:

- CloudWatch preserves metric data for up to 2 weeks, after which it is deleted
- The maximum period value that you can specify is 1 day or 86,400 seconds
- You can create up to 5,000 alarms per AWS account, with each alarm supporting up to five actions

Keeping these things in mind, let's go ahead and create our very first alarm with CloudWatch!

Getting started with CloudWatch

In this section, we are going to carry out two tasks. First up, we will check out some simple steps, using which you will be able to create your very first billing alarm, followed by creating a few simple alarms for an instance using both the AWS Management Console as well as the AWS CLI. So, without further ado let's get started on some CloudWatch!

Monitoring your account's estimate charges using CloudWatch

CloudWatch provides a really simple alarm setup using which you as an end user can monitor your account's estimated costs and usage. To work with this, you need to log in to your AWS account as the root user and not as an IAM user, even if you are the administrator. I know I'm not following my own rules here by using the root user, but hey, that's what AWS says! Log in to your AWS account using your root credentials. Once logged in, select the **Billing & Cost Management** option highlighted under your account's name, as shown in the following screenshot:

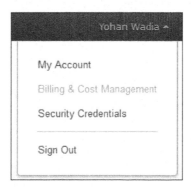

This will pop up your account's management dashboard, using which you can view your account's **Bills**, set new **Payment Methods**, view past **Payment History**, and so on so forth. For now, select the **Preferences** option from the navigation page to bring up the Preferences dashboard, as shown in the following screenshot:

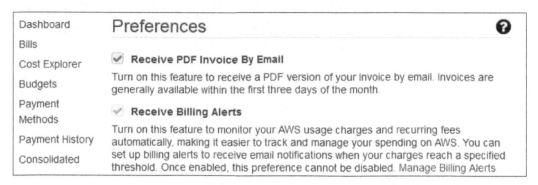

Select the **Receive Billing Alerts** checkbox to enable monitoring of your account's usage. It's important to, however, note that once you enable this checkbox, there is no going back! You will not be able to uncheck this option afterward!

Click on the **Save Preferences** option to save your new settings and then select the **Manage Billing Alerts** link to bring up CloudWatch's **Create Alarm** wizard, as shown in the following screenshot. This option is available from the CloudWatch dashboard to billing in the N. Virginia region.

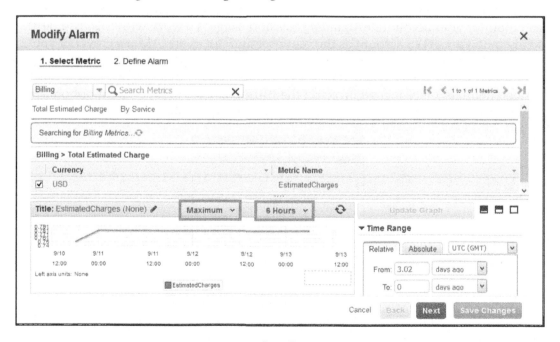

The wizard will walk you through some simple steps to configure your first billing alarm. Select the checkbox adjoining to the **EstimatedCharges** option and click on **Next** to continue with the process. You can optionally change the statistic and period; however, I have gone ahead with the default values which is **Maximum** and **6 Hours** respectively.

 AWS does not allow the billing alarm's period to be set less than 6 hours.

Moving on to the final step of your **Create Alarm** wizard, provide a suitable **Name** and **Description** for your billing alarm, as shown in the following screenshot. Next, configure the threshold for your alarm by selecting the **>=** (greater than or equal to) option and providing a threshold monetary amount such as $2 or $200, whichever is applicable to you. You can even set the threshold to $0.01, which will notify you the moment you start going out of the free tier eligibility. In either case, the alarm will only trigger when the actual cost of usage exceeds the monetary threshold that you have set. You can verify the setting by looking at the **Alarm Preview graph** as well. The red line indicates the threshold value set by you, whereas the blue highlighted portion is your account's current estimate bill:

With the **Alarm's threshold set**, the final thing that you need to do is define what action the alarm must take when it is triggered. From the **Notification** section, fill out the required details, as mentioned in the following:

- **Whenever this alarm**: This option will allow you to determine when the alarm will actually perform an action. There are three states of an alarm out of which you can select any one at a single time:
    - **State is ALARM**: Triggered when the metric data breaches the threshold value set by you

- **State is OK**: Triggered when the metric data is well within the supplied threshold value

- **State is INSUFFICIENT**: Triggered when the alarm generally doesn't have enough data with itself to accurately determine the alarm's state.

For this scenario, I have selected the **State is ALARM** option as I want to get notified as soon as my threshold limit is breached.

- **Send notification to**: As discussed earlier, CloudWatch leverages Amazon SNS to send notifications to a particular set of users and e-mail IDs. Since this is our first SNS topic, go ahead and select the **New List** option, as shown in the following screenshot. Provide a suitable SNS topic name against the send notification to option and a valid e-mail address in the **Email list** field, as shown in the following screenshot:

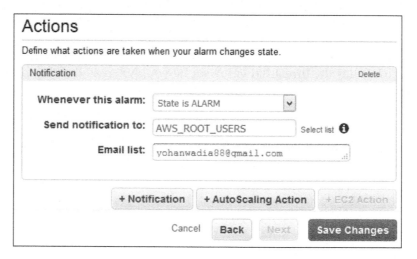

You can add multiple e-mail IDs in the **Email list** field by separating them with commas. Once done, click on **Save Changes** to complete the alarm's creation process.

The alarm will take a few seconds to change from the **INSUFFICIENT** state to **OK,** as shown in the following screenshot. This is normal behavior as the alarm generally takes a few seconds to gather the metric data and verify it against the set threshold value.

You can view additional details about your newly created alarm by simply selecting it and checking out the **Details** and **History** tab provided in the following:

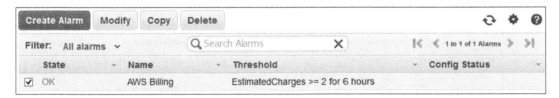

Oh! And one very important thing I almost forgot to mention! There is a catch to creating alarms, specifically billing ones, using CloudWatch. Don't worry, it's nothing serious! It's just that by design, the billing metric data of your entire account, which includes all your regions and AWS services, is collected and stored only in the US East (N. Virginia) region. So if you want to create or update this billing alarm at a later stage, you will have to change your default operating region to US East (N. Virginia) and then view and edit the billing alarm as required. You can, however, create EC2, ELB, RDS, and other AWS services related alarms from any particular region that you are operating from.

Monitoring your instance's CPU Utilization using CloudWatch

With the billing alarm created, let's try out something even more exciting! In this section, we will be creating a simple alarm to monitor an instance's CPU utilization. If the CPU utilization breaches a certain threshold, say 75 percent, then the alarm will trigger an e-mail notification as well as perform an additional task such as stop the instance.

To begin with, AWS makes creating alarms a really simple and straightforward process. The easiest way to do this is by selecting your individual instances from the **EC2 Management Dashboard** and selecting the **Monitoring** tab, as shown in the following screenshot. Each instance is monitored on a five-minute interval by default. You can modify this behavior and set the time interval as low as one minute by selecting the **Enable Detailed Monitoring** option.

 Enabling detailed monitoring for you instance will incur additional costs.

Each instance, by default, gets its own set of performance graphs as well, which can be viewed in the **Monitoring** tab. These graphs generally include and display important metric information such as CPU utilization, disk Read/Writes, bytes transferred in terms of network IO, and so on. You can expand on each of the graphs by simply selecting them. This gives you a much better and detailed view of your instance's performance, as shown in the following image:

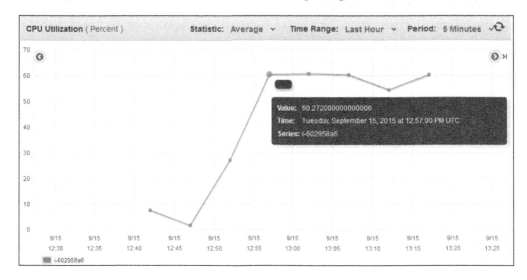

This is an example of an enhanced graph view of the CPU utilization metric. The x axis displays the CPU utilization in percent whereas the y axis display the time as per the current period's settings. You can view the individual data points and their associated values by simply hovering over them on the graph. Alternatively, you can also switch between the **Statistics**, **Time Range,** and **Period** as per your requirements. Once you have viewed your instance's performances, you can create a simple alarm by selecting the **Create Alarm** option provided in the **Monitoring** tab. This method is great if you want to set alarms for your instances on an individual basis, alternatively you can use the CloudWatch dashboard as well.

To view the CloudWatch Dashboard, from the AWS Management Console's home page, select the **CloudWatch** option, as shown in the following screenshot:

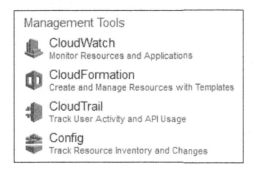

This will bring up the CloudWatch dashboard for the particular region in which you are currently operating. The dashboard is divided into two sections, a navigation pane to the left that groups and lists out your alarms based on their current state, for example, **ALARM, OK,** or **INSUFFICIENT**. It also provides access to the CloudWatch **Logs** and **Metrics,** as shown in the following screenshot:

Let's go ahead and check out the steps required to create our very first instance-based alarm. To get started, select the **Create Alarm** option. This will bring up the **Create Alarm** wizard, as shown in the following screenshot. The wizard is a simple two-step process that will help you with the necessary steps required to create your alarm.

First up, we need to select the correct metric that needs to be monitored. You can use the **Browse Metrics** or the search bar to filter out the particular metric, which in this case is **CPU Utilization**.

Next, select the particular instance for which you want to set this alarm. You can select multiple instances here as well. Selecting the instance will view its CPU utilization graph which you can modify using the statistics (**Average**) as well as the period (5 **Minutes**) dropdown lists. For now, click on **Next** to continue with the wizard.

The second step of the wizard is where you actually define the alarm, including its threshold value, as well as what actions have to be performed in case the alarm is triggered. For starters, provide a suitable **Name** and **Description** for your alarm. In this case, I provided the alarm with a name **US-WEST-PROD-WEBSERVER-CPU** — now that's pretty self-explanatory!

Moving on, the next part of your alarm's configuration is the threshold setting. As per our scenario, this alarm has to be triggered when the CPU utilization of the instance breaches 75 percent. Select the **>=** (greater than equal to) option from the **is** dropdown list and provide the value 75 in its adjoining textbox, as shown in the following screenshot. You can check your alarm's threshold settings in the **Alarm Preview** box.

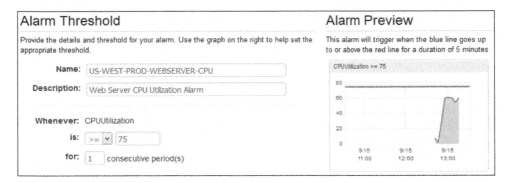

With the threshold value set, the final thing to do is create the actions that will get triggered when the alarm is raised. There are three basic action items that you can create for each of your EC2 alarms described as follows:

- **Notification**: This option will generate a simple e-mail-based notification using the Amazon SNS service.

- **AutoScaling Action**: This option is useful when we want to trigger an auto-scaling event. We will be looking at AutoScaling a bit more in detail in the coming chapter.

- **EC2 Action**: This option allows you perform a set of EC2 related actions on your instance. These actions can stop, terminate, reboot, or even recover an instance.

For this particular scenario, we need to generate an e-mail-based notification when the alarm is raised and perform an EC2 action on the instance as well. Let's first create the notification action.

In the **Notification** section, select the option **State is ALARM** from the **Whenever this alarm** dropdown list. Next, click on the **new list** option to create a new SNS topic. Provide a suitable **SNS Topic name** is the **Send notification to** text field along with a list of comma separated e-mail addresses in the **Email list,** as shown in the following screenshot:

When the alarm is triggered, you will start receiving e-mails on the supplied e-mail list stating the nature of the alarm as well as the instance's metric data points at that particular time. You will receive these mails as long as the threshold value is breached or until the alarm state changes back to **OK**.

To add an additional EC2 action to this alarm, simply click on the **+EC2 Action** option. Follow the same process of setting the alarm's trigger state by selecting the **State is ALARM** option, as shown in the following screenshot. Next, select the particular EC2 action that you want to perform on this alarm's breach. In this case, I have opted for the instance to be stopped by selecting the **Stop this instance** option. Do remember that stopping an instance is only possible when your instances are backed by EBS volumes!

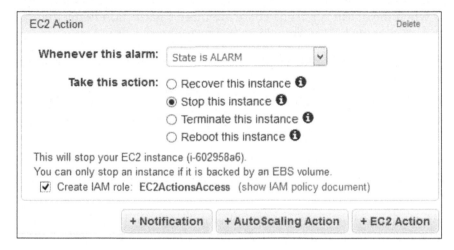

Now, here's something new for you. You will need to assign an IAM Role that will basically allow AWS to perform the EC2 actions on your instance. The alarm will auto-create an `EC2ActionsAllow` IAM Role for your convenience. The following is the code sample of the IAM Role for your reference. You can optionally create and assign your own IAM Roles as well use the **IAM Management Dashboard** (*Chapter 2, Security and Access Management*); however, this basic role should suffice for the time:

```
{
  "Version": "2012-10-17",
  "Statement": [
    {
      "Effect": "Allow",
      "Action": [
        "cloudwatch:Describe*",
        "ec2:Describe*",
        "ec2:RebootInstances",
```

```
        "ec2:StopInstances",
        "ec2:TerminateInstances"
      ],
      "Resource": "*"
    }
  ]
}
```

Select the **Create IAM Role** checkbox and verify the newly created IAM role. You can optionally even create additional action items that can get triggered when the alarm's threshold value changes to **OK**. Simply select the **+Notification** option and provide the details, as shown in the following screenshot. Remember, you can only create up to five actions for each alarm, so use them wisely!

Click on **Create Alarm** to complete the alarm's creation process. You can test your alarm's functionality by generating CPU load on your instance using a variety of tools such as Stress (`http://people.seas.harvard.edu/~apw/stress/`), Lookbusy (`https://www.devin.com/lookbusy/`), an so on. I personally use Lookbusy to generate artificial loads on my instances as it's pretty straightforward and easy to use. Do remember that these tools should only be used for testing and in no way are these tools recommended to be deployed on production workloads or instances. With this basic alarm created and tested, go ahead and create similar alarms for monitoring your instances disk as well as network utilization and performance!

Monitoring your instance's memory and disk utilization using CloudWatch Scripts

Although CloudWatch does an excellent job at monitoring your instance's performance and status, it still has a few short comings to it. For starters, CloudWatch monitors your instance's CPU utilization, but cannot measure its load. Similarly, it can monitor the instance's memory size or a disk's IO performance, but cannot tell you the exact memory usage or the disk usage of a particular partition or layout. Why not? Well, simply because CloudWatch gets its monitoring metrics directly from the Xen hypervisors which host your instances. As a result, you don't get to see the performance and utilization of your instances at a very granular level. Luckily, CloudWatch is designed to accept metric values from other sources as well as from the hypervisor. These metrics are called as **Custom Metrics** and can be pushed into CloudWatch using a variety of ways. In this section, we are going to send custom metrics to CloudWatch using a set of simple Perl scripts provided by CloudWatch itself. These scripts have to be installed in your instance and are designed to send metric data periodically to CloudWatch. But before you begin, let's go through a few necessary prerequisite steps as follows.

Creating CloudWatch access roles

Just as with the alarm actions, the instances need to be provided with a special set of permissions to write to CloudWatch. There are two ways to go about this. The first method is to copy your secret and access keys to your instance, which let's face it is not the best of options! The second method is to create a role using IAM and assign your instances that role during their launch. The role will provide the instance with the necessary access rights to CloudWatch without having to expose any of your keys.

So, let's go ahead and create a simple access role for our instance using the **IAM Management Dashboard**.

From the **IAM Management Dashboard**, select **Roles** from the **navigation pane**. Next, select the option **Create New Role**. Provide a suitable **Role Name** for your new role and select **Next Step** to continue with the process:

Set Role Name

Enter a role name. You cannot edit the role name after the role is created.

Role Name   CloudWatch_FullAccess

Maximum 64 characters. Use alphanumeric and '+=,.@-_' characters

Cancel   Next Step

Next up, from the **Select Role Type** page, select the **Amazon EC2** option. This will bring up the **Attach Policy** page, as shown in the following screenshot. Using the **Filter**, search and select the **CloudWatchFulllAccess** policy as shown. You can alternatively create your very own custom CloudWatch access policy and attach that to your role if you want or use this default policy, which is the easier of the two. Click on **Next Step** to proceed with the wizard.

Review your role's information and finally select the **Create Role** option to complete the process.

Once your role is defined, go ahead and launch a new instance using the EC2 Management dashboard. Remember to assign this new role to your instance using the **IAM role** dropdown list, as shown in the following screenshot :

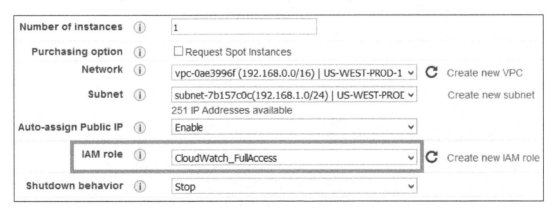

 A role is only assigned to an instance during its launch phase. You cannot assign roles to instances that are already running. To know more about IAM roles, refer to http://docs.aws.amazon.com/IAM/latest/UserGuide/id_roles.html.

With your instance launched, SSH into it using any of the options discussed in *Chapter 3*, *Images and Instances*. You are now ready to go ahead and install the necessary CloudWatch scripts!

Installing the CloudWatch monitoring scripts

Installing the CloudWatch scripts is a fairly straightforward process. The Perl scripts report an instance's memory, swap, and disk utilization metrics to CloudWatch. You can run these scripts off any Linux operating system, including the Amazon Linux AMI as well.

Run the following command in your instance's terminal to install and configure certain pre-requisite software:

```
# sudo yum install perl-DateTime perl-Sys-Syslog perl-LWP-Protocol-https
```

Once completed, download the latest copy of the CloudWatch monitoring scripts using the following command:

```
# wget http://aws-cloudwatch.s3.amazonaws.com/downloads/
CloudWatchMonitoringScripts-1.2.1.zip
```

 The current version of the CloudWatch monitoring scripts is 1.2.1.

Next, unzip the contents of the downloaded Zip file using the following command:

```
# unzip CloudWatchMonitoringScripts-1.2.1.zip
```
```
# cd aws-scripts-mon
```

The output of the preceding commands is as follows:

```
[ec2-user@ip-192-168-1-116 ~]$
[ec2-user@ip-192-168-1-116 ~]$ cd aws-scripts-mon/
[ec2-user@ip-192-168-1-116 aws-scripts-mon]$
[ec2-user@ip-192-168-1-116 aws-scripts-mon]$ ll
total 96
-rw-r--r-- 1 ec2-user ec2-user    30 Mar  6 2015 awscreds.template
-r--r--r-- 1 ec2-user ec2-user 17021 Mar  6 2015 AwsSignatureV4.pm
-r--r--r-- 1 ec2-user ec2-user 22487 Mar  6 2015 CloudWatchClient.pm
-rw-r--r-- 1 ec2-user ec2-user  9124 Mar  6 2015 LICENSE.txt
-rwxr-xr-x 1 ec2-user ec2-user  9739 Mar  6 2015 mon-get-instance-stats.pl
-rwxr-xr-x 1 ec2-user ec2-user 18144 Mar  6 2015 mon-put-instance-data.pl
-rw-r--r-- 1 ec2-user ec2-user   138 Mar  6 2015 NOTICE.txt
[ec2-user@ip-192-168-1-116 aws-scripts-mon]$
```

The following are some of the important files that the CloudWatch monitoring script ZIP contains:

- `CloudWatchClient.pm`: This is a shared Perl module file that is used to make remote procedure calls to Amazon CloudWatch from other scripts.
- `mon-put-instance-data.pl`: This Perl script is responsible for collecting your instance's metrics (memory, swap, disk space utilization) and sending them to Amazon CloudWatch for processing.
- `mon-get-instance-stats.pl`: This Perl script is used to query CloudWatch and display the most recent utilization statistics for the EC2 instance on which this script is executed.
- `awscreds.template`: This file is used to store your AWS Secret and Access Keys. We will not be requiring this file as we have opted to use an IAM Role instead.

With this basic understanding in mind, let's use the `mon-put-instance-data.pl` script to view the instance's memory utilization (`mem-util`). Run the following command as shown here:

```
# ./mon-put-instance-data.pl --mem-util --verify --verbose
```

Note that this command will not publish any metrics to CloudWatch because of the `--verify` attribute. Instead, it will only output the instance's memory utilization on the terminal, as shown in the following:

The script will initially search for the presence of the secret and access keys in the `awscreds.template` file. Since we have not provided the keys explicitly in the instance, the script then resorts to using the IAM role which we created earlier. Make sure that you receive confirmation from the script of its successful verification before you move on to the next steps.

You can additionally use the `--mem-used` (memory used) and `--mem-avail` (memory available) metrics to query your instance's memory performance as well.

Next, run the following command to collect all your instance's memory related metrics and send them to CloudWatch:

```
# ./mon-put-instance-data.pl --mem-util --mem-used --mem-avail
```

You can even create a cron job and schedule the `mon-put-instance-data.pl` script to collect and send metric data over a period of time using the following set of commands. First, create a new file and save the following cron task in it:

```
# vi /etc/cron.d/Monitor_MEM
```

Add the following lines to your cron file:

```
*/5 * * * * ~/aws-scripts-mon/mon-put-instance-data.pl --mem-util --mem-used --mem-avail --from-cron
```

The cron will execute every five minutes and send the instance's memory details over to CloudWatch:

```
ec2-user@ip-192-168-1-116:~

[ec2-user@ip-192-168-1-116 ~]$
[ec2-user@ip-192-168-1-116 ~]$ cat /etc/cron.d/Monitor_CPU
*/5 * * * * ~/aws-scripts-mon/mon-put-instance-data.pl --mem-util --mem-
avail --mem-used --from-cron
[ec2-user@ip-192-168-1-116 ~]$
[ec2-user@ip-192-168-1-116 ~]$ sudo chmod +x /etc/cron.d/Monitor_CPU
[ec2-user@ip-192-168-1-116 ~]$
[ec2-user@ip-192-168-1-116 ~]$ sudo service crond restart
Stopping crond:                                      [  OK  ]
Starting crond:                                      [  OK  ]
[ec2-user@ip-192-168-1-116 ~]$
[ec2-user@ip-192-168-1-116 ~]$
```

You can create additional cron files to monitor the instance's disk utilization as well. For example, if you want to be notified when the instance's root (/) or /var partition starts to fill up. In that case, create a simple cron task with the following information in it:

```
*/5 * * * * ~/aws-scripts-mon/mon-put-instance-data.pl --disk-space-avail --disk-path=/ --disk-path=/var --from-cron
```

You can optionally even use the `--disk-space-util` (disk utilization) and the `--disk-space-used` (disk space used) metrics to query your instance's disk performance as well.

Viewing the custom metrics from CloudWatch

You can view your custom metrics from the CloudWatch management dashboard as well. Simply select the **Metrics** option from the CloudWatch navigation pane. Next, browse the listed metrics for a Linux System metrics, as shown in the following screenshot. You can optionally even use the **Browse Metrics** search bar to filter out the required metrics.

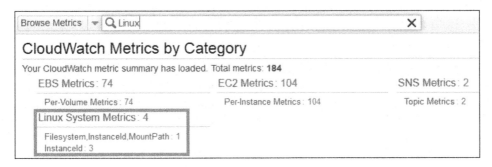

Select the **Linux System Metrics** option to view your instance's memory and disk utilizations, as shown in the following screenshot. You can use these metrics to list and create your very own custom alarms, as well use the **Create Alarm** option.

For example, raise an alarm when **Memory Utilization** of the instance crosses a threshold of 75 percent, or send a notification alert to the concerned sysadmins when the root (/) partition's available disk space is below 10 percent, and so on. With this, we have now successfully started monitoring our instance's memory and disk utilizations as well! Next up, let's look at how you can leverage CloudWatch to monitor your instance's or your application's log files using CloudWatch Logs!

Monitoring logs using CloudWatch Logs

Imagine that you have a bunch of web server instances with some web applications running on top of them. Now, what if you wanted to collect the log files off these instances and the web app and store it in a central repository such that you can troubleshoot errors and faults more effectively? That's precisely what CloudWatch Logs is all about!

CloudWatch Logs basically allows you to monitor custom application log files as well as log files generated by your EC2 instances in real time. You can even create and associate CloudWatch alarms which can send you notifications in case a particular log file displays errors. For example, you can monitor your application's logs for `NullPointerExceptions` or even your classical `404` status codes provided by your Apache web servers log files. You can additionally even store your log files to S3 for further analysis or to be loaded into some other log processing system.

In this section, we will learn how to monitor our application's web server (Apache HTTP) logs using CloudWatch Logs; however, before we proceed with that, let's first have a look at some of CloudWatch Log's concepts and terminologies.

CloudWatch Log concepts and terminologies

The following are some important concepts and terms that you will come across while using CloudWatch Logs:

- **Log events**: A log event is an activity that is recorded by either your OS or your application. It consists of two main parts: a timestamp entry that signifies when the log event was generated and a raw message that describes the logging event. For example, a simple log event for an HTTP web server would look like: `[17/Sept/2015:14:44:54 +0000] "GET /index.html HTTP/1.1 404"`.

- **Log stream**: A sequence of log events generated from the same source is called as a log stream.

- **Log groups**: A log group is a collection of log streams that share some common set of properties together. For example, an HTTP log group can contain log streams for Apache's HTTP as well as Nginx web servers.

- **Metric filters**: Metric filters are responsible for extracting certain key pieces of information from your log files and then converting them into CloudWatch metrics.

- **Retention policies**: Retention policies dictate how long a particular log event has to be retained. Retention policies are applied to log groups and thus are inherited by log streams as well.

- **Log agent**: Log agents are small agent based software that you need to install on your individual EC2 instances. Each log agent is responsible for storing and pushing the log events to CloudWatch.

So, how does all this work? Well for starters, we will need to allow our instances to communicate with CloudWatch Logs just as we did with the custom metrics. You can go ahead and create a different role or use the **CloudWatchFullAccess** role as we did before.

Once a role is associated to your instances, the next steps require us to configure CloudWatch Logs and install the log agent on the instance itself. Let's go ahead and get started with the CloudWatch Logs dashboard first.

Getting Started with CloudWatch Logs

CloudWatch Logs can be accessed from the CloudWatch management dashboard itself. Select the **Logs** option from the navigation pane to bring up the CloudWatch Logs dashboard. From the main page, select the option **Create Log Group**, as shown in the following screenshot:

In this scenario, we are going to monitor the HTTP logs of our web server instance, so go ahead and provide a suitable name for the log group, as shown in the following. Click on **Create Log Group** when done. In this case, I have named my log group as **HTTP_LOG_GROUP**.

With the log group now created, the next step is to create a log stream associated with it. From the log groups dashboard, select the name of your newly created log group. Here, you can create different log streams for your applications or OSs based on your requirements. Next, click on the **Create Log Stream** option. Provide a suitable name for your log stream and select the **Create Log Stream** button to complete the process. In this case, I have named my log stream as **HTTP_LOG_STREAM**, as shown in the following screenshot:

With these basic steps out of the way, now comes the fun part where we actually get to install and configure the log agent on the instance. To do so, launch a new Linux-based instance (I would recommend the Amazon Linux AMI or the Private Web Server AMI that we created in *Chapter 4, Security, Storage, Networking, and Lots More!*) and associate the CloudWatch access role with it. SSH into the instance and type in the following command to install the log agent:

```
# sudo yum install awslogs
```

With the log agent now installed, there are just a couple of files that you need to edit in order for the agent to work. The first file is the awscli.conf file. Open the file using any text editor of your choice and in the [*default*] section and specify the region where you want to view the log data. Since I am operating my instance out of the US-WEST (Oregon) region, I have provided us-west-2 as the region of my choice. You can provide either of these values as per your requirements: us-east-1, us-west-1, us-west-2, eu-west-1, eu-central-1, ap-southeast-1, ap-southeast-2, or ap-northeast-1. Now, run the following command:

```
# vi /etc/awslogs/awscli.conf
```

Once done, save the file and exit the editor:

```
[root@ip-192-168-1-116 ~]# cat /etc/awslogs/awscli.conf
[plugins]
cwlogs = cwlogs
[default]
region = us-west-2
[root@ip-192-168-1-116 ~]#
```

 You can optionally provide your AWS secret key and access key information in the awscli.conf file; however, we have not done that as our instance is already associated with an IAM role.

The next file that you will need to edit is the awslogs.conf file. This is the primary log agent configuration file, using which you can define one or more log streams as well as define the logs that you want to track. Open the file using any text editor of your choice and paste the following lines toward the end of the file:

```
# vi /etc/awslogs/awslogs.conf
[/etc/httpd/logs/access_log]
file = /etc/httpd/logs/access_log
datetime_format = %b %d %H:%M:%S
initial_position = start_of_file
log_group_name = HTTP_LOG_GROUP
log_stream_name = HTTP_LOG_STREAM
```

What do all these lines mean? Here's a quick look at the `awslogs.conf` file's parameters:

- `file`: The file parameter specifies the log file whose contents you want to push on to the CloudWatch Logs. In my case, I want to specify the HTTP web server's access log file, hence the path of the Apache web server's access log file (`/etc/httpd/logs/access_log`).

- `datetime_format`: This parameter specifies how the timestamp value is extracted from supplied log file.
    - `%b` specifies month as in Jan, Feb, and so on.
    - `%d` specifies day of month in numbers as in 1,2,3,...31.
    - `%H` specifies hour in a 24 hour clock format.
    - `%M` specifies minutes.
    - `%S` specifies seconds.

  The access_log file's log entries have the timestamp of `%b %d %H:%M:%S` which translates to `Sep 9 18:45:59`.

- `Initial_position`: This parameter specifies where to start to read the log data from the log file. It supports two values: `start_of_file and end_of_file`.

- `log_group_name`: As the name implies, this parameter refers to the log group name that you created in CloudWatch Logs earlier.

- `log_stream_name`: This parameter refers to the destination log stream name.

Besides these standard parameters, the `awslogs.conf` file supports a few additional parameters as well. A complete list can be found at `http://docs.aws.amazon.com/AmazonCloudWatch/latest/DeveloperGuide/AgentReference.html`.

With the necessary entry made in the `awslogs.conf` file, we are now ready to start the log agent. Type in the following command in your instance's terminal screen to start the log agent service:

```
# sudo service awslogs start
# sudo chkconfig awslogs on
```

Viewing the logs

With the log agent up and running, you can now go ahead and view the HTTP logs from the CloudWatch Logs UI. Select the particular log group for which you want to view the log data. Next, select the appropriate log stream for the same. In this case, I had to select **HTTP_LOG_GROUP** as my log group and **HTTP_LOG_STREAM** as its associated log stream. You should see a bunch of log statements, as shown in the following screenshot:

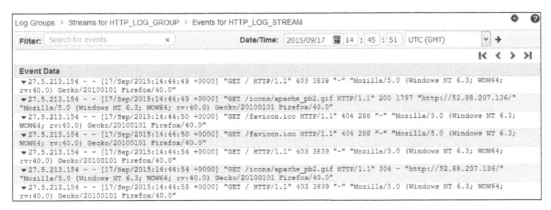

You can use the **Filter** option to search for particular errors or status events from your log data. Alternatively, you can also use the **Date/Time** adjustor to view log data from a particular time period. With this step, we are now ready to go ahead and create a few metric filters for our log data.

Creating metric filters and alarms

CloudWatch Logs provide a really awesome method, using which you can filter and search out patterns, phrases, and even values from your log data. For example, you can create and set a filter that will raise an alarm when it encounters the words **FATAL** or **ERROR** from your application logs or even create a filter that searches for any 4XX-based errors from your HTTP logs such as 400 - Bad Request, 401 - Unauthorized, 403 - Forbidden, 404 - Not Found, and so on. Each time any of these values are found, CloudWatch registers them as a metric value, which can then be compared with the rest of the log data.

To create a metric filter, select your log group's name from the CloudWatch Log dashboard and select the **Create Metric Filter** option. This will bring up the **Metric Filter** wizard, as shown in the following screenshot:

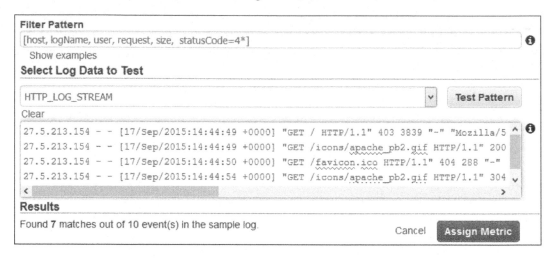

Provide a suitable pattern to filter your log stream in the **Filter Pattern** field. In my case, I have created a simple filter that will extract the **host**, **logName**, **user**, **request**, **size**, and the **status_code** option if the status code has any 4XX values in it, which includes 401,403, 404, and so on.

 You can read more about filter patterns and how to use them at http://docs.aws.amazon.com/AmazonCloudWatch/latest/DeveloperGuide/FilterAndPatternSyntax.html.

Next, select the correct log stream on which you wish to test this filter pattern. In my case, I selected the **HTTP_LOG_STREAM** option. Next, select the **Test Pattern** option to test your filter pattern. You should see a few results show up in the **Results** section if your filter pattern is accurate. This validates that the filter patter is correct, so move on to the next phase of the wizard where we assign a metric to this filter. Click on **Assign Metric** to continue. You should see the **Create Metric Filter and Assign a Metric** page, as shown in the following screenshot:

Using this page, you can assign a metric to your filter that can be used to graph as well as set alarms. Provide a suitable **Filter Name** for your newly created filter pattern. In my case, I have used the default values itself. Next, in the **Metric Details** section, provide an appropriate **Metric Namespace**, **Metric Name,** as well as a **Metric Value** for your filter. Click on **Create Filter** to complete the metric filter creation process. You should receive a confirmation box, as shown in the following screenshot. Click on **Create Alarm** to create and assign an alarm to this newly created metric filter.

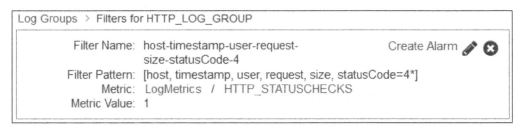

That's all there is to it! You can refer to some interesting and easy to follow metric filter examples by following http://docs.aws.amazon.com/AmazonCloudWatch/ latest/DeveloperGuide/MonitoringPolicyExamples html.

Planning your next steps

Well, we have covered a lot about CloudWatch in this chapter; however, there are a few things that I would really recommend you to try out next. First off is exporting your log data to S3. Although an optional step, exporting your logs over to S3 can be really beneficial in terms of analyzing and monitoring your application's as well as your instance's performance and trends. How do you get started with this? Well, it's very simple!

You will need to first create an S3 bucket in the same region as that of your log data. Next, provide a set of permissions to your S3 bucket so that it and its contents are writeable by CloudWatch Logs. You can use an IAM policy or even use S3's access polices for the same. Finally, create a CloudWatch Logs Export task that includes your log group's name as the input and the S3 bucket's destination as the output. That's it! You can read more about the detailed steps required for exporting logs to S3 at `http://docs.aws.amazon.com/AmazonCloudWatch/latest/DeveloperGuide/S3ExportTasks.html`.

The second thing worth trying out is log data processing using Amazon Kinesis. Why is this so important? Well to be honest, CloudWatch Logs is a good tool, but it is not designed to process and handle large log files that too close to real time. That's where Amazon Kinesis comes into play! Kinesis is a managed service used for the rapid processing of large amounts of data, particularly logs, application usage statistics, and so on. Working with Kinesis is pretty straightforward. To begin with, you will first need to create a Kinesis stream. This is where your log events will be delivered to for processing. Next, you will need to create something called as a subscription filter using CloudWatch. A subscription filter basically will filter out the required log events from your log data using a defined filter pattern. These log events are then sent to the Amazon Kinesis stream for further analysis and processing. You can read more about subscription filters and Amazon Kinesis at `http://docs.aws.amazon.com/AmazonCloudWatch/latest/DeveloperGuide/Subscriptions.html`.

Recommendations and best practices

The following are some key recommendations and best practices to keep in mind when working with CloudWatch:

- Create a monitoring plan for your infrastructure and abide by it. Note down all the metrics that you need to collect along with the method of its collection before actually deploying your infrastructure on the cloud.

- Monitor each and every aspect of your infrastructure, including EC2 instances, EBS volumes, Elastic Load Balancers, and so on. Create specific alarms for monitoring each AWS resource independently

- Avoid storing secret and access keys in your instances, and instead create and use specific IAM roles for permitting the instances to communicate with CloudWatch.

- Create and check log files periodically for application or instance related faults
and alerts.

- Perform stress tests on your application and instances and create alarms that respond accordingly.

Summary

Phew! This has been a long but interesting and worthwhile chapter indeed! Let's quickly recap the things we learnt so far!

First up, we started off with a quick introduction to Amazon CloudWatch, its features, concepts, and terminologies. Next, we went ahead and created our very first alarm in the form of an estimate billing alarm. We then even saw how to create alarms for monitoring the performance of our EC2 instances, as well as how to perform certain actions when the alarms are triggered. Toward the end of this chapter, we looked at CloudWatch Logs and how you can leverage it to monitor your web server's logs. And, finally, we finished the chapter with a brief look at custom metrics and metric filters and how we can use them effectively to monitor our instances and applications.

In the next chapter, we will be taking CloudWatch and monitoring to the next level by exploring the awesome concept of auto scaling, so stay tuned!

7
Manage Your Applications with Auto Scaling and Elastic Load Balancing

In the previous chapter, you learnt a lot about monitoring our AWS infrastructure, especially the EC2 instances using Amazon CloudWatch. We also created our very first alarms using CloudWatch and monitored our instance's CPU, memory, and disk utilization and performance using the same.

In this chapter, we are going continue where we last dropped off and introduce an amazing and awesome concept called **Auto Scaling**! AWS has been one of the first public cloud providers to provide this feature and really it is something that you must try out and use in your environments! This chapter will teach you the basics of Auto Scaling, its concepts and terminologies, and even how to create an auto scaled environment using AWS. It will also cover **Amazon Elastic Load Balancers** and how you can use them in conjunction with Auto Scaling to manage your applications more effectively! So without wasting any more time, let's first get started by understanding what Auto Scaling is and how it actually works!

An overview of Auto Scaling

We have been talking about AWS and the concept of dynamic scalability, also known as **Elasticity** in general throughout this book; well now is the best time to look at it in depth with the help of Auto Scaling!

Auto Scaling basically enables you to scale your compute capacity (*EC2 instances*) either up or down, depending on the conditions you specify. These conditions could be as simple as a number that maintains the count of your EC2 instances at any given time, or even complex conditions that measure the load and performance of your instances such as CPU utilization, memory utilization, and so on. But a simple question that may arise here is why do I even need Auto Scaling? Is it really that important? Let's look at a dummy application's load and performance graph to get a better understanding of things; let's take a look at the following screenshot:

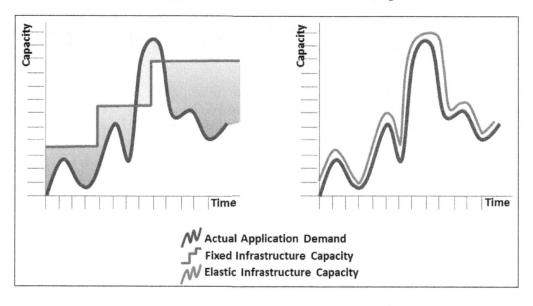

The graph to the left depicts the traditional approach that is usually taken to map an application's performance requirements with a fixed infrastructure capacity. Now, to meet this application's unpredictable performance requirements, you would have to plan and procure additional hardware upfront, as depicted by the red line. And since there is no guaranteed way to plan for unpredictable workloads, you generally end up procuring more than you need. This is a standard approach employed by many businesses and it doesn't come without its own set of problems. For example, the region highlighted in red is when most of the procured hardware capacity is idle and wasted as the application simply does not have that high a requirement. Whereas there can be cases as well where the procured hardware simply did not match the application's high performance requirements, as shown by the green region. All these issues, in turn, have an impact on your business, which frankly can prove to be quite expensive. That's where the elasticity of a cloud comes into play. Rather than procuring at the nth hour and ending up with wasted resources, you grow and shrink your resources dynamically as per your application's requirements, as depicted in the graph on the right. This not only helps you in saving overall costs but also makes your application's management a lot more easy and efficient. And don't worry if your application does not have an unpredictable load pattern! Auto Scaling is designed to work with both predictable and unpredictable workloads so that no matter what application you may have, you can rest assured that the required compute capacity is always going to be made available for use when required. Keeping that in mind, let us summarize some of the benefits that AWS Auto Scaling provides:

- **Cost savings**: By far the biggest advantage provided by Auto Scaling, you can actually gain a lot of control over the deployment of your instances as well as costs by launching instances only when they are needed and terminating them when they aren't required.

- **Ease of use**: AWS provides a variety of tools using which you can create and manage your Auto Scaling, such as the AWS CLI and even the EC2 Management Dashboard. Auto Scaling can be programmatically created and managed via a simple and easy to use web service API as well.

- **Scheduled scaling actions**: Apart from scaling instances as per a given policy, you can additionally even schedule scaling actions that can be executed in the future. This type of scaling comes in handy when your application's workload patterns are predictable and well known in advance.

- **Geographic redundancy and scalability**: AWS Auto Scaling enables you to scale, distribute, and load balance your application automatically across multiple availability zones within a given region.

- **Easier maintenance and fault tolerance**: AWS Auto Scaling replaces unhealthy instances automatically based on predefined alarms and thresholds.

With these basics in mind, let us understand how Auto Scaling actually works out in AWS.

Auto scaling components

To get started with Auto Scaling on AWS, you will be required to work with three primary components, each described briefly as follows.

Auto scaling groups

An Auto Scaling group is a core component of the Auto Scaling service. It is basically a logical grouping of instances that share some common scaling characteristics between them. For example, a web application can contain a set of web server instances that can form one Auto Scaling group and another set of application server instances that become a part of another Auto Scaling group and so on. Each group has its own set of criteria specified that includes the minimum and maximum number of instances that the group should have, along with the desired number of instances that the group must have at all times.

 The desired number of instances is an optional field in an Auto Scaling group. If the desired capacity value is not specified, then the Auto Scaling Group will consider the minimum number of instance values as the desired value instead.

Auto Scaling Groups are also responsible for performing periodic health checks on the instances contained within them. An instance with degraded health is then immediately swapped out and replaced by a new one by the Auto Scaling Group, thus ensuring that each of the instances within the Group works at optimum levels.

Launch configurations

A launch configuration is a set of blueprint statements that the Auto Scaling Group uses to launch instances. You can create a single launch configuration and use it with multiple Auto Scaling Groups; however, you can only associate one Launch Configuration with a single Auto Scaling Group at a time. What does a Launch Configuration contain? Well to start off with, it contains the AMI ID using which Auto Scaling launches the instances in the Auto Scaling Group. It also contains additional information about your instances such as instance type, the security group it has to be associated with, block device mappings, key pairs, and so on. An important thing to note here is that once you create a Launch Configuration, there is no way you can edit it again. The only way to make changes to a Launch Configuration is by creating a new one in its place and associating that with the Auto Scaling Group.

Scaling plans

With your Launch Configuration created, the final step left is to create one or more scaling plans. Scaling Plans describe how the Auto Scaling Group should actually scale. There are three scaling mechanisms you can use with your Auto Scaling Groups, each described as follows:

- **Manual scaling**: Manual scaling by far is the simplest way of scaling your resources. All you need to do here is specify a new desired number of instances value or change the minimum or maximum number of instances in an Auto Scaling Group and the rest is taken care of by the Auto Scaling service itself.

- **Scheduled scaling**: Scheduled scaling is really helpful when it comes to scaling resources based on a particular time and date. This method of scaling is useful when the application's load patterns are highly predictable, and thus you know exactly when to scale up or down. For example, an application that process a company's payroll cycle is usually load intensive during the end of each month, so you can schedule the scaling requirements accordingly.

- **Dynamic scaling**: Dynamic scaling, or scaling on demand is used when the predictability of your application's performance is unknown. With dynamic scaling, you generally provide a set of scaling policies using some criteria; for example, scaling the instances in my Auto Scaling Group by 10 when the average CPU utilization exceeds 75 percent for a period of 5 minutes. Sounds familiar, right? Well that's because these dynamic scaling policies rely on Amazon CloudWatch to trigger scaling events. CloudWatch monitors the policy conditions and triggers the auto scaling events when certain thresholds are breached. In either case, you will require a minimum of two such scaling policies: one for scaling in (*terminating instances*) and one for scaling out (*launching instances*).

Before we go ahead and create our first Auto Scaling activity, we need to understand one additional AWS service that will help us balance and distribute the incoming traffic across our auto scaled EC2 instances. Enter the Elastic Load Balancer!

Introducing the Elastic Load Balancer

The **Elastic Load Balancer** or **ELB** is a web service that allows you to automatically distribute incoming traffic across a fleet of EC2 instances. In simpler terms, an ELB acts as a single point of contact between your clients and the EC2 instances that are servicing them. The clients query your application via the ELB; thus, you can easily add and remove the underlying EC2 instances without having to worry about any of the traffic routing or load distributions. It is all taken care of by the ELB itself!

Coupled with Auto Scaling, ELB provides you with a highly resilient and fault tolerant environment to host your applications. While the Auto Scaling service automatically removes any unhealthy EC2 instances from its group, the ELB automatically reroutes the traffic to some other healthy instance. Once a new healthy instance is launched by the Auto Scaling service, ELB will once again re-route the traffic through it and balance out the application load as well. But the work of the ELB doesn't stop there! An ELB can also be used to safeguard and secure your instances by enforcing encryption and by utilizing only HTTPS and SSL connections. Keeping these points in mind, let us look at how an ELB actually works.

Well to begin with, when you create an ELB in a particular AZ, you are actually spinning up one or more ELB nodes. Don't worry, you cannot physically see these nodes nor perform any actions on them. They are completely managed and looked after by AWS itself. This node is responsible for forwarding the incoming traffic to the healthy instances present in that particular AZ. Now here's the fun part! If you configure the ELB to work across multiple AZs and assume that one entire AZ goes down or the instances in that particular AZ become unhealthy for some reason, then the ELB will automatically route traffic to the healthy instances present in the second AZ:

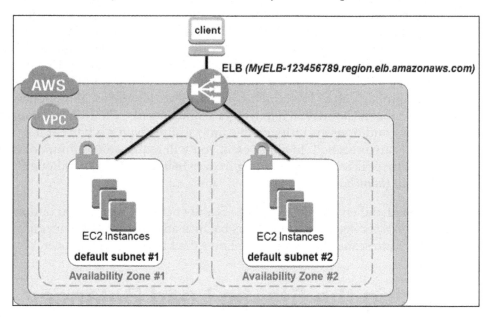

How does it do the routing? The ELB, by default, is provided with a public DNS name, something similar to MyELB-123456789.region.elb.amazonaws.com. The clients send all their requests to this particular Public DNS name. The AWS DNS servers then resolve this public DNS name to the public IP addresses of the ELB nodes. Each of the nodes has one or more listeners configured on them which constantly check for any incoming connections. Listeners are nothing but processes that are configured with a combination of protocols; for example, HTTP and a port, for example, 80. The ELB node that receives the particular request from the client then routes the traffic to a healthy instance using a particular routing algorithm. If the listener was configured with an HTTP or HTTPS protocol, then the preferred choice of routing algorithm is the least outstanding requests routing algorithm.

 If you have configured your ELB with a TCP listener, then the preferred routing algorithm is **Round Robin**.

Confused? Well don't be, as most of these things are handled internally by the ELB itself. You don't have to configure the ELB nodes nor the routing tables. All you need to do is set up the listeners in your ELB and point all client requests to the ELB's Public DNS name, and that's it! Keeping these basics in mind, let us go ahead and create our very first ELB!

Creating your first Elastic Load Balancer

Creating and setting up an ELB is a fairly easy and straightforward process provided you have planned and defined your Elastic Load Balancer's role from the start. The current version of ELB supports HTTP, HTTPS, and TCP, as well as SSL connection protocols; however, for the sake of simplicity, we will be creating a simple ELB for balancing HTTP traffic only. I'll be using the same VPC environment that we have been developing since *Chapter 5*, *Building Your Own Private Clouds Using Amazon VPC*; however, you can easily substitute your own infrastructure in this place as well.

To access the ELB Dashboard, you will have to first access the
EC2ManagementConsole. Next, from the navigation pane, select the **LoadBalancers**
option, as shown in the following screenshot. This will bring up the ELB Dashboard
as well, using which you can create and associate your ELBs. An important point
to note here is that although ELBs are created using this particular portal, you can,
however, use them for both your EC2 and VPC environments. There is no separate
portal for creating ELBs in a VPC environment:

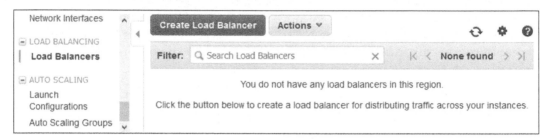

Since this is our first ELB, let us go ahead and select the **Create Load Balancer**
option. This will bring up a seven-step wizard using which you can create and
customize your ELBs.

Step 1 – Defining the Load Balancer

To begin with, provide a suitable name for your ELB in the **Load Balancer name**
field. In this case, I have opted to stick to my naming convention and name the
ELB US-WEST-PROD-LB-01. Next up, select the **VPC** option in which you wish
to deploy your ELB. Again, I have gone ahead and selected the US-WEST-PROD-1
(192.168.0.0/16) VPC that we created in *Chapter 5, Building Your Own Private
Clouds Using Amazon VPC*. You can alternatively select your own VPC environment
or even select a standalone EC2 environment if it is available. Do not check the
Create an internal load balancer option as in this scenario, we are creating an
Internet-facing ELB for our Web Server instances.

There are two types of ELB that you can create and use based on your requirements.
The first is an Internet-facing Load Balancer, which is used to balance out client
requests that are inbound from the Internet. Ideally, such Internet-facing load
balancers connect to the public subnets of a VPC. Similarly, you also have something
called as Internal Load Balancers that connect and route traffic to your private
subnets. You can use a combination of these depending on your application's
requirements and architecture; for example, you can have one Internet-facing ELB as
your application's main entry point and an internal ELB to route traffic between your
public and private subnets; however, for simplicity, let us create an Internet-facing
ELB for now.

With these basic settings done, we now provide our ELB's Listeners. A Listener is made up of two parts: a protocol and port number for your frontend connection (*between your client and the ELB*), and a protocol and a port number for a backend connection (*between the ELB and the EC2 instances*).

In the **Listener Configuration** section, select **HTTP** from the **Load Balancer Protocol** drop-down list and provide the port number 80 in the **Load Balancer Port** field, as shown in the following screenshot. Provide the same protocol and port number for the **Instance Protocol** and **Instance Port** fields as well:

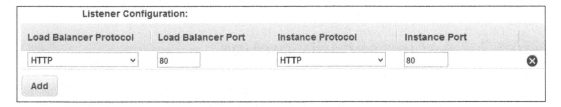

What does this mean? Well, this listener is now configured to listen on the ELB's external port (**Load Balancer Port**) 80 for any client's requests. Once it receives the requests, it will then forward it out to the underlying EC2 instances using the **Instance Port**, which in this case is port 80 as well. There is no rule of thumb as such that both the port values must match; in fact, it is actually good practice to keep them different. Although your ELB can listen on port 80 for any client's requests, it can use any ports within the range of 1-65,535 for forwarding the request to the instances. You can optionally add additional listeners to your ELB such as a listener for the HTTPS protocol running on port 443 as well; however, that is something that I will leave you do to later.

The final configuration item left in step 1 is where you get to select the **Subnets** option to be associated with your new Load Balancer. In my case, I have gone ahead and created a set of subnets each in two different AZs so as to mimic a high-availability scenario:

Select Subnets

VPC vpc-0ae3996f (192.168.0.0/16) | US-WEST-PROD-1
Available Subnets

Actions	Availability Zone	Subnet ID	Subnet CIDR	Name
⊕	us-west-2a	subnet-70157c07	192.168.5.0/24	US-WEST-PROD-DB-1
⊕	us-west-2c	subnet-c472f99d	192.168.6.0/24	US-WEST-PROD-DB-2

Selected Subnets

Actions	Availability Zone	Subnet ID	Subnet CIDR	Name
⊖	us-west-2a	subnet-7b157c0c	192.168.1.0/24	US-WEST-PROD-WEB-1
⊖	us-west-2c	subnet-cc72f995	192.168.2.0/24	US-WEST-PROD-WEB-2

Cancel   Next: Assign Security Groups

Select any particular subnets and add them to your ELB by selecting the adjoining + sign. In my case, I have selected two subnets, both belonging to the web server instances; however, both present in two different AZs.

 You can select a single subnet as well; however, it is highly recommended that you go for a high available architecture, as described earlier.

Once your subnets are added, click on **Next: Assign Security Groups** to continue over to step 2.

Step 2 – Assign security groups

Step 2 is where we get to assign our ELB with a security group. Now, here's the catch: You will not be prompted for a Security Group if you are using an EC2-Classic environment for your ELB. This Security Group is only necessary for VPC environments and will basically allow the port you designated for inbound traffic to pass through:

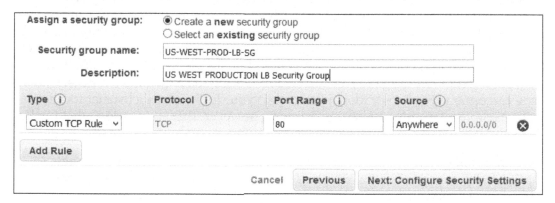

In this case, I have created a new dedicated Security Group for the ELB. Provide a suitable **Security group name** as well as a **Description**, as shown in the preceding screenshot. The new security group already contains a rule that allows traffic to the port that you configured your Load Balancer to use; in my case it's port 80. Leave the rule at its default value and click on **Next: Configure Security Settings** to continue.

Step 3 – configure security settings

This is an optional page that basically allows you to secure your ELB by using either the HTTPS or the SSL protocol for your frontend connection. But since we have opted for a simple HTTP-based ELB, we can ignore this page for now. Click on **Next: Configure Health Check** to proceed to the next step.

Step 4 – Configure Health Check

Health checks are a very important part of an ELB's configuration and hence you have to be extra cautious when setting them up. What are health checks? To put it in simple terms, these are basic tests that the ELB conducts to ensure that your underlying EC2 instances are healthy and running optimally. These tests include simple pings, attempted connections, or even some send requests. If the ELB senses either of the EC2 instances in an unhealthy state, it immediately changes its Health Check Status to OutOfService. Once the instance is marked as OutOfService, the ELB no longer routes any traffic to it. The ELB will only start sending traffic back to the instance only if its Health Check State changes to InService again.

To configure the health checks for your ELB, fill in the following information as described here:

- **Ping protocol**: This field indicates which protocol the ELB should use to connect to your EC2 instances. You can use the TCP, HTTP, HTTPS, or the SSL options; however, for simplicity, I have selected the **HTTP** protocol here.

- **Ping port**: This field is used to indicate the port which the ELB should use to connect to the instance. You can supply any port value from the range 1 to 65,535; however, since we are using the HTTP protocol, I have opted to stick with the default value of port 80. This port value is really essential as the ELB will periodically ping the EC2 instances on this port number. If any instance does not reply in a timely fashion, then that instance will be deemed unhealthy by the ELB.

- **Ping path**: This value is usually used for the HTTP and HTTPS protocols. The ELB sends a simple GET request to the EC2 instances based on the Ping Port and Ping Path. If the ELB receives a response other than an OK, then that particular instance is deemed to be unhealthy by the ELB and it will no longer route any traffic to it. Ping paths generally are set with a forward slash, /, which indicates the default home page of a web server. However, you can also use a /index.html or a /default.html value as you see fit. In my case, I have provided the /index.php value as my dummy web application is actually a PHP app.

Besides the ping checks, there are also a few advanced configuration details that you can configure based on your application's health check needs:

- **Response time**: The Response Time is the time the ELB has to wait in order to receive a response. The default value is **5** seconds with a maximum value up to 60 seconds. Let's take a look at the following screenshot:

- **Health Check Interval**: This field indicates the amount of time (in seconds) the ELB waits between health checks of an individual EC2 instance. The default value is **30** seconds; however, you can specify a maximum value of 300 seconds as well.

- **Unhealthy Threshold**: This field indicates the number of consecutive failed health checks an ELB must wait before declaring an instance unhealthy. The default value is **2** with a maximum threshold value of **10**.

- **Healthy Threshold**: This field indicates the number of consecutive successful health checks an ELB must wait before declaring an instance healthy. The default value is **2** with a maximum threshold value of **10**.

Once you have provided your values, go ahead and select the **Next: Add EC2 Instances** option.

Step 5 – Add EC2 instances

In this section of the wizard, you can select any running instance from your Subnets to be added and registered with the ELB. But since we are setting this particular ELB for use with Auto Scaling, we will leave this section for now. Click on **Next: Add Tags** to proceed with the wizard.

Step 6 – Add tags

We already know the importance of tagging our AWS resources, so go ahead and provide a suitable tag for categorizing and identifying your ELB. Note that you can always add/edit and remove tags at a later time as well using the ELB Dashboard. With the tags all set up, click on **Review and Create**.

Step 7 – Review and Create

The final step of our ELB creation wizard is where we simply review our ELB's settings, including the Health Checks, EC2 instances, tags, and so on. Once reviewed, click on **Create** to begin your ELB's creation and configuration.

The ELB takes a few seconds to get created, but once it's ready, you can view and manage it just like any other AWS resource using the ELB dashboard, as shown in the following screenshot:

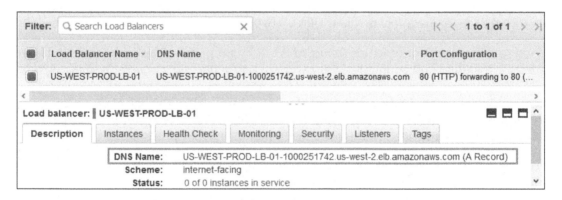

Select the newly created ELB and view its details in the **Description** tab. Make a note of the ELB's public **DNS Name** as well. You can optionally even view the **Status** as well as the **ELBScheme** (*whether Internet-facing or internal*) using the **Description** tab. You can also view the ELB's **Health Checks** as well as the **Listeners** configured with your ELB.

Before we proceed with the next section of this chapter, here are a few important pointers to keep in mind when working with ELB. Firstly, the configurations that we performed on our ELB are all very basic and will help you to get through the basics; however, ELB also provides us with additional advanced configuration options such as Cross-Zone Load Balancing, Proxy Protocols, Sticky Sessions, and so on, which can all be configured using the ELB dashboard. To know more about these advanced settings, refer to `http://docs.aws.amazon.com/ElasticLoadBalancing/latest/DeveloperGuide/elb-configure-load-balancer.html`. Second important thing worth mentioning is the ELB's costs. Although it is free (*Terms and Conditions apply*) to use under the Free Tier eligibility, ELBs are charged approximately $0.025 per hour used. There is a nominal charge on the data transferring as well, which is approximately $0.008 per GB of data processed.

With these points in mind and our ELB all prepped, let us go ahead and get started with the fun part of Auto Scaling!

Getting started with Auto Scaling

With your ELB all set up, you are now ready to go ahead and start configuring the Auto Scaling service. As discussed earlier, there are basically three parts to Auto Scaling: The Launch Configurations, the Auto Scaling Group, and, finally, the Scaling Triggers. In this section, we are going to check out some simple steps using which you will be able to create and configure your own auto scaled environment; but before that, here are a few tips and tricks worth mentioning!

First up, prepare your Machine Image or AMI. By prepare I mean make sure you have already installed and configured your web server (*in my case, I'm using a simple Apache HTTP web server*) to start on instance boot up as well as place your application's code or website files in the correct directories. Additionally, you can even install and configure the CloudWatch Log agent in your AMI such that it captures the essential web server logs and sends them to CloudWatch for further processing.

The second most important part of any Auto Scaling activity is planning and understanding instance quantity, that is, what is the desired capacity of your Auto Scaling Group and what are the minimum and maximum number of instances you want your application to scale to. Since we are just starting off, I would really recommend doing the basics. Have a desired capacity set to 1 instance, which means that there will be a single instance hosting your web server at all times. Next, set up a minimum instance value of 1 and a maximum instance value of, say, 5. Remember that you can always change the Auto Scaling Group values but not the Launch Configuration details.

The third and final thing that I would like to mention is the famous moto: *Plan for failure, and nothing will fail*. Although you can set up Auto Scaling using a single AZ, it is highly recommended that you distribute your workloads across AZs as much as possible. The following is a look at my simple Auto Scaling example:

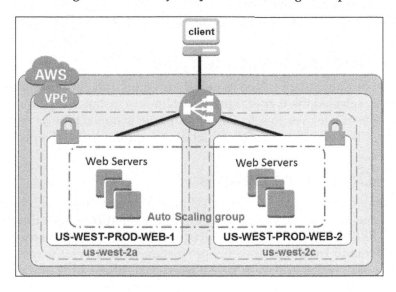

In this case, we have already deployed and configured our ELB, and the only thing remains is the Auto Scaling configuration. So without further ado, let's get started!

Creating the Launch Configuration

The first step to setting up an Auto Scaling activity is to create and configure a Launch Configuration. To do so, from the **EC2 Management Dashboard** option, select the **AutoScaling Groups** option from the navigation pane as shown in the following screenshot. This will bring up the **Auto Scaling Groups** dashboard. Next, select the **Create Auto Scaling group** option to bring up the Auto Scaling setup wizard.

The wizard is a simple six-step process that will first enable you to create and configure a Launch Configuration, followed by a five-step process to associate an Auto Scaling Group with it. Let us go through each of the steps in detail.

Step 1 – Choose AMI

From the **Choose AMI** page, select your choice of AMI for your Launch Configuration. You can either select the Amazon Linux AMI to get started with or even select the custom AMI that we created back in *Chapter 4, Security, Storage, Networking, and Lots More!,* by selecting the **My AMIs** option and then selecting your particular custom AMI.

Step 2 – Choose Instance type

Select the appropriate instance type required for your Launch Configuration. In my case, I have selected the **General purpose t2.micro** instance type for my demo purposes; however, feel free to select an appropriate instance type as per your requirements. Click on **Next: Configure details** to continue with the process.

Step 3 – Configure details

Provide a suitable **Name** for your Launch Configuration. In my case, I have named it using the same naming convention that I'm following throughout this book, that is, *US-WEST-PROD-WEB-LC-1*. You can **Request Spot Instances** instead of the default **On-Demand Instances** as well. Spot instances are a great way to save costs compared to your on-demand instances; however, use them with caution. Spot instances are spun up the moment your bid price rises above the instance's market value and are terminated when the market value exceeds your spot price.

You can optionally even assign a particular **IAM Role** for your Auto Scaled instances by selecting an appropriate Role name from the **IAM role** drop-down list. In this case, I have not provided any roles to my Launch Configuration. Select the **Enable CloudWatch detailed monitoring** checkbox if you wish to have your instances monitored for a duration of 60 seconds. By default your instances will be monitored by CloudWatch for a minimum period of 300 seconds (five minutes) for no charge at all. Selecting **detailed monitoring** will incur additional charges, so use it with caution.

 Note: Enabling the **CloudWatch detailed monitoring** option is highly recommended in case the instances belong to a production environment.

1. Choose AMI	2. Choose Instance Type	3. Configure details	4. Add Storage	5. Configure Security Group	6. Review

Create Launch Configuration

Name ⓘ	US-WEST-PROD-WEB-LC-1	
Purchasing option ⓘ	☐ Request Spot Instances	
IAM role ⓘ	None ▾	
Monitoring ⓘ	☐ Enable CloudWatch detailed monitoring	
	Learn more	

Once your basic details are filled out, you can even set the instance's IP addressing scheme by selecting the **Assign a public IP address** to every instance option from the **Advanced Details** section. This option comes in handy when you wish to connect and log into to your VPC instances from your home network.

Step 4 – Add storage

With your Launch Configuration created, you can now continue to adding and configuring the remaining elements of your instances, which includes the Storage and Security Groups. You can add an optional **Volume** to your instances by selecting the **Add NewVolume** button on the **Add Storage** page. The rest of the fields are pretty self-explanatory, so I'm really not going to talk about them here. In my case, I have not provided any additional volumes to my instances and opted for only a single EBS root volume (`/dev/xvda`). Click on **Next: Configure Security Group** to either create or select an existing security group for your auto scaled instances.

Step 5 – Configure Security Group

From the **Configure Security Group** page, select an appropriate **Security Group** for your Auto Scaled instances. Since we are working with web server instances, I have selected my **US-WEST-PROD-WEB-SG** (*Web Server Security Group*). The group has the following set of inbound rules:

Web Server Inbound Security Rules			
Source	**Protocol**	**Port Range**	**Remarks**
0.0.0.0/0	TCP	22	Permit inbound SSH access to web server instance
0.0.0.0/0	TCP	80	Permit inbound HTTP access to web server instance
0.0.0.0/0	TCP	443	Permit inbound HTTPS access to web server instance

You can optionally even create a new Security Group as per your requirements; however, make sure to have the SSH as well as the HTTP ports opened up before you proceed with the next steps.

Step 6 – Review

Phew! After all those intense configurations, we are now officially ready to review and create our Launch Configuration. Make sure the **AMI details**, **Instance Type**, and your **Launch Configuration** settings are correct. Once verified, click on **Create Launch Configuration** to complete the process.

The wizard will now automatically set and create a new Launch Configuration based on your specifications. You can create as many Launch Configurations as you need; however, you will be able to specify only a single LC for an Auto Scaling Group at a time. Also, once a LC is created, there is no way you can edit its configurations. The only way to do so is by creating a new LC and associating that with your Auto Scaling Group. Instances that were launched as a part of the old LC remain unaffected by this change; however, any new instances that are created will use the new LC as their blueprint for the Auto Scaling activity.

Creating the Auto Scaling Group

With your Launch Configuration ready, the next and final stage of creating your first Auto Scaling task involves the setting up of an Auto Scaling Group. We have already talked about Auto Scaling Groups in the beginning of this chapter, so let's have a quick recap of the same.

As discussed previously, an Auto Scaling Group is nothing more than a logical grouping of instances that share some common scaling characteristics between them. Each group has its own set of criteria specified which includes the minimum and maximum number of instances that the group should have along with the desired number of instances which the group must have at all times. Besides these, an Auto Scaling group also helps us to create and define scaling triggers which, when triggered, result in either instances getting added or removed from the group. These scaling triggers rely on CloudWatch Metrics and periodic health checks to determine whether a particular instance is unhealthy or unresponsive. If such an instance is found, then the Auto Scaling service will automatically terminate the unhealthy instance and replace it with a brand new one! Awesome, isn't it!

With these basics in mind, let us go ahead and continue where we left off from the Launch Configurations stage. Log in to your AWS account using your IAM credentials and select the **EC2** option from the **AWS Management Console**. Next, from the navigation pane provided, select the **Auto Scaling Groups** option. This will bring up the **Auto Scaling Group dashboard,** as shown in the following screenshot. Select the **Create Auto Scaling Group** option to get started:

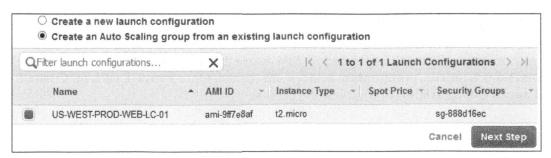

Here, you will be provided with two options: either create a new launch configuration or create an Auto Scaling Group out of an existing one. Since we have already created our LC, select the **Create an Auto Scaling group from an existing launch configuration** option. Select the newly created LC and click on **Next Step** to proceed. Now comes the fun part where we actually get to configure the Auto Scaling Groups. Follow the next steps carefully and fill out the required fields as per your requirements:

Step 1 – Configure Auto Scaling group details

The first step in creating your Auto Scaling Group requires you to provide a suitable name for your Auto Scaling Group as well as its **Network** and **Load Balancing** details.

Fill in the required fields as per your requirements:

- **Group name**: Provide a suitable name for your Auto Scaling Group. In this case, I have used the name US-WEST-PROD-WEB-ASG-1.

- **Group size**: Here, enter the desired capacity for your Auto Scaling Group. Remember that the value entered here represents the number of instances Auto Scaling must have at all times, so choose a smaller number to start with. In my case, I have chosen **1** as this is just a demo:

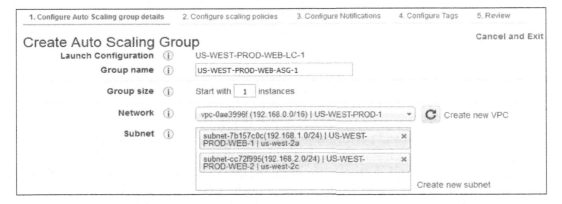

- **Network**: From the **Network** drop-down list, select your appropriate VPC in which you wish to enable Auto Scaling.

- **Subnet**: Once your **Network** is selected, you can now select your corresponding subnets. Auto Scaling will then launch the instances based on the subnet that you select here. In my case, I have selected two subnets, each created in a different AZ. This setup maximizes the availability of your application while minimizing any unwanted downtime.

Each instance in this Auto Scaling Group will be provided with a public IP address.

With these basic settings filled out, we now move on to the **Advanced Details** section of our Auto Scaling Group:

- **Load Balancing**: These are optional settings that you can configure to work with your Auto Scaling Group. Since we have already created and configured our ELB, we will be using that itself to balance out incoming traffic for our instances. Select the **Receive traffic from Elastic Load Balancer(s)** option, as shown in the following screenshot. Next, type in the name of your **ELB** (US-WEST-PROD-LB-01) in the **Load Balancing** text field:

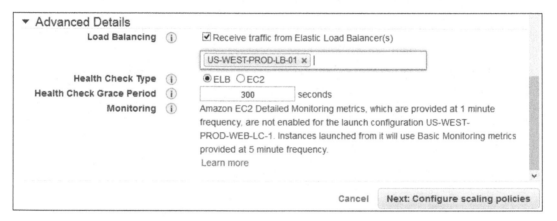

- **Health Check Type**: You can use either your EC2 instances or even your ELB as a health check mechanism to make sure that your instances are in a healthy state and performing optimally. By default, Auto Scaling will check your EC2 instances periodically for their health status. If an unhealthy instance is found, Auto Scaling will immediately replace that with a healthy one. Here, I have selected **ELB** as my health check type, so all the instance health checks are now going to be performed by the ELB itself.

- **Health Check Grace Period**: Enter the health check's grace period in seconds. By default, this value is set to **300** seconds.

Once your Auto Scaling Group's basic configuration is complete, the next step is where you actually get to create and define the scaling policies. Click on **Next: Configure scaling policies** to continue with the process.

Step 2 – Configure scaling policies

The second most important part of creating any Auto Scaling Group is defining its scaling policies. A scaling policy is a set of instructions used by the Auto Scaling service to make adjustments in your Auto Scaling group's size (*number of instances*). Each Scaling Policy is attached with a CloudWatch alarm and a notification action. When the alarm is breached, the appropriate scaling policy is triggered, which will either add or remove instances from your Auto Scaling Group depending on its definition. Let us go ahead and create a few such scaling policies for our own use.

First up, we need to define whether this particular scaling policy will be used to maintain the Auto Scaling Group's initial size (*desired capacity*) only or whether you wish to adjust the Group's size by adding or removing instances. In this case, I have selected the **Use scaling policies to adjust the capacity of this group** option, as shown in the following screenshot. I have also provided the minimum (1 instance) and maximum number (5 instances) of instances I want to the group to scale between. You can provide your own set of values here as per your needs; however, stick to the basics if this is your first time:

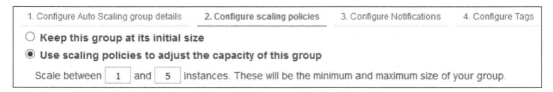

Next, we define and create our scaling policies. There are two policies that are used by an Auto Scaling Group: one to increase the instance count based on certain alarms and the other to decrease the instance count. To begin with, let us first go ahead and populate the **Increase Group Size** policy, as shown in the following screenshot:

- **Name**: Provide a suitable name for your scale-out policy.

- **Execute policy when**: In this field, you have to select a pre-configured alarm using which the policy will get triggered. Since this is our first time configuring, select the **Add new alarm** option. This will pop up the **Create Alarm** dialog, as shown in the following screenshot:

Filling out and creating the alarm is a very simple process; for example, we want our Auto Scaling Group to be monitored based on the **CPU Utilization** metric for an interval of **5 minutes**. If the **average CPU Utilization** is greater than or equal to 50 percent for at least one consecutive period, then send a notification mail to the specified **SNS Topic** (in this case, **All-About-Dogs-Admins**). You can verify your alarm's configuration by comparing it to the Alarm Graph as well. Once you are satisfied with your settings, click on **Create Alarm**.

- **Take the action**: With your basic alarm now set, you can further tell your policy what action it has to take if the particular threshold is breached. Select **Add** from the dropdown list and provide a suitable number of instances that you wish to add when a certain condition matches. For example, I have created a four-step scaling policy that first adds one instance to the group when the average CPU utilization is within a particular threshold range, such as 50-55 percent. Next, another instance is added when the CPU utilization increases even further to 55-65 percent, and so on so forth. You can add multiple such steps by selecting the **Add step** option, as shown in the following screenshot. Once the steps are added, your Increase Group Size policy should look something like the following:

Adding steps in a policy is an optional setting and is only meant to provide you with finer grained control over when exactly your instances are to be launched.

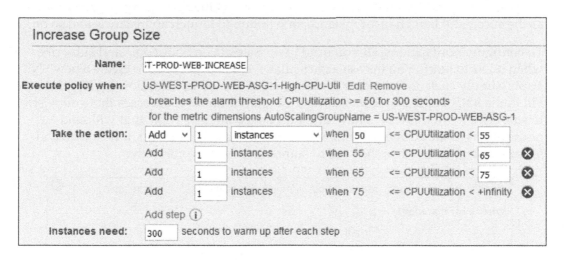

- **Instances need**: With the steps added, the final field left is the Cooldown period. By default, this value is set to **300** seconds and can be changed as per your requirements. What is this cooldown period and why is it important? Well, a Cooldown period is kind of like a grace period that we assign to the Auto Scaling Group to ensure that we don't launch or terminate any more resources before the effects of previous scaling activities are completed. It is just a way of telling the Auto Scaling Group to wait for a short period of time before initiating another scaling event. Ideally, this field is very important and should not be taken for granted. There have been cases where the Auto Scaling activity goes into a loop-like condition where an instance is launched and terminated repeatedly, only because the cooling period and the ELB health check timeout did not match, so use this value with utmost care!

Once the Increase Group Size policy is created, you can conversely create and configure the **Decrease Group Size policy** as well. Follow the same steps by first creating and assigning an alarm that now triggers when the average CPU Utilization is less than or equal to 75 percent. Next, add the scaling steps that will remove one instance from the Auto Scaling Group at a time depending on the alarm's threshold ranges, such as removing one instance from the group when the average CPU utilization is between 65 percent and 75 percent and so on so forth. Once configured, click on **Next: Configure Notifications** to proceed with the next steps.

Step 3 – Configure notifications

Notifications play a very important role in an Auto Scaling activity. You can basically configure your Auto Scaling Group to send notifications out to any particular endpoint, such as an e-mail address, whenever a specified event gets triggered, such as the successful launch of an instance, or a failure to launch an instance, and so on.

To configure notifications, all you need to do is create an SNS Topic and subscribe when it has to notify you in case a particular event is triggered. To create a new SNS Topic, simply click on the **create topic** option, as shown in the following screenshot. Fill in the **SNS Topic Name** as well as the required **Email Addresses** that you wish to subscribe to. In this case, I have already created an SNS Topic that will send notifications to the administrators whenever the instances successfully launch and terminate as well as when they fail to launch or terminate correctly:

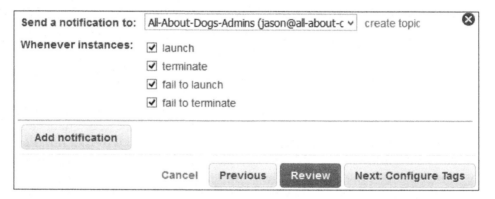

You can optionally add more notifications to your Auto Scaling Group by selecting the **Add notification** option as well. Once done, click on **Next: Configure Tags** to proceed.

Step 4 – Configure tags

We do know the importance of tags and tagging from our previous chapters. Tagging helps us organize, manage, and identify our resources more effectively and efficiently by specifying one or more metadata in the form of a **key** and a **value** pair. Auto Scaling Groups too can be assigned tags using the **Configure Tags** page. Provide a suitable **Key** and **Value** for your new Auto Scaling Group. You can optionally even tag your instances that will be launched by your Auto scaling Group by selecting the **Tag New Instances** checkbox, as shown in the following screenshot:

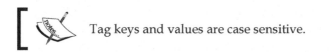 Tag keys and values are case sensitive.

Remember, you can add up to 10 tags for each Auto Scaling Group that you create as well as remove them at any time. Once you have tagged your Auto Scaling Group, move on to the final step of the process by clicking on the **Review** option.

Step 5 – Review

Congratulations if you made it this far! You are almost done with your first fully functional Auto Scaling Group, but before you finish, review the settings once more and make sure that all the configuration settings and auto scaling values are correct. Once satisfied with the checks, click on **Create Auto Scaling Group**. The group will first check the number of desired instances that you have specified. In our scenario, we specified one as the desired value, so Auto Scaling will automatically launch one instance in either of the subnets that we specified during the group's configuration stage. You can view and verify the instance launch from the **EC2 Management Dashboard** as well. With the instance successfully launched, we now move on to an important part of verifying and actually testing the Auto Scaling configurations.

Verifying and testing Auto Scaling

Once your Auto Scaling configuration and deployment is completed, you are now ready to go ahead and verify its validity. The first step to do so is by checking the instance deployment itself using the ELB dashboard. Select the **Elastic Load Balancer** option from the **EC2 dashboard** and select your **ELB,** as shown in the following screenshot. Next, select the **Instances** tab and make a note of the instance's **Status** column. It should display the status as **InService** as shown in the following screenshot. This basically means that the instance is associated with the ELB and that its health status is being continuously monitored by the ELB as well. In some cases, your **Status** column may show the status as **Pending**, so don't worry, give it a bit more time and the status should change back to **InService** again. You can optionally even view the number of instances launched as well as the overall health of your AZ by viewing the **Instance Count** as well as the **Health** columns highlighted in the following:

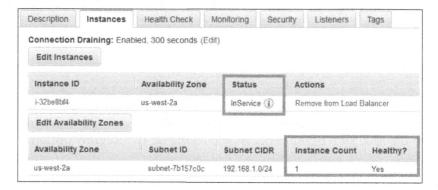

The next way to verify the Auto Scaling configuration as well as the ELB is by actually viewing the ELB's DNS name in a local web browser. If all goes well, you should see your application's landing page, or in this case the index.php page. Make a note of the ELB's public DNS name and copy it over to any web browser of your choice. Don't forget to append the /index.php landing path to the public DNS as well, as shown in the following screenshot:

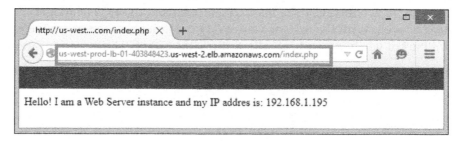

Now in my case, the `index.php` file is nothing more than a simple PHP page that displays the IP address of the running underlying instance along with a simple welcome message.

The code for the `index.php` file is as follows:

```php
<?php
echo "Hello! I am a Web Server instance and my IP address is:
".$_SERVER['SERVER_ADDR']; ?>
```

This IP address is actually a part of the Web Server Subnet (us-west-2a) that we created back in *Chapter 5*, *Building Your Own Private Clouds Using Amazon VPC*. If you got it till this far, then you are on the right track! However, in case you don't see your application's landing page here, then I might suggest changing your instance's cooldown period as well as the ELB's Health Check period to suit your needs.

Once the verification is completed, you can go ahead and test your Auto Scaling configuration. To do so, simply SSH into your launched instance and increase its load using any load synthesizer tool you can find. I personally like **Stress** as well as **Lookbusy** as they are really simple and easy to use. For this scenario, I used Lookbusy to increase the instance's CPU Utilization to 60 percent. After a good 5 minutes of continuously loading the instance, the Increase Capacity scaling policy was triggered and a new instance was automatically created to balance out the application's load. You can verify this newly added instance by once again checking your **Instances** tab from the ELB dashboard. You should see two instances now, as shown in the following screenshot:

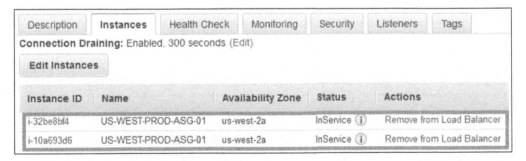

Similarly, gradually increase the CPU utilization of your instances from 60 percent to 70 percent and, finally, to 85 percent. If all goes well, you should see instances launch up as per your increase scaling policy. Once the instances are all added, gradually reduce the CPU utilization and watch the instances terminate automatically as well. This is one of the real reasons why I love AWS so much! It's simple and so easy to use! Once configured properly, your Auto Scaling service as well as ELB can run completely independently from all manual interventions, so you can concentrate on your business while the heavy lifting is taken care of by AWS itself!

Suspend, resume and delete Auto Scaling

Yup! You heard it right! You can additionally even suspend and resume an Auto Scaling activity in your Auto Scaling Group. Why would someone want to do that? Well, at times, you may want to run some minor configuration changes in your instances but don't want that to trigger an auto scaling event; or there may be a configuration issue in your Auto Scaling Group, or some problem with your application and you want to investigate it but without starting up the Auto Scaling process, and so on. In such cases, suspending an Auto Scaling process comes in really handy!

There is a small catch though! You cannot suspend or resume an Auto Scaling activity using the EC2 Management Console; you have to use the AWS CLI to get this done. Let us go through few commands and see how easy it is to put an Auto Scaling Group in a suspended state.

First up, let us describe our Auto Scaling Group using the AWS CLI. Type in the command as shown in the following and substitute the Auto Scaling Group's name with your own:

```
# aws autoscaling describe-auto-scaling-groups --auto-scaling-group-
names US-WEST-PROD-WEB-ASG-1
```

Now go ahead and suspend the Auto Scaling Group using the following command:

```
# aws autoscaling suspend-processes --auto-scaling-group-name US-
WEST-PROD-WEB-ASG-1
```

Verify the status of your Auto Scaling Group by running the describe-auto-scaling-groups command once again. You should see its status shown as **SUSPENDEDPROCESSES**:

To resume an Auto Scaling Group, type in the following command as shown in the following:

```
# awsautoscaling resume-processes --auto-scaling-group-name US-WEST-PROD-WEB-ASG-1
```

Once again, check the status of your Auto Scaling Group to make sure that the process has indeed been initiated. Both the `suspend-processes` and `resume-processes` commands can be used to suspend and resume, respectively, the entire scaling activity in one go; however, if you wish to suspend or resume only a particular process from the entire Auto Scaling activity, then you will have to use the `--scaling-processes` attribute along with your `suspend-processes` and `resume-processes` commands.

For example, consider the following example that suspends an Auto Scaling's Health Check process:

```
# awsautoscaling suspend-processes --auto-scaling-group-name US-WEST-PROD-WEB-ASG-1  --scaling-processes HealthCheck
```

You can use the following set of processes with the `suspend`/`resume` commands: `Launch`, `Terminate`, `HealthCheck`, `ReplaceUnhealthy`, `AZRebalance`, `AlarmNotification`, `ScheduledActions`, and `AddToLoadBalancer`.

> Tip: To know more about each of these individual processes, refer to `http://docs.aws.amazon.com/AutoScaling/latest/DeveloperGuide/US_SuspendResume.html`.

With your process suspend and resume operations done, the final thing left to do is clean up your Auto Scaling Group. To delete your Auto Scaling Group, you first need to make sure that it has no running instances in it. To do so, simply set the minimum and maximum number of instances to zero! You can edit the group's size by using either the Auto Scaling Group Dashboard or the AWS CLI using the following set of commands:

First, set the minimum and maximum size to zero using the following command:

```
# awsautoscaling update-auto-scaling-group --auto-scaling-group-name US-WEST-PROD-WEB-ASG-1 --max-size 0 --min-size 0
```

```
[root@YoYoNUX ~]#
[root@YoYoNUX ~]# aws autoscaling update-auto-scaling-group \
> --auto-scaling-group-name US-WEST-PROD-WEB-ASG-1 \
> --max-size 0 --min-size 0 \
> --profile jason
[root@YoYoNUX ~]#
```

Before you proceed with the deletion of the group, check the status of the group using the `describe-auto-scaling-groups` command. Make sure there are no instances running at all. Next, type in the following command to delete your Auto Scaling Group:

```
# awsautoscaling delete-auto-scaling-group --auto-scaling-group-name
US-WEST-PROD-WEB-ASG-1
```

Once the Auto scaling Group is deleted, you can optionally go ahead and delete the Launch Configuration as well as the ELB using the following set of commands:

```
# awsautoscaling delete-launch-configuration --launch-configuration-
name US-WEST-PROD-WEB-LC-1
```

Similarly, delete the ELB as well using the following command:

```
# awselb delete-load-balancer US-WEST-PROD-LB-01
```

To know more about the various additional Auto Scaling CLI commands and their usage, refer to `http://docs.aws.amazon.com/cli/latest/reference/autoscaling/index.html`.

Planning your next steps

Well, we covered a lot about Auto Scaling and ELB in this chapter; however, there are a few things that I would really recommend you try out next. First up, let's have a look at ELB! In this chapter, we have looked only at how to set up and configure a very basic HTTP-based ELB. However, in a real production scenario, this just doesn't cut it. That's where you need to deploy your ELB using HTTPS and SSL-like secure protocols. To know more about how you can create and leverage ELBs securely, refer to `http://docs.aws.amazon.com/ElasticLoadBalancing/latest/DeveloperGuide/elb-https-load-balancers.html`.

With your ELB securely configured, there's one additional step that you can configure to enable easier access to your applications hosted on AWS. Route 53 is a highly scalable and available DNS service provided by AWS that can be leveraged to replace the long and complicated public DNS name of an ELB with something a bit more convenient and easier to remember, such as `all-about-dogs.com`. Amazon Route 53 effectively connects your user requests to infrastructure running in AWS, whether it is your EC2 instances, or ELB, or even your S3 bucket. It can also be used as a health check mechanism to periodically monitor the health of your application and its endpoints. To know more about Route 53 and how you can leverage it with your applications, refer to `http://docs.aws.amazon.com/Route53/latest/DeveloperGuide/routing-to-elb-load-balancer.html`.

On a similar note, there are a couple of things that you can try out for Auto Scaling as well. First up is Scheduled Auto Scaling. We have already talked about it in the beginning of this chapter, so I'll not dwell on it for long. Just a few pointers that you should keep in mind when working with Scheduled Auto Scaling: Each scheduled scaling action has to have a unique date and time provided to it in the UTC format that is generally represented as *YYYY-MM-DDThh:mm:ssZ*. You can create a recurring scheduled scaling activity as well; however, note that this will not work side by side with a onetime scheduled activity. Last but not the least, AWS currently does not support scheduled scaling using the EC2 Management Console, which means that you will have to use the AWS CLI for it. To know more on how to leverage Scheduled Auto Scaling for your environments, refer to `http://docs.aws.amazon.com/AutoScaling/latest/DeveloperGuide/schedule_time.html`.

> Note: Auto scaling can also be applied to AWS SQS. I think it is nice to just mention it and point to further reading at:
>
> `http://docs.aws.amazon.com/AutoScaling/latest/DeveloperGuide/as-using-sqs-queue.html`.

The final recommendation with regard to Auto Scaling is something a bit new and is called as Lifecycle Hooks. Hooks basically allow you to add a custom event to your instances before they are actually terminated or added to the Auto Scaling Group by the Auto Scaling service. These events can be anything from retrieving logs from your instances to installing and configuring software, and so on. The main idea behind hooks is very similar to the concept of suspending and resuming Auto Scaling processes; however, here we don't suspend the Auto Scaling activity but just put the instance into a definite `wait` state. It is during this `wait` state that you get to perform your selected action on your instance. Do note, however, that the default wait period is only an hour. So if you do not perform any action over your instances during this period, Auto Scaling will automatically terminate the instances once the time has passed. And very similar to Schedule Auto Scaling, you cannot perform Lifecycle Hooks using the EC2 Management Console. You can use the AWS CLI or the AWS API to perform the same.

Recommendations and best practices

Now that we have come to the end of this chapter, let us look at some key recommendations and best practices that you need to keep in mind when working with ELBs and Auto Scaling:

- Plan and provide the ELB with enough of a grace period (by default its *300 seconds*) so that it does not put an instance in the unhealthy state even before the application has had time to initialize completely.

- Use Amazon Route 53 and provide a suitable domain name for your applications. Additionally, leverage Route 53 to balance your application's load across multiple regions as well.

- Although ELBs can handle large loads (up to *20k/sec*), they can only do so if the load increases gradually, say over a period of several hours. If your application spikes in load in minutes rather than hours, then you are better off by using pre-warmed ELBs. To know more about pre-warmed ELBs and how to get them, refer to `http://aws.amazon.com/articles/1636185810492479#pre-warming`.

- Configure HTTPS and SSL listeners for your ELB whenever possible.

- Plan your Auto Scaling well in advance. This includes deciding on the number of instances that will be required for your application as well as the type of instance family.

- Plan on which monitoring metrics (*CPUUtilization*, *MemoryUtilization*, *Disk Space used*, and so on) you tend to use and set up the scaling policies accordingly.

- Deploy your Auto Scaling Groups across multiple AZs. This provides an additional layer of high availability in case an entire AZ should fail.

- Prepare, test, and bootstrap your application on an AMI before adding it to the Auto Scaling activity. Try and keep your application as decoupled as possible.

- Always monitor and set up notifications for your Auto Scaling activity. This will help you track and maintain your application's as well as instances' performance.

Summary

So it's been a really long but interesting chapter and I really hope that you have got to learn about Amazon ELB as well as Auto Scaling as much as possible. Let's quickly recap all the things covered so far in this chapter.

To begin with, we talked about the importance of Auto Scaling and how it proves to be super beneficial when compared to the traditional mode of scaling infrastructure. You then learnt a bit about AWS Auto Scaling and its core components. Next, you learnt about a new service offering called Elastic Load Balancers and saw how easy it is to deploy one for your own use. Toward the end of this chapter, we also deployed our first Launch Configuration and an Auto Scaling Group and, finally, topped it all off with some simple steps to help verify and test the entire setup.

In the next chapter we are going to dive into the amazing world of databases and learn how AWS provides some simple and easy to use database services, so stay tuned for lots more coming your way!

8
Database-as-a-Service Using Amazon RDS

In the previous chapter, you learnt a lot about the concepts of Auto Scaling and Elastic Load Balancing, and how you can leverage them to host highly scalable and fault tolerant applications.

In this chapter, we are going to shift our attention from all those web servers and EC2 instances and talk about more on the database offerings provided by AWS, with some special emphasis on Amazon RDS. This chapter will help you understand the overall concept of RDS and even demonstrate how you can leverage RDS in your own application's hosting environment. We will also be studying some of AWS's other popular database-as-a-service options along the way; so let's get started without any further ado!

An overview of Amazon RDS

Before we go ahead and dive into the amazing world of RDS, it is essential to understand what exactly AWS provides you when it comes to database-as-a-service offerings and how can you effectively use them. To start off, AWS provides a bunch of awesome and really simple-to-use database services that are broadly divided into two classes: the relational databases, which consist of your MySQL and Oracle databases, and the non-relational databases, which consist of a propriety NoSQL database similar to MongoDB. Each of these database services is designed by AWS to provide you with the utmost ease and flexibility of use along with built-in robustness and fault tolerance. This means that all you need to do as an end user or a developer is simply configure the databases service once, run it just as you would run any standard database without worrying about the internal complexities of clustering, sharding, and so on, and only pay for the amount of resources that you use! Now that's awesome, isn't it!

However, there is a small catch to this! Since the service is provided and maintained by AWS, you as a user or developer are not provided with all the fine tuning and configuration settings that you would generally find if you were to install and configure a database on your own. If you really want to have complete control over your databases and their configurations, then you might as well install them on EC2 instances directly. Then you can fine-tune them just as you would on any traditional OS, but remember that in doing so, you will have to take care of the database and all its inner complexities.

With these basic concepts in mind, let us go ahead and learn a thing or two about Amazon **Relational Database Service (RDS)**. Amazon RDS is a database service that basically allows you to configure and scale your popular relational databases such as MySQL and Oracle based on your requirements. Besides the database, RDS also provides additional features such as automated backup mechanisms, point-in-time recovery, replication options such as multi-AZ deployments and Read Replicas, and much more! Using these services you can get up and running with a completely scalable and fault tolerant database in a matter of minutes, all with just a few clicks of a button! And the best part of all this is that you don't need to make any major changes to your existing applications or code. You can run your apps with RDS just as you would run them with any other traditional hosted database, with one major advantage: you don't bother about the underlying infrastructure or the database management. It is all taken care of by AWS itself!

RDS currently supports five popular relational database engines, namely MySQL, Oracle, Microsoft's SQL Server, PostgreSQL, and MariaDB as well. Besides these, AWS also provides a MySQL-like propriety database called Amazon Aurora. Aurora is a drop-in replacement for MySQL that provides up to five times the performance that a standard MySQL database provides. It is specifically designed to scale with ease without having any major consequences for your application or code. How does it achieve that? Well, it uses a combination of something called as an Aurora Cluster Volume, as well as one Primary Instance and one or more Aurora Replicas. The Cluster Volume is nothing more than virtual database storage that spans across multiple AZs. Each AZ is provided with a copy of the cluster data so that the database is available even if an entire AZ goes offline. Each cluster gets one Primary Instance that's responsible for performing all the read/write operations, data modifications, and so on. With the Primary Instance, you also get a few Aurora Replicas (also like Primary Instances). A Replica can only perform read operations and is generally used to distribute the database's workload across the Cluster. You can have up to 15 Replicas present in a Cluster besides the Primary Instance, as shown in the following image:

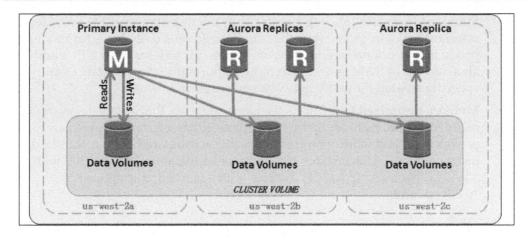

You can also read more on Amazon Aurora at
`http://docs.aws.amazon.com/AmazonRDS/`
`latest/UserGuide/CHAP_Aurora.html`.

With this basic information in mind, let us now understand some of RDS's core components and take a look at how RDS actually works.

RDS instance types

To begin with, RDS does operate in a very similar way as EC2. Just as you have EC2 instances configured with a certain amount of CPU and storage resources, RDS too has instances that are spun up each time you configure a database service. The major difference between these instances and your traditional EC2 ones is that they cannot be accessed remotely via SSH even if you want to. Why? Well, since it's a managed service and everything is provided and maintained by AWS itself, there is no need for you to SSH into them! Each instance already has a particular database engine preinstalled and configured in it. All you need to do is select your particular instance type and assign it some storage, and voila! There you have it! A running database service of your choice in under 5 minutes! Let's have a quick look at some of the RDS instance types and their common uses:

- **Micro instances** (`db.t1.micro`): Just as we have micro instances in our EC2 environments, the same is also provided for RDS as well. Each database micro instance is provided with just 1 CPU and approximately 600 MB of RAM, which is good enough if you just want to test RDS or play around with it. This instance type, however, is strictly not recommended for any production-based workloads at all. Along with this particular micro instance, RDS also provides a slightly better instance type in the form of a `db.m1.small`, which provides 1 CPU with a slightly better 1.7 GB RAM.

- **Standard instances (**db.m3**)**: Besides your micro instances, RDS provides a standard set of instance types that can be used on a daily basis for moderate production workloads. This class of instance provides up to 8 CPUs and about 30 GB of RAM as well, but more importantly, these instances are specially created for better network performance as well.

- **Memory optimized (**db.r3**)**: As the name suggests, this instance class provides really high-end, memory optimized instances that are capable of faster performance and more computing capacity as compared to your standard instance classes. This instance class provides a maximum of 32 CPUs with a RAM capacity of up to 244 GB along with a network throughput of 10 GB/second.

> The db.r3 DB instance classes are not presently available in the South America (Sao Paulo) and AWS GovCloud (US) regions.

- **Burst capable (**db.t2**)**: This instance class provides a baseline performance level with the ability to burst to full CPU usage if required. This particular class of database instance, however, can only be launched in a VPC environment. The maximum CPU offered in this category is up to 2 CPUs with approximately 8 GB of RAM.

Along with an instance type, each RDS instance is also backed by an EBS volume. You can use this EBS volume for storing your database files, logs, and lots more! More importantly, you can also select the type of storage to go with your instances as per your requirements. Here's a quick look at the different storage types provided with your RDS instances:

- **Magnetic (standard)**: Magnetic storage is an ideal choice for applications that have a light to moderate I/O requirement. A magnetic volume can provide up to 100 IOPS approximately on average with burst capability of up to hundreds of IOPS. The disk sizes can range anywhere between 5 GB to 3 TB. An important point to note here, however, is that since magnetic storage is kind of shared, your overall performance can vary depending on the overall resource usage by other customers as well.

- **General purpose (SSD)**: These are the most commonly used storage types from the lot and are generally a good choice of storage if you are running a small to medium-sized database. General purpose or SSD-backed storage can provided better performance as compared to your magnetic storage at much lower latencies and higher IOPs. General purpose storage volumes can provide a base performance of three IOPS/GB and have the ability to burst up to 3,000 IOPS as per the requirements. These volumes can range in size from 5 GB to 6 TB for MySQL, MariaDB, PostgreSQL, and Oracle DB instances, and from 20 GB to 4 TB for SQL server DB instances.

- **Provisioned IOPs**: Although general purpose volumes are good for moderate database workloads, they are not a good option when it comes to dedicated performance requirements and higher IOPs. In such cases, provisioned IOPs are the best choice of storage type for your instances. You can specify IOPs anywhere between the values 1,000 all the way up to 30,000 depending on the database engine you select as well as the amount of disk size that you specify. A MySQL, MariaDB, PostgreSQL, or Oracle database instance with approximately 6 TB of storage can get up to 30,000 IOPs. Similarly, an SQL server DB instance with approximately 4 TB of disk size can get up to 20,000 IOPs.

 You cannot decrease the storage of your RDS instance once it is allocated to it.

With the RDS instance types in mind, let's now look at some of the key services as well as processes provided by Amazon RDS.

Multi-AZ deployments and Read Replicas

We all know the importance and the hard work needed to keep a database, especially the one running a production workload up and running at all times. This is no easy feat, especially when you have to manage the intricacies and all the tedious configuration parameters. But thankfully, Amazon RDS provides us with a very simple and easy-to-use framework, using which tasks such as providing high availability to your databases, clustering, mirroring, and so on are all performed using just a click of a button!

Let's take high availability for example. RDS leverages your region's availability zones and mirrors your entire primary database over to some other AZ present in the same region. This is called as a **Multi-AZ deployment** and it can easily be enforced using the RDS database deployment wizard. How does it work? Well it's quite simple actually. It all starts when you first select the Multi-AZ deployment option while deploying your database. At that moment, RDS will automatically create and maintain another database as a standby replica in some different AZ. Now if you use a MySQL, MariaDB, Oracle, or PostgreSQL as your database engine, then the mirroring technology used by RDS is AWS propriety. Whereas, if you go for an SQL server deployment, then the mirroring technology used is SQL server mirroring by default. Once the standby replica database instance is created, it continuously syncs up with the primary database instance from time to time, and in the event of a database failure or even a planned maintenance activity, RDS will automatically failover from the primary to the standby replica database instance within a couple of minutes:

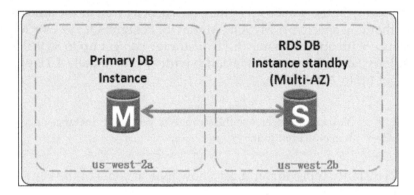

 Amazon RDS guarantees an SLA of 99.95 percent! To know more about the RDS SLA agreement, refer to http://aws.amazon.com/rds/sla/.

However remarkable and easy multi-AZ deployment may be, it still has some minor drawbacks of its own. Firstly, you can't use a multi-AZ deployment for scaling out your databases, and, secondly, there is no failover provided if your entire region goes down. With these issues in mind, RDS provides an additional feature for our database instances called as Read Replicas.

Read Replicas are database instances that enable you to offload your primary database instance's workloads by having all the read queries routed through them. The data from your primary instance is copied asynchronously to the read replica instance using the database engine's built-in replication engine. How does it all work? Well it's very similar to the steps required for creating an AMI from a running EC2 instance! First up, RDS will create a snapshot based on your primary database instance. Next, this snapshot is used to span a read replica instance. Once the instance is up and running, the database engine will then start the asynchronous replication process such that whenever a change is made to the data in the primary, it gets automatically replicated over to the read replica instance as well. You can then connect your application to the new read replica and offload all your read queries to it! As of date, RDS supports only MySQL, MariaDB, and PostgreSQL database engines for read replicas:

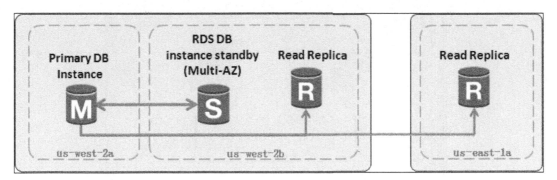

You can create up to five Read Replicas for a given database instance.

You can additionally use these Read Replicas as a failover mechanism as well by deploying read replicas in a different region altogether. The only downside to this is that you will have to manually promote the replica as a primary when the latter fails. We will be creating and promoting a Read Replica later on in this chapter, but for now let's look at how you can create and get started with your first database using RDS.

Working with Amazon RDS

In this section, we are going to create our very first scalable database using the Amazon RDS service. For simplicity, I will be deploying a simple MySQL database using the RDS Management Console; however, you can use any of the database engines provided by RDS for your testing purposes, including Oracle, MariaDB, PostgreSQL, as well as SQL Server. Let's first examine our use case up to now:

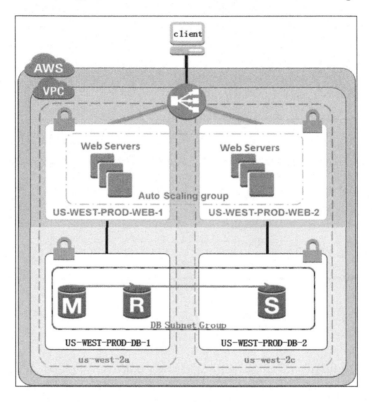

For starters, we have already set up Auto Scaling and Load Balancing for our application's web server instances (see *Chapter 7, Manage Your Applications with Auto Scaling and Elastic Load Balancing*), as shown in the preceding image. We have also created a separate private subnet in each AZ for hosting our database instances. These subnets are named US-WEST-PROD-DB-1 (192.168.5.0/24) and US-WEST-PROD-DB-2 (192.168.6.0/24), respectively. Another extremely important point here is that the communication between the public subnets and the private subnets is also set up using a combination of network ACLs as well as security groups that can be found in *Chapter 5, Building Your Own Private Clouds Using Amazon VPC*. Now, if you haven't been following this book from the very beginning, you might find all these things a bit vague to set up all over again, but don't worry! You can replicate the next steps even with a standalone VPC subnet as well.

With our subnets in place, the next thing to do is jot down the database's essential configuration parameters as well as plan whether you want to leverage a Multi-AZ deployment and Read Replicas for your deployment or not. The configuration parameters include the database name, the database engine's version to use, the backup and maintenance window details, and so on. For this deployment, I will be deploying my database using the Multi-AZ deployment option as well. Do note, however, that the Multi-AZ deployment scheme is not included in the AWS Free Tier eligibility and, hence, you will be charged for the same. To know more about the costs associated with your RDS services, refer to https://aws.amazon.com/rds/pricing/. Once you have thoroughly planned out these details, you can go ahead and start off with the actual deployment of the database.

Getting started with MySQL on Amazon RDS

You can access and manage your RDS deployments by using the AWS CLI, the AWS SDK, as well as the AWS Management Console. For this activity, we will be using the AWS Management Console. Log on to your AWS account using the IAM credentials, and from the AWS Management Console, select the **RDS** option from the **Database** group, as shown in the following screenshot:

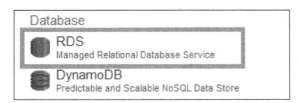

Next, from the RDS Management Dashboard, select the option **Subnet Groups** from the navigation pane. A **Subnet Group** is an essential step toward setting up the security of your database. For starters, a subnet group is a logical grouping or cluster of one or more subnets that belong to a VPC; in this case, the cluster is of our two database subnets (US-WEST-PROD-DB-1 and 2).When we first launch a DB Instance in a VPC, the subnet group is responsible for providing the database instance with an IP address from a preferred subnet present in a particular availability zone.

To get started, provide a suitable **Name** and **Description** for your DB Subnet Group as shown in the following screenshot. Next, from the **VPC ID** drop-down list, select a VPC of your choice. In my case, I have selected the **US-WEST-PROD-1** VPC (**192.168.0.0/16**). Once your VPC is selected, you can now add the required set of subnets to your DB Subnet Group. To do so, first select the preferred **Availability Zone** and its corresponding **Subnet ID**. Click on **Add** to add your subnet to the DB Subnet Group:

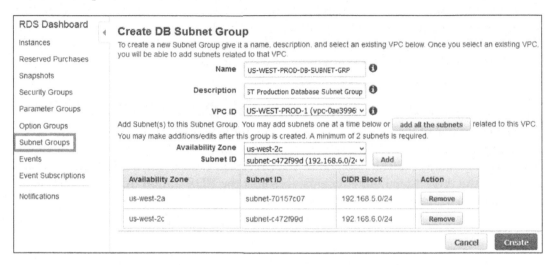

Now as a good practice, provide at least two subnets that are present in different AZs for your DB Subnet Group. For example, in my case, I have provided two private subnets that are present in us-west-2a (**US-WEST-PROD-DB-1**) and us-west-2c (**US-WEST-PROD-DB-2**), respectively. Click on **Create** when done. With this step complete, you can now go ahead and create your first RDS database instance in your VPC!

Creating a MySQL DB instance

Creating an RDS database instance involves a simple four-step process. To begin with, select the **Instances** option from the navigation pane, as shown in the following screenshot. Next, select the **Launch DB Instance** button to bring up the **DB Launch Wizard**:

Step 1 – Select Engine

To get started, select the appropriate database engine of your choice. For our scenario, I have selected the MySQL database; however, feel free to select any of the database engines as per your requirements.

Step 2 – Production?

Now here comes the fun part! RDS basically allows you to create a database based on your requirements; for example, a production database with multi-AZ support and provisioned IOPS storage or a simpler database that has none of these add-on features. With Multi-AZ deployments, your DB instance is guaranteed with a monthly uptime SLA of 99.95 percent! However, because of such high SLAs, Multi-AZ deployments are not covered under the AWS Free Tier usage scheme. Click on **Next Step** to continue, as shown in the following screenshot:

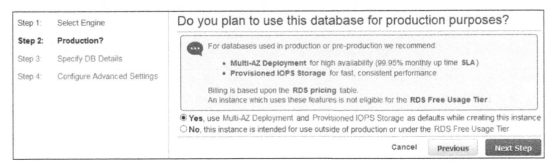

Step 3: Specify DB Details

The next page of the wizard will help you configure some important settings for your DB instance:

- **License Model**: Select the appropriate database **License Model** as per your database engine's selection. MySQL databases have only one license model; that is, general-public-license. Other propriety databases such as Oracle and SQL servers offer two license modes: Licenses Included and the BYOL (*Bring Your Own Licenses*) model. With licenses included, AWS provides the required license keys for your databases, so you don't have to separately purchase one. Alternatively, you can even use the BYOL model to provide your own licenses or obtain new ones from the database provider itself.

- **DB Engine Version**: Select the appropriate **DB Engine Version** as per your requirements. RDS provides and supports a variety of database engine versions that you can choose from. In this case, I have selected the MySQL database engine version **5.6.23** as shown:

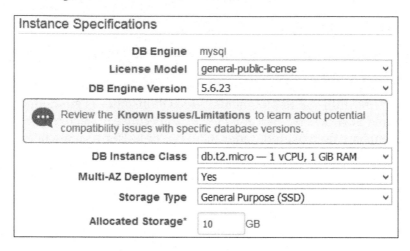

- **DB Instance Class**: From this dropdown list, select the appropriate class of DB instance you wish to provide for your DB instance. For a complete list of supported instance class types, refer to `http://docs.aws.amazon.com/AmazonRDS/latest/UserGuide/Concepts.DBInstanceClass.html`.

- **Multi-AZ Deployment**: Select **Yes** from the dropdown list to ensure a multi-AZ deployment for your database. Selecting **No** will create your DB instance only in a single availability zone.

- **Storage type**: Select an appropriate storage option from the dropdown list. In this case, I have opted for **General Purpose (SSD)**; however, you can also select between **Magnetic** and **Provisioned IOPS** as well.

- **Allocate storage**: Allocate some storage for your database instance. You can provide anywhere between 5 GB to 6 TB.

With these basic configurations out of the way, configure your database's settings as shown in the following screenshot:

Here are the parameters you need to provide in **Settings** panel:

- **DB Instance Identifier**: Provide a suitable name for your DB instance. This name will be a unique representation of your DB instance in the region it is getting deployed in. In my case, I have provided the name **US-WEST-PROD-DB**.

- **Master Username**: Provide a suitable username for your MySQL database. You will use this username to log in to your DB instance once it is deployed.

- **Master Password**: Provide a strong password for your DB instance. You will use this password to log in to your DB instance once it is deployed. You can provide a password that's up to 41 characters long; however, do not provide the following characters in it: (@, " , /).

With the settings configured, click on **Next Step** to proceed with your database's configuration.

Step 4: Configure Advanced Settings

The final step of configuring your database instance can be split up into three parts. The first part involves the setting up of the DB instance's **Network & Security**, that includes selecting the **VPC** along with the **Subnet Group** that we created a while back. The second part involves configuring various database options such as the database name, the database port number on which the application can connect to it, and so on. The final part consists of the database's **Backup** and **Maintenance** window details. Let's have a quick look at each part a bit more in detail:

- **VPC**: Select the name of the VPC that will host your MySQL DB instance. You can optionally select the option **Not** in **VPC** as well if you wish to deploy your DB instance in a standard EC2 Classic environment.

- **Subnet Group**: Select the newly created Subnet Group from the dropdown list, as shown in the following screenshot:

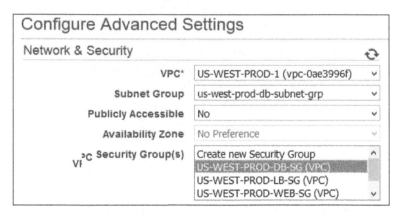

- **Publicly Accessible**: You can optionally set your DB instance to have public connectivity by selecting **Yes** from the **Publicly Accessible** dropdown list; however, as best practice, avoid making your DB instances public at all times.

- **Security Group(s)**: There are two levels of security group that you can use here. The first is a DB security group that is basically used to control access to your DB instances that are outside a VPC. When working with DB security groups, you only need to specify the subnet CIDR associated with your DB instance, and no DB port or protocol details are required. The second is your traditional VPC security group that can be used to control access to your DB instances that are present in a VPC. Here, however, you need to specify both inbound and outbound firewall rules, each with associated port numbers and supported protocols.

You can select one or more security groups here for your DB instance; in my case, I have selected a VPC security group as shown in the previous screenshot. Just remember to open up only the required ports whenever you work with VPC security groups. In this case, I have opened up ports **3306 (MySQL)** and **1433 (SQL Server)**.

Moving on to the second part of the **Advanced Settings**, we will now set up the **Database Options** as shown in the following:

- **Database Name**: Provide a suitable database name here. RDS will not create and initialize any database unless you specify a name here.

- **Database Port**: Provide the port number using which you wish to access your database. MySQL's default port number is **3306**:

 You will not be able to change the database port number once the DB instance is created.

- **DB Parameter Group**: DB parameter groups are logical groupings of database engine configurations that you can apply to one or more DB instances at the same time. RDS creates a default DB parameter group that contains mostly AWS specific configuration settings and default values. You cannot edit the default DB parameter group, so in order to make changes, you will have to create a DB parameter group of your own. In this case, I have left it as the default value.

- **Option Group**: This option is similar to DB parameter groups in that they too provide and support few additional configuration parameters that make it easy to manage databases; for example, MySQL DB Instances support for Memcached and so on. RDS currently supports option groups for Oracle, MySQL, and SQL Server database engines. To know more about option groups, refer to `http://docs.aws.amazon.com/AmazonRDS/latest/UserGuide/USER_WorkingWithOptionGroups.html`.

- **Enable Encryption**: RDS provides standard AES-256 encryption algorithms for encrypting data at rest. This includes your DB instance, its associated Read Replicas, DB Snapshots, as well as the automated backups. An important point to note here is that encryption is not supported on the `t2.micro` DB instances.

For encryption to work, you will need your DB instance to be one of the following instance classes:

Instance Type	Supported Instance Class
General purpose (M3) current generation	`db.m3.medium`
	`db.m3.large`
	`db.m3.xlarge`
	`db.m3.2xlarge`

Instance Type	Supported Instance Class
Memory optimized (R3) current generation	`db.r3.large`
	`db.r3.xlarge`
	`db.r3.2xlarge`
	`db.r3.4xlarge`
	`db.r3.8xlarge`
Burst capable (T2) current generation	`db.t2.large`

In this case, we are not going to encrypt our DB instance, so select **No** from the **Enable Encryption** field as shown in the previous screenshot.

The final part of the **Advance Settings** page is the **Backup** and **Maintenance** window selection. Using this section, you can configure automated backups for your database as well as provide designated maintenance windows for the same. You can set the **Backup Retention Period** as well as the **Backup** window's **Start Time** and **Duration**, as shown in the following screenshot. In my case, I have opted for the backups to be taken at **12:00AM UTC**. If you do not supply a backup window time, then RDS will automatically assign a 30-minute backup window based on your region. For example, the default backup time block for the US West (Oregon) region is 06:00 to 14:00 UTC. RDS will select a 30-minute backup window from this block on a random basis:

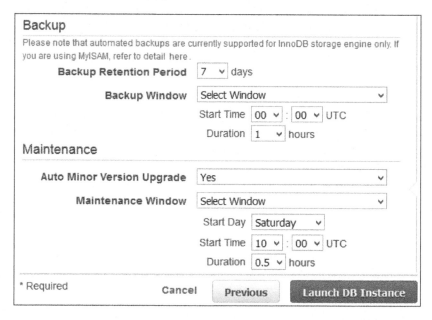

The same can be set for your **Maintenance** window as well. An additional feature provided here is that you can choose whether or not the database should receive automated minor version updates from AWS or not. These minor updates for the database engine will be automatically installed on the database based on their availability as well as the maintenance window's time frame. You can make changes in these settings even after your DB instance is created; however, remember that the backup window should not overlap the weekly maintenance window for your DB instance. Once you have configured the settings, click on **Launch DB Instance** to complete the launch process.

The DB instance will take a good 2 to 3 minutes to spin up depending on whether you have opted for the Multi-AZ deployment or not. You can check the status of your newly created DB instance using the RDS management dashboard, as shown in the following screenshot. Simply check the **Status** column for all the stat us changes that occur while your DB instance is created:

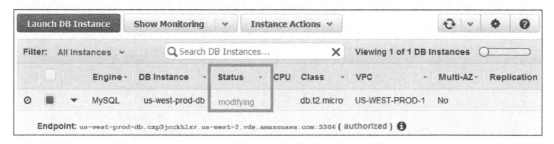

Let's take a quick look at some of the states that a DB instance goes through during its lifecycle:

- **Creating**: This is the first stage of any DB instance's lifecycle where the instance is actually created by RDS. During this time, your database will remain inaccessible.

- **Modifying**: This state occurs whenever the DB instance enters any modifications either set by you or by RDS itself.

- **Backing-up**: RDS will automatically take a backup of your DB instance when it is first created. You can view all your DB instance snapshots using the Snapshots option on the navigation pane.

- **Available**: This status indicates that your DB instance is available and ready for use. You can now access your database remotely by copying the database's endpoint.

To read the complete list of DB instance status messages, refer to http://docs.aws.amazon.com/AmazonRDS/latest/UserGuide/Overview.DBInstance.Status.html.

Connecting remotely to your DB instance

Once your DB Instance is in the Available state, you can now access your database remotely from any other EC2 instance or even remotely from your desktop if you have set the security groups right. In my case, I have launched a new EC2 instance in my VPC, as shown in the following screenshot. This instance is a part of the Web ServerSubnet (US-WEST-PROD-WEB-1) we used in the previous chapter:

```
root@ip-192-168-1-254:~                                                       _ □ ×
[root@ip-192-168-1-254 ~]#
[root@ip-192-168-1-254 ~]# mysql -u admin -h us-west-prod-db.cxp3jcckhlxr.us-west-2.rds.amazonaws.com -p
Enter password:
Welcome to the MySQL monitor.  Commands end with ; or \g.
Your MySQL connection id is 18
Server version: 5.6.23-log MySQL Community Server (GPL)

Copyright (c) 2000, 2015, Oracle and/or its affiliates. All rights reserved.

Oracle is a registered trademark of Oracle Corporation and/or its
affiliates. Other names may be trademarks of their respective
owners.

Type 'help;' or '\h' for help. Type '\c' to clear the current input statement.

mysql>
mysql>
```

The first thing to do is make sure you have the required MySQL client packages installed on your web server EC2 instance. To do so, simply type in the following commands as shown:

```
# sudo yum install mysql
```

With the client installed, you can now access your remote RDS database using the following command:

```
# mysql -u <USERNAME> -h <DATABSE_ENDPOINT> -p
```

Substitute the values with your master username and password that you set for the database during the Create DB Instance phase. Here, <DATABSE_ENDPOINT> is the Endpoint (<DB_IDENTIFIER>.xxxxxxxxxxxx.us-west-2.rds.amazonaws.com:3306) that is provided by each DB instance when it is created. If all goes well, you should see the MYSQL command prompt. Go ahead and run a few MYSQL commands and check whether your database was created or not:

```
> show databases;
```

You can additionally connect your database with tools such as the MySQL workbench as well. Just remember to provide your database's endpoint in the **hostname** field followed by the master username and password. With the database connected successfully, you can now run a few simple tests just to make sure that the DB instance is accessible and working as expected.

Testing your database

In this section, I'm going to show you a simple exercise, using which you can test the configurations and the working of your database, as well as your DB instance. First up, log in to your database using the following command as done earlier:

```
# mysql -u <USERNAME> -h <DATABSE_ENDPOINT> -p
```

Next, let's go ahead and create a simple dummy table called doge. Type the following command in your MySQL prompt:

```
CREATE TABLE doge
(
idint(11) NOT NULL auto_increment,
namevarchar(255),
description text,
sizeenum('small','medium','large'),
date timestamp(6),
  PRIMARY KEY (id)
);
```

Fill in some data in your newly created table using the following INSERT commands:

```
INSERT INTO doge (name,description ,size,date) VALUES('Xena','Black
Labrador Retreiver','medium',NOW());

INSERT INTO doge (name,description ,size,date) VALUES('Betsy','Browndachs
hund','medium',NOW());

INSERT INTO doge (name,description ,size,date) VALUES('Shark','Mix bread-
Half dachshund','small',NOW());
```

With your basic table and data created, you can now access the same using your Web Server Instances. In my case, I'm using a simple PHP script (index.php) that is installed on the web server instance itself to print the database name as well as the table's data. Remember that as per our use case scenario, the web server instances are isolated from the database instances by different subnets as well as security groups and network ACLs, so make sure your subnets can communicate with each other correctly before testing. If all goes well, you should see your database, as well as the newly created table and its data, as shown in the following screenshot:

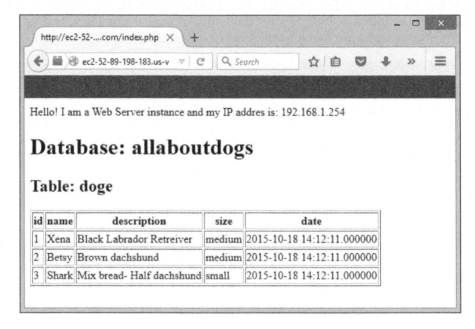

Modifying your DB instances

Once your DB Instances are created and launched, you can further modify them using two methods. The first method is by using the AWS CLI, where you can use the modify-db-instance command along with a bunch of options to specify and assign new parameters and values to your DB instances. For example, we need to expand the storage as well as the instance class of our DB instance so that it can accommodate the growing database's needs. To do so, type in the following command:

```
# aws  modify-db-instance --db-instance-identifier us-west-prod-db \
--allocate-storage 100 \
--db-instance-class db.m1.large
```

The preceding command will update the DB instance with the identifier `us-west-prod-db` with 100 GB of disk space and change its instance class to `db.m1.large` as well. The CLI provides a host of additional parameters as well which you can use to configure almost any aspect of your DB Instance, such as the master user's password, the preferred backup and maintenance window, the database engine versions, and so on. You can find the complete list of parameters and their descriptions at `http://docs.aws.amazon.com/cli/latest/reference/rds/modify-db-instance.html`.

 Changing the instance class of a DB instance will result in an outage, so plan the changes in advance and perform them during the maintenance window only.

The second method of modifying the DB instances is by using the RDS Management dashboard itself. Select your DB instance, and from the **Instance Actions** dropdown list, select the **Modify** option, as shown in the following screenshot:

Using the **Modify** page, you can change almost all configuration parameters of your DB instance just as you would by using the CLI. You can optionally set the changes to take effect immediately as well by selecting the **Apply Immediately** checkbox. Note, however, that by doing so, your DB instance will try to accept the made changes instantly, which can cause outages and even performance degradation at certain times. So as good practice, avoid setting this checkbox unless absolutely necessary. Changes made otherwise are reflected in your DB instance during its next scheduled maintenance window.

Backing up DB instances

RDS provides two mechanisms using which you can perform backups of your database instances as per your requirements. The first is an automated backup job that can be scheduled to run at a particular backup job interval, preferably when the database is at its least utilization point. This is something that we configured sometime back while creating our DB Instance. The second is a manual database instance snapshot that you can perform at any point in time. Here's a look at both the techniques in a bit more detail:

- **Automated backup**: Automated backups are conducted periodically by RDS on a daily user configured backup window. These backups are kept stored by RDS until the backup's retention period doesn't expire. By default, your first new database instance will have these backups enabled for ease of use. You can use these backups to restore your database to any point in time, down to the last second. The only thing that you need to be aware of is the slight freeze in storage IO operations that occurs when RDS actually performs the backups.

- **DB snapshots**: DB snapshots are point in-time snapshots that are created by you as and when required. To create a DB Instance snapshot, select the **Take Snapshot** option from the **Instance Actions** dropdown list, as shown in the following screenshot:

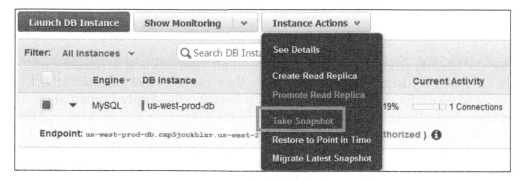

This will bring up the **Take Snapshot** page where all you need to do is provide a suitable name for your snapshot and click on **Take Snapshot** to complete the process.

Alternatively, you can also use the AWS CLI for performing a manual DB instance snapshot. Type in the following command:

```
# aws rds-create-db-snapshot -i<DB_IDENTIFIER> -s <SNAPSHOT_NAME>
```

Once you have taken your DB instance snapshot, you can view them on the RDS Management dashboard under the **Snapshots** page, as shown in the following screenshot:

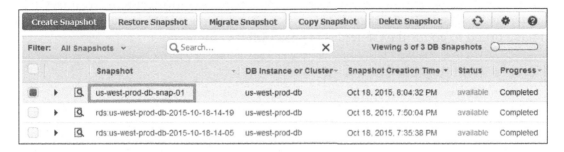

The snapshot dashboard allows you to perform various operations on your DB snapshots including copying DB snapshots from one region to another for high availability, restoring the state of a DB instance based on a particular snapshot, as well as options to migrate your MySQL database completely over to the Amazon Aurora database engine!

Creating Read Replicas and promoting them

We have already discussed the concept of read replicas in some depth, and how they can be useful for offloading the read operations from your primary DB instance as well as providing a mechanism using which you can create and set up Read Replicas across AWS regions. In this section, we are going to check out a few simple steps using which you can create and set up read replicas for your own environment using the RDS Management dashboard.

To get started, first select your newly created database from the RDS dashboard, as shown in the following screenshot. Next, using the **Instance Actions** tab, select the **Create Read Replica** option:

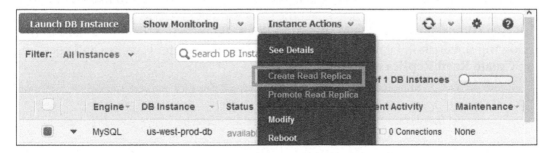

This will bring up the **Create Read Replica DB Instance** page, as shown in the following screenshot. The page is pretty self-explanatory and easy to configure. Start off by selecting an appropriate **DB Instance Class** from the dropdown list. You can alternatively select a high-end DB instance class here as compared to the primary DB instance. Next, select a **Storage Type** for your Read Replica DB instance. In this case, I have opted to go for the **General Purpose (SSD)** volumes:

Create Read Replica DB Instance

You are creating a replica DB Instance from a source DB Instance. This new DB Instance will have the source DB Instance's DB Security Groups and DB Parameter Groups.

Instance Specifications

DB Instance Class	db.t2.micro — 1 vCPU, 1 GiB RAM ⌄
Storage Type	General Purpose (SSD) ⌄

Settings

Read Replica Source	us-west-prod-db ⌄
DB Instance Identifier*	US-WEST-PROD-DB-READ-REPLICA

DB Instance identifier. This is the unique key that identifies a DB Instance. This parameter is stored as a lowercase string (e.g. mydbinstance).

Next, select your primary DB instance as the source for your Read Replica using the **Read Replica Source** dropdown list, and provide a suitable and unique name for your Read Replica in the **DB Instance Identifier** field, as shown in the preceding screenshot.

Now comes the fun part where you actually get to specify where you wish to deploy your Read Replica DB instance. Remember that you can have a maximum of five read replicas for a single primary DB instance, so ideally have your replicas spread out across the AZs that are present in your operating region or even have them residing in a different region altogether. Select an appropriate **Destination Region** and its corresponding **Availability Zone**. In this case, I have opted for the same region (**US West (Oregon)**) as well as same **AZ (us-west-2a)** as my primary DB instance.

Besides the placement of your replica instance, you will also need to make it a part of your existing DB Subnet Group. Select the same subnet group as provided for your primary DB instance from the **Destination DB Subnet Group** field, as shown in the following screenshot. Leave the rest of the fields to their default values and click on the **Create Read Replica** option:

Here's what will happen next. First up, RDS will start off by taking a snapshot of your primary DB instance. During this process, the DB instance will face a brief moment of IO freeze which is an expected behavior. Here's a handy tip that you can use to avoid the IO freeze! Deploy your DB instances using the multi-AZ deployment. Why? Well, because when it comes to taking the snapshot, RDS will perform the snapshot on the primary DB instance's standby copy, thereby not affecting any performance on your primary DB instance. Once the snapshot is taken, RDS will start to spin up a new Read Replica based on your specified configurations, as shown in the following screenshot.

During the replica's creation phase, your primary DB instance will change from a backing up state to modifying, and ultimately back to **available** status once the Replica is launched. Each Replica will behave as a DB instance on its own; hence, each of them will be provided with a unique DB endpoint as well. Refer to the following screenshot as an example of multiple Replicas:

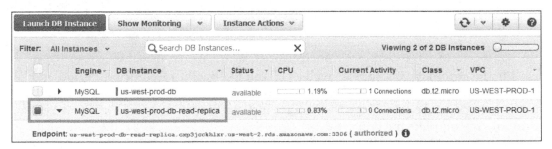

In case you create multiple Replicas at the same time using the same primary DB instance, then RDS will only perform the snapshot activity once, and that too at the start of the first replica's creation process. You can even perform the same process using the AWS CLI's `rds-create-db-instance-read-replica` command, as shown in the following:

```
# rds-create-db-instance-read-replica <REPLICA_NAME> -s <DATABASE_
IDENTIFIER>
```

In this case, RDS will create a new Replica DB instance based on your supplied database identifier value while keeping all the configurations same as that of the primary DB instance. To know more about the various options and related operations that you can perform using this command, refer to http://docs.aws.amazon.com/AmazonRDS/latest/CommandLineReference//CLIReference-cmd-CreateDBInstanceReadReplica.html.

Once your Read Replica instance is created and functioning, you can promote it as a primary DB instance as well. This feature comes in real handy when you have to perform a DB failure recovery, where your primary DB instance fails and you need to direct all traffic to the newly promoted Read Replica, and so on. To promote any Read Replica instance, all you need to do is select it from the RDS Management dashboard and select the **Promote Read Replica** option from the **Instance Action** drop-down list. This will bring up the **Promote Read Replica** page, as shown in the following screenshot:

Enable the automatic backups as well as fill out the **Backup Retention Period** and **Backup Window** details as per your requirements. Click on **Continue** to proceed to the next page. Acknowledge the Replica instance's promotion and click on **Yes, Promote** to complete the process.

 As a good practice, always enable the automatic backups option for your DB Instances.

During this process, your Read Replica instance will reboot itself once, post which it will become available as a standalone DB instance. You can then perform all sorts of activities on this DB instance, such as taking manual snapshots and creating new Read Replica instances from it as well.

You can promote a Read Replica using the AWS CLI as well. Type in the following command while replacing the <REPLICA_NAME> value with your own Replica instance's name:

```
# rds-promote-read-replica <REPLICA_NAME> \
--backup-retention-period 7 \
--preferred-backup-window 00:00-00:30
```

The preceding command will promote the <REPLICA_NAME> to a standalone primary DB instance. It will also set the automated backup retention period to 7 and configure the backup window for half an hour between 00:00 UTC and 00:30 UTC.

Logging and monitoring your DB instance

AWS provides a variety of tools and services to track and monitor the performance of your DB instances — the most popular and commonly used being Amazon CloudWatch itself. Besides this, RDS, too, comes with a list of simple tools that you can use to keep an eye on your DB instances. For example, you can list and view the DB instance's alarms and events by simply selecting the DB instance from the RDS Management dashboard, as shown in the following screenshot:

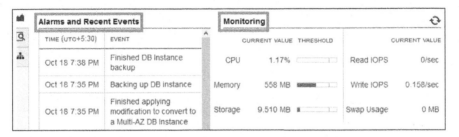

You can additionally view the DB instance's security group and snapshot events using this page as well. RDS will store the events for a period of 14 days, after which they are deleted. The **DB instance quick view** page also displays the DB instance's memory as well as storage utilization in near real time. Each of these fields has a custom threshold that RDS sets. If the threshold value is crossed, RDS will automatically trigger notifications and alarms to inform you about the same. You can also view the database's Read/Write IOPS value using this page.

RDS also provides a page using which you can view the DB Instance's real time performance graphs. To do so, simply select **Launch DB Instance** and the **Show Monitoring** option, as shown in the following screenshot:

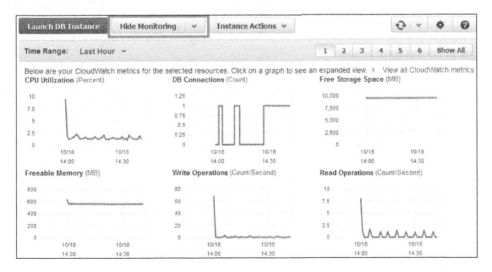

Each graph can be further expanded by selecting it. You can optionally view graphs for the past hour or a later duration by selecting the appropriate time from the **Time Range** dropdown list.

Furthermore, RDS also allows you to view your database's essential logs using the RDS Management dashboard. Select your DB instance, and from the dashboard, select the **Logs** option. This will bring up the **Logs** page, as shown in the following screenshot:

You can use this page to view as well as **download** the appropriate logs as per your requirements. RDS obtains logs from the database at short, regular intervals (mostly 5 minutes) and stores them in files that rotate as well. Selecting the **Watch** option adjoining a log file will display the log file in real time within your browser. You can view up to 1,000 lines of your logs at a time using this feature.

Cleaning up your DB instances

Once you have completed work with your DB instances, it is equally important to clean up your environment as well. You can delete a DB instance at any time you want using both the RDS Management dashboard and the AWS CLI.

To delete a DB instance using the RDS Management dashboard, select the **Delete** option from the **Instance Actions** dropdown list. You will be prompted to **Create a final Snapshot?** for your DB instance before you proceed, as shown in the following screenshot:

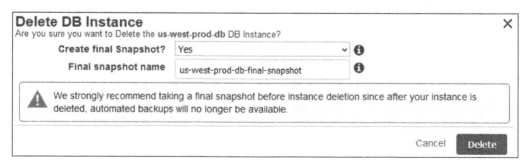

It is strongly recommended that you create a snapshot of your DB instance before you go ahead and delete it. Once you select the **Delete** option, RDS will delete the DB instance along with all the automated backups that were taken earlier. The manual snapshots, however, are not deleted and thus can be used to restore your DB instance to its original state if you want to revert to your original settings.

To delete a DB instance using the AWS CLI, simply type in the following command and replace <DATABASE_IDENTIFIER> with the name of your DB instance:

```
# aws rds-delete-db-instance <DATABASE_IDENTIFIER> \
--final-db-snapshot-identifier MyFinalDBSnapshot
```

The command will delete your DB Instance but will additionally first create a snapshot for it by the name of MyFinalDBSnapshot.

Planning your next steps

There are a ton of amazing things that you can do besides the steps that we have covered in this chapter. To begin with, try out encrypting your databases using the Encryption facility provided by RDS itself. RDS encrypts as well as decrypts data without any major impact on your DB instance's performance. The encryption process can only be set up during the DB instance's initial deployment phase, so plan and use the facility before you actually deploy your database. An important point to remember here, though, is that encryption is not supported on the t1.micro instance class. You will have to use the memory optimized (R3) or burst capable (T2) for the same. To know more about how you can use and set up the encryption on your DB instances, refer to http://docs.aws.amazon.com/AmazonRDS/latest/UserGuide/Overview.Encryption.html.

Besides RDS, AWS also provides a host of other database-related services that you can try out depending on your application's needs. For example, if you are looking for a high performance and low cost non-relational database, then Amazon DynamoDB is your obvious choice! With DynamoDB you can actually set up and start using a NoSQL database in a matter of minutes! Plus, you don't have to worry about any of the management overheads such as clustering or scaling. RDS automatically replicates and synchronizes your data across multiple AZs present in a region, thereby providing high availability and durability.

AWS also provides a highly scalable caching service in the form of Amazon ElastiCache. You can use this service as an in-memory caching service for your web applications and improve their overall performance by retrieving information much faster than a disk-based database. Along with this, AWS also provides a petabyte scalable data warehousing service called as **RedShift** that you can use to query extremely large datasets. It's easy to set up and the best part is that it scales as per your needs! The more data you feed it, the larger it grows, and all this without any upfront costs or commitments! To know more about these services and how to use them, refer to `https://aws.amazon.com/running_databases`.

Recommendations and best practices

Here are some key recommendations and good practices to keep in mind when working with RDS:

- To begin with, always monitor your DB instances for overall performance and usage. Leverage CloudWatch and its metrics to set thresholds and customized alarms that notify you in case of any issues.

- Additionally, you can also enable event notifications for your DB instance that will inform you of all the events that occur with your instance.

- Leverage Multi-AZ deployments in conjunction with Read Replicas to increase the overall availability of your database along with its performance.

- Always enable automatic snapshots for your DB instances. Also take manual snapshots of your DB instances before performing any maintenance activities on them.

- For a small to medium-sized database, set the storage type of your DB instance to General Purpose (SSD).

- If your database has a high performance requirement, then do use the DB instances with Provisioned IOPS.

- Tune your options group as well as your parameters group to improve your database's overall performance.

- Secure your DB instances with a proper security group and encryption facilities. Also remember to assign and use IAM users with specific rights and privileges.

Summary

With this we come to the end of yet another chapter and yet another awesome AWS service. Let's quickly recap all the things covered so far. First up, we started off by understanding and learning what RDS is all about, followed by an in-depth look at DB instances and how RDS actually works. Next, you learnt about how you can leverage high availability for your databases by using something called as Multi-AZ deployments and Read Replicas. You also learnt a lot of basic actions that you can perform on a database using RDS, such as creating a DB instance, connecting to one, testing it, and so on. Toward the end, we topped it all off with some easy-to-remember recommendations and best practices that you should keep in mind when working with RDS!

In the next chapter, we are going to look at yet another AWS core service that provides us with virtually unlimited storage for all our needs! So stick around, there's more to learn just around the corner!

9
Working with Simple Storage Service

In the previous chapter, we covered a lot about Amazon RDS and how you can leverage it to host highly scalable and fault-tolerant databases.

In this chapter, we will be exploring yet another popular and widely used AWS core service, that is, the **Simple Storage Service (S3)**. This chapter will cover many important aspects of S3, such as its use cases, its various terms and terminologies, along with a few steps on how to use S3 to store and retrieve objects. It will also go through few simple steps using which you can archive your data using both the AWS Management Console and the AWS CLI. So, buckle up and get ready for an awesome time.

Introducing Amazon S3

Ever used Dropbox to store and back up your important data and files? Or how about Netflix to watch your favorite TV shows online? Both Dropbox and Netflix have one very interesting thing in common, which you may have guessed already! They are both using Amazon S3 to store and retrieve data. How much data are we talking about here? Well, way back in 2008, S3 was storing approximately 30 billion objects or unique data elements in it. This number has grown exponentially ever since with approximately 2 trillion objects reportedly stored in S3 as of April 2013, so no prizes for guessing what this number has gone up to today! But enough numbers, let's learn a bit more about what Amazon S3 actually is.

To begin with, Amazon S3 is a highly scalable, durable, and low cost storage as a service option provided by AWS for everyone to use. Using S3, you can upload virtually any file, folder, or data from anywhere on the web and retrieve it just as easily all the while paying only for the storage that you use! Now that's amazing, isn't it!

How much of data can you upload to S3? Well, its virtually unlimited, so you can feel free to upload your songs, movies, high-resolution pictures, anything and everything goes! S3 will treat each of the files that you upload as individual objects and store them redundantly across the underlying secure hardware. You don't have to worry about the replication process or even for the hardware's scalability, it is all taken care of by AWS itself.

You can leverage S3 for a variety of purposes; a few listed as follows:

- S3 serves as an ideal place to store and back up all your data, including pictures, videos, documents, and so on
- Since each object in S3 is provided and accessed by a web URL, you can actually host a website on it as well, provided your website is completely static by design

> You can upload objects as small as 1 KB or as large as 5 TB at a time to Amazon S3, with virtually unlimited storage capacity.

How does it all work? Well, to begin with, you first need to create something called as a Bucket. A Bucket is a top level entity in S3 and acts as a logical container that will hold all your objects. You can create multiple buckets and store various objects in them as you please; however, there are a few pointers that you must always keep in mind when working with them:

- Bucket names have to be unique across your entire AWS account.
- Bucket names always start in lowercase. Although you can specify uppercase letters in your names, it is advised that you avoid doing so.
- Buckets can be accessed globally; however, they are still created and located within a particular region.

It is equally important to note that S3 is not some hierarchical organization of objects, although you can create folders and store objects in them. Folders are just a logical representation that AWS provides you with for easier object storing and arrangement, but underneath all this, S3 really does not use any hierarchy at all as it is a flat storage system. This enables S3 to add new storage and scale virtually without any limits, without having to worry about the objects that already reside in it.

Buckets also provide us with some simple access control mechanisms, using which you can restrict users to operations such as create, delete, or list all the objects present in the bucket. You can even assign the bucket permissions that govern who can upload or even download data from it.

S3 also provides different storage classes for the objects that you store on it. Each storage class has its own performance and cost associated with it, as described here:

- **Standard**: This is the default storage class used to store all your objects unless you specify a different value. This storage class comes in really handy for common S3 workloads where data is accessed on a frequent basis. For the first 1 TB that you use per month, the Standard storage class will cost about $0.0300 per GB of data stored on S3.

- **Standard_IA**: This is a special storage class used to store objects that are less frequently accessed. You can transition an object to move from the Standard to the Standard_IA storage class after say a period of 30 days. This helps you save on the costs as Standard_IA will cost you about $0.0125 per GB. However, note that there is a separate minimal retrieval fee in case you use Standard_IA as your storage class.

- **Glacier**: Glacier is yet another less frequently accessed storage class, with a retrieval time of nearly 2 to 3 hours. You cannot assign an object with the Glacier storage class directly. The object has to be transitioned from Standard or Standard_IA to Glacier and vice versa when it comes to retrieving as well. Glacier storage is by far the cheapest, costing about $0.007 per GB of data stored in S3.

- **Reduced Redundancy Storage (RRS)**: Each of the previous storage classes are designed to sustain data losses by replicating data across multiple data centers. RRS, however, is designed for non-critical data and also maintains fewer redundant copies of data compared to its counterparts. This enables you to reduce costs, however, with less durability (only 99.99%).

With this basic understanding in mind, let's see how we can use the AWS Management Console to create and upload a few objects to a bucket of our choice.

Getting started with S3

Getting started with S3 is by far the simplest and most straightforward thing you will ever do! Simply log in to your AWS account using your IAM credentials and select the S3 option:

This will bring up the S3 Management Dashboard as shown in the following screenshot. You can use this dashboard to create, list, upload, and delete objects from buckets as well as provide fine-grained permissions and access control rights as well. Let's start off by creating a simple bucket for our demo website `all-about-dogs.com`.

Creating buckets

To get started with your first bucket, simply select the **Create Bucket** option from the S3 dashboard. Provide a suitable name for your new bucket. Remember, your bucket name will have to be unique and will have to start with a lowercase character. Next, select a particular **Region** where you would like your bucket to be created. Although buckets are global entities in AWS, you still need to provide it with a **Region** option. This comes in handy, especially when you wish to create a bucket close to your location to optimize latency or meet certain regulatory compliances. Also keep in mind that you are not allowed to change the bucket's name after it has been created, so make sure you provide it a correct and meaningful name before you proceed. In this case, I opted to create my bucket in the Oregon region, as shown:

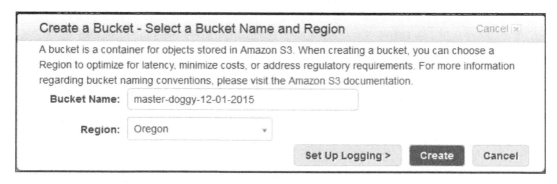

You are not charged for creating a bucket; you are charged only for storing objects in the bucket and for transferring objects in and out of the bucket.

You can optionally enable logging for your bucket as well, by selecting the **Set Up Logging** option. This will store detailed access logs of your bucket to a different bucket of your choice. By default, logging of a bucket is disabled; however, you can always re-enable it even after your bucket is created. AWS will not charge you for any of the logging that it will perform; however, it will still charge you for the storage capacity that your logs will consume on S3.

 Log records are delivered by S3 on a best effort basis. This means that most records will be delivered to your bucket within a few hours of their creation. However, not all logs may be delivered on time, depending on the overall traffic your bucket handles.

Once your details are in place, select the **Create** option to create your new bucket. The bucket is created within a few seconds, and you should see the following landing page for your bucket as shown here:

You can even create one or more folders in your bucket by selecting the **Create Folder** option. Folders are just a nice way to represent and categorize your objects more effectively. You can even perform additional operations on your bucket using this dashboard, such as assign permissions, enable logging, versioning, cross-region replication, and so on. We shall be exploring each of these operations in detail throughout this chapter, but for now, let's upload some objects to our newly created bucket.

Uploading your first object to a bucket

With your bucket now created, you can easily upload any object to it. But first, let's take a closer look at what an S3 object actually comprises:

- **Key**: This is nothing but the unique name using which you upload objects into S3. Each object has its own key, which can be used to identify and retrieve the object when necessary.

- **Value**: This can be defined as a sequence of bytes used to store the object's content. As discussed previously, an object's value can range anywhere between zero bytes to 5 TB.

- **Version ID**: This is yet another entity that in conjunction with a key can be used to uniquely identify an object by S3. Version ID is equally important for maintaining an object's version count. Using S3, you can keep multiple versions of an object in a single bucket. Versioning helps protect your objects against accidental overwrites as well as deletions by maintaining a separate version number for each new object that you upload into the bucket. By default, versioning is disabled on your bucket and thus your objects get the version ID Null. It is your responsibility to enable versioning on your buckets in case you wish to protect them against accidental deletions and overwrites.

- **Metadata**: These are nothing but simple name-value pairs that define some information regarding a given object. There are two types of metadata provided in S3: the first is system-defined metadata, which is generated by S3 itself when an object is first uploaded and it generally contains information such as the object's creation date, version ID, storage class, and so on. The second is user-defined metadata, which, as the name suggests, requires you as a user to provide some additional name-value information to your objects when they are uploaded.

- **Sub resources**: Sub resources are a set of resources that can be associated with either objects or buckets. S3 currently supports two sub resources with objects. The first is an **Access Control List** (**ACL**), which consists of a list of users and permissions that are granted access over the object. The second sub resource is called torrent and is used to return the torrent file associated with any particular object.

 Apart from the traditional client-server model, S3 also supports the BitTorrent protocol that you can use to distribute your objects over a large number of users. To know more about BitTorrent protocol and how you can leverage it using S3, go to http://docs.aws.amazon.com/AmazonS3/latest/dev/S3Torrent.html.

- **Access control**: This provides the access information of a particular object. You can control access to your objects that are stored in S3 using a combination of access control mechanisms that are discussed briefly in the later parts of this chapter.

With this basic understanding in mind, we are now ready to upload our first object into S3. You can upload objects directly into your buckets or within sub folders that you may have created. To get started, simply select the **Upload** option from your bucket or folder. In the **Upload–Select Files and Folders** dialog box, shown in the following screenshot, you can browse and select any video, document, media file, and so on, of your choice and upload it to S3. The wizard also provides you with an advanced enhanced uploader that is basically a Java applet that can help you upload entire folders into S3 with ease.

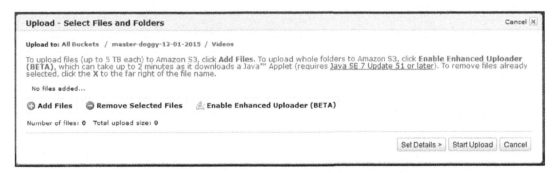

The enhanced uploader will be installed on your local machine's browser only once per console session. In my case, I opted to upload a single video file to my S3 bucket, and hence opted to select the **Add Files** option rather than **Enhanced Uploader**.

Once your required files are loaded into the wizard, start the upload process by selecting the **Start Upload** button. You can view the transfer process of your individual files by selecting the transfer panel shown here:

Keep in mind though that you can upload files up to 5 TB in size at any given point in time using the **Upload**—Select the **Files and Folders** dialog box. Once the file is uploaded to S3, you are ready to view it!

Viewing uploaded objects

Each uploaded object in S3 is provided with a URL that you can use to view your object using a browser of your choice. The URL is in the following format: `https://s3.amazonaws.com/<BUCKET_NAME>/<OBJECT_NAME>`. You can view the URL of your object by simply selecting your object from the dashboard and the **Properties** option, as shown in the following screenshot. Copy the URL presented against the **Link** attribute and paste it into a web browser of your choice:

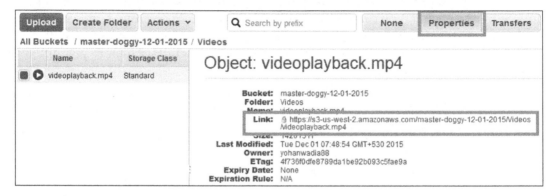

But wait! That's really not going to help you much. In fact if you did try and access your object's URL from a browser, you make have ended up with an XML-based access denied warning! Well, that's because all buckets and objects in S3 are set to private by default. You can change this default behavior by simply selecting the **Make Public** option from the **Actions** tab. This will modify your object's permissions and enable everyone to view as well as download your object. You can even perform the same action by selecting the **Permissions** option from the object's **Properties** tab. Once the object is made public, you can view it using the URL copied earlier.

Accessing buckets and objects using S3CMD

Now here's the fun part! S3 provides a wide variety of CLI tools using which you can manipulate your buckets and objects; one of the popular ones being S3CMD. In this section, we will walk through some simple steps to install S3CMD on a local Linux box and then check out some cool commands using which you can work with S3.

So what is S3CMD? In simple words it's a Python-based open source tool used to query any cloud storage service that supports and uses the S3 protocol, including Amazon S3 and even Google's cloud storage. S3CMD can be installed and configured on any major Linux OS, such as CentOS, RHEL, Ubuntu, and so on, and even comes with Windows OS support in the form of a commercial tool called S3Express. The main reason I'm talking about S3CMD here is because of its high versatility and use. If you are capable of writing bash scripts and cron jobs, then you can easily perform automated backups of your files and folders in S3 using S3CMD in a few easy steps.

> To know more about S3CMD, check http://s3tools.org/s3cmd.

First off, let's get started by installing S3CMD on our trusty Linux box. To do so, simply type in the following command. However, S3CMD requires Python Version 2.6 and above, so make sure this prerequisite is met before you proceed further:

```
# wget http://sourceforge.net/projects/s3tools/files/s3cmd/1.6.0/s3cmd-1.6.0.tar.gz
```

Here as a screenshot of the preceding command:

Once the tar is downloaded, extract its contents using the following command:

```
# tar -xvfs3cmd-1.6.0.tar.gz
```

Next, install S3CMD on your Linux box by executing the following command:

```
# cd s3cmd-1.6.0
# python setup.py install
```

With this, S3CMD is now successfully installed. The next step is to configure it to work with your Amazon S3. To do so, type in the following command and follow the on screen instructions provided:

```
# s3cmd --configure
```

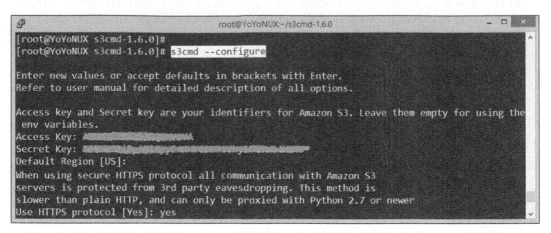

The configuration utility will request an AWSaccess and Secret Key. It will also prompt you to set your operating region, which is set to US by default. You can even enable S3CMD to communicate with Amazon S3 using the https protocol; however, do note that this setting can have a slight impact on S3CMD's overall performance. The entire configuration is saved locally in the Linux user's home directory in a file called `.s3cfg`. Once done, you are now ready to test your S3CMD! Here are some basic commands that you can use to query your Amazon S3. First up, let's list our Buckets using the following S3CMD command:

```
# s3cmdlss3://<BUCKET_NAME>
```

You should see the contents of your bucket listed using this command. If you do not specify the bucket name, then by default the `s3cmdls` command will print out all the buckets present in that particular region. Next, let's try to upload some data to our bucket. Uploading is performed using the `s3cmd put` command and conversely, downloads are performed using the `s3cmd get` command. Type in the following command in your Linux terminal:

```
# s3cmd put -r /opt s3://<BUCKET_NAME>
```

This command will recursively upload all the contents present in the `/opt` directory to the bucket name that you specify. Remember one important thing though! Trailing slashes after the `/opt` directory would have copied only the directory's content over to the bucket, but not the directory itself.

To know more about the usage of various s3cmd commands visit http://s3tools.org/usage.

On a similar note, you can perform a wide variety of operations using the s3cmd tool. For example, you can upload your instance log files to an S3 bucket on a periodic basis. Here is a base snippet of the /etc/logrotate.d/httpd file where we use the s3cmd command with the sync attribute. The sync attribute is a really useful tool for transferring files over to Amazon S3. sync performs conditional transfers, which means that only files that don't exist at the destination in the same version are transferred.

In this snippet, we are assuming that a bucket with the name httpd-logger has already been created in S3. The code will sync the instance's httpd error log file (/etc/httpd/logs/error_log) and the httpd access log file (/etc/httpd/logs/access_log) and transfer them to their respective folders:

```
BUCKET=httpd-logger
INSTANCE_ID=`curl --silent http://169.254.169.254/latest/meta-data/instance-id`

  /usr/bin/s3cmd -m text/plain sync /etc/httpd/logs/access_log*
s3://${BUCKET}/httpd/access_log/instance=${INSTANCE_ID}/

  /usr/bin/s3cmd -m text/plain sync /etc/httpd/logs/error_log*
s3://${BUCKET}/httppd/error_log/instance=${INSTANCE_ID}/
```

Managing an object's and bucket's permissions

Just like we talked about IAM permissions and policies back in *Chapter 2*, *Security and Access Management*, security and access management, S3 too provides permissions and policies using which you can control access to both your buckets and the objects they contain. In this section, we will have a quick look at two such methods provided by S3, namely resource-based policies and user-based policies, as follows:

- **Resource-based policies**: Resource-based policies are simple Json-based policies that are generally created and enforced on S3 resources by the bucket or the resource owner themselves. These S3 resources include the object lifecycle management configuration information, the versioning configuration, the website config details, and a few other parameters. Resource-based policies can be further sub-classified into two types: Bucket Policies and **Access Control Lists** (**ACLs**).

- **Bucket policies**: These are enforced on the bucket level or on the individual objects contained within it. Here is a simple example of a Bucket Policy that basically will allow any user to perform any operation on the specified bucket name, provided the request source is generated from the IP address specified in the condition (23.226.51.110):

```
{
"Id": "Policy1448937262025",
"Version": "2012-10-17",
"Statement": [
    {
"Sid": "Stmt1448937260611",
"Effect": "Allow",
"Principal": "*",
"Action": "s3:*",
"Resource": "arn:aws:s3:::<BUCKET_NAME>/*",
"Condition": {
"IpAddress": {"aws:SourceIp": "23.226.51.110"}
        }
      }
    ]
}
```

You will notice that a lot of the syntax actually matches up with what we have already seen in *Chapter 2*, *Security and Access Management*, while discussing the building blocks of an IAM policy. Well, here, most of the things remain the same. The only notable difference will be the inclusion of the Principal element, which lists the principals or owners that bucket policy controls access for. The Principal element is not mandatory when creating an IAM policy as it is by default the entity to which the IAM policy is going to be attached. The best part of all this is that AWS provides a really easy to use policy generator tool that you can use to interactively set and create your S3 policies with. You can try out and create your own policies at http://awspolicygen.s3.amazonaws.com/policygen.html.

How do you apply bucket policies? Well that's really simple! Select your bucket from the S3 dashboard and from the **Properties** panel, select the **Permissions** drop-down menu, as shown in the following screenshot. Here, select the **Add bucket policy** option. This will bring up a **Bucket Policy Editor** dialog box using which you can type in your policy or even use the AWS policy generator to create one for yourself interactively.

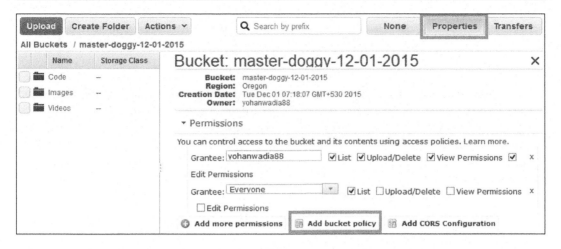

Remember to save your policy in the Bucket Policy Editor before closing the dialog box.

ACLs are very similar to bucket policies. An ACL is basically a list of grant operations comprising a grantee and a set of permissions granted. Every bucket that you create in S3 along with each object that you upload gets a set of ACLs with them. ACLs are a great way to control which users get access to your buckets and resources, whether they are AWS users or even some random normal user. To view your bucket's or object's ACLs, simply select the bucket or object from the S3 dashboard and select the **Properties** option. There, select the **Permissions** drop-down to view the associated ACLs, as shown here:

A default ACL is provided with each object that you upload into S3. This default ACL has one grant attribute set for the owner of the bucket.

ACLs have a predefined set of user groups created using which you can configure access control for your buckets. These user groups include **Everyone**, **Any Authenticated AWSUser**, **Log Delivery**, along with your bucket's creator. ACLs can enforce the following set of permissions (read/write) over an object as well as bucket. On the basis of these permissions, a user can perform operations such as uploading new files or delete existing objects. Here's a quick look at the ACL permissions provided by S3 and how they are associated with both buckets and objects:

Permissions	Associated with Buckets	Associated with Objects
READ	Users can list the object names, their size, and last modified date from a Bucket.	Users can download the object.
WRITE	Users can upload new objects in your Bucket. They can also delete files on which they don't have permission.	Users can replace the object or delete it.
READ_ACP	Users can read the ACL associated with a Bucket, but cannot make any writes to it.	Users can read the ACL associated with that object but cannot make writes to it.
WRITE_ ACP	Users can modify the ACL associated with the bucket.	Users can modify the ACL associated with the object.
FULL_ CONTROL	Users get READ, WRITE, READ_ACP, and WRITE_ACP permissions on the associated bucket.	Users get READ, READ_ACP, and WRITE_ACP permissions on the associated object.

 Bucket ACLs are completely independent from Object ACLs. This means that bucket ACLs can be different from ACLs set on any Object contained in a bucket.

Now the obvious question running through your mind right now is what do I use for my S3 buckets and objects? ACLs or bucket policies? The answer for this is two folds. First off, understand that the main difference between an ACL and a bucket policy is that an ACL grants access permissions to buckets or objects individually, whereas a bucket policy will help you write a policy that will either grant or deny access to a bucket or its objects. Ideally, you can use ACLs when each object in the bucket needs to be provided with some explicit grant permissions. You will also need to use ACLs instead of bucket policies when your policy's size reaches 20 KB. Bucket policies have a size limit of 20KB, so if you have a very large number of objects and users to grant access to, you might want to consider the use of ACLs.

User-based policies, perhaps the most simple and easy to use, the user-based policies are nothing more than simple IAM policies that you can create and use to manage access to your Amazon S3 resources. Using these policies, you can create users, groups, and roles in your account and attach specific access permissions to them.

Consider this simple example IAM policy in which we grant the user-specific rights to put objects into S3, to get objects, list them, as well as delete them. Notice the syntax remains quite the same as we have seen throughout this book. You can create multiple such IAM policies and attach them to your users and groups as described here in the AWSS3 documentation page: `http://docs.aws.amazon.com/AmazonS3/latest/dev/example-policies-s3.html`.

The following is an example of the IAM policy:

```
{
"Statement": [
        {
"Effect":"Allow",
"Action": [
"s3:PutObject",
"s3:GetObject",
"s3:DeleteObject",
"s3:ListBucket"
            ],
"Resource":"arn:aws:s3:::<BUCKET_NAME>/*"
        }
    ]
}
```

Using buckets to host your websites

Yes! Believe it or not, you can actually use Amazon S3 to host your websites, provided that they are static in nature. How does it work? Well, its quite simple and easy, actually! All you need to do is create a bucket and enable the website hosting attribute on it. Once done, you can easily upload the website's `index.html` page along with the other static web pages and voila! You got yourself a really simple website up and running in a matter of minutes.

Here's a simple example in which I used my previously created bucket as a website host. All you need to do is select your bucket and from the **Properties** panel select the **Static Website Hosting** option as shown here:

Here, you will see an Endpoint (**http://<BUCKET_NAME>.s3-website-<REGION>. amazonaws.com**) provided to you. This is your website's end URL, which you can copy and paste in a web browser to view your website; however, before you do that, don't forget to make your website public! To do so, copy and paste the following bucket policy in your bucket's **Policy Editor** dialog box:

```
{
"Version":"2012-10-17",
"Statement":[
{
    "Sid":"BucketWebsiteHostingPolicy",
"Effect":"Allow",
    "Principal": "*",
"Action":["s3:GetObject"],
"Resource":["arn:aws:s3:::<BUCKET_NAME>/*"
      ]
    }
  ]
}
```

Save the policy in the bucket policy editor, and then upload your **index.html** file as well as an optional **error.html** file to your bucket. Type your endpoint URL in a web browser of your choice, and you should see your website's landing (**index.html**) page.

Using static website hosting, you can also redirect all requests to an alternate DNS hostname or even to an alternate bucket. Simply select the **Redirect all requests to another host name** option and provide an alternative bucket's name in the **Redirect all requests to** field, as shown in the following screenshot. Alternatively, you can even setup Amazon Route53 to act as your DNS provider by providing a few DNS records and a valid new domain name for your website, such as **all-about-dogs.com**:

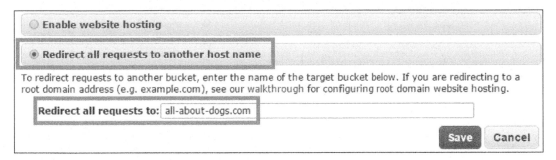

S3 events and notification

Amazon S3 provides an easy-to-use notification feature that can send notifications in case a certain event gets triggered in your bucket. Currently, S3 supports notifications on the following set of events:

- **Object created**: This event includes PUT, POST, and COPY operations and even something called as Complete Multi-part Uploads. Multi-part uploads is a feature leveraged by S3 where a large object is broken down into smaller, more manageable chunks (approx 10 MB), and then each chunk is uploaded to an S3 bucket in a parallel fashion, thereby cutting down on the overall upload time as well as costs.

- **Objects removed**: This event includes any delete operations that are performed either on the bucket or on the objects contained within it.

- **Object lost**: Don't worry! We are not talking about S3 misplacing any of your objects here! This event is raised only when an object of the RRS storage class has been lost.

To enable the notification service, select your bucket and from the **Properties** panel, select the **Events** drop-down menu, as shown. Fill in the required details and click on **Save** once done to enable the notification service:

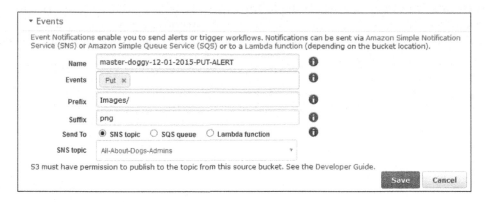

The parameters are as follows:

- **Name**: Provide a suitable name for your notification alert. In this case, I named my alert `<BUCKET_NAME>-PUT-ALERT` for notifying me against any PUT operations that are performed on the bucket.

- **Events**: Type in the event for which you wish to get notified. Here I have specified the **PUT** event, but you can specify anything from POST, COPY, CompleteMultiPartUpload, to DELETE, based on your requirements.

- **Prefix**: This is an optional attribute and is used to limit the notifications of an object based on its matching characters. For example, notify me in case any PUT operation is performed in the Images directory.

- **Suffix**: Once again this is an optional attribute that is used to limit the notifications of an object based on its suffix. For example, notify me in case any PUT operation is performed and the key contains a `.png` as a suffix.

- **Send To**: Currently, S3 supports sending notifications to three AWS services, namely SNS, SQS, and Amazon Lambda.

- **SNS topic**: Select a **SNS topic** using which S3 will send notifications to. You can optionally create a new SNS topic here as well.

Once all the fields are filled in, click on **Save** to enable the notification service. Remember to alter the Bucket's access policy to allow S3 to publish statements to SNS using the sample policy snippet provided here. Replace `<SNS_TOPIC_ARN>` with an actual SNS Topic ARN value (`arn:aws:sns:aws-region:account-id:topic-name`) and `<BUCKET_NAME>` with your bucket name:

```
{
"Version": "2008-10-17",
```

```
"Id": "Policy1448937262025",
"Statement": [
    {
"Sid": "Stmt1448937260611",
"Effect": "Allow",
"Principal": {
"Service": "s3.amazonaws.com"
    },
"Action": [
"SNS:Publish"
    ],
"Resource": "<SNS_TOPIC_ARN>",
"Condition": {
"ArnLike": {
"aws:SourceArn": "arn:aws:s3:*:*:<BUCKET_NAME>"
    }
    }
    }
 ]
}
```

Bucket versioning and lifecycle management

Versioning is perhaps the most important and useful feature provided by S3. In a way, it is a means to create and maintain multiple copies of a single object present in a bucket. Each copy of the same object that you upload into the bucket receives a unique version ID, which can later be used to retrieve and restore the object in case of an accidental deletion or failure. To enable versioning on a bucket, all you need to do is select the particular bucket from the S3 dashboard, and from the **Properties** panel, select the **Versioning** drop-down menu, as shown here:

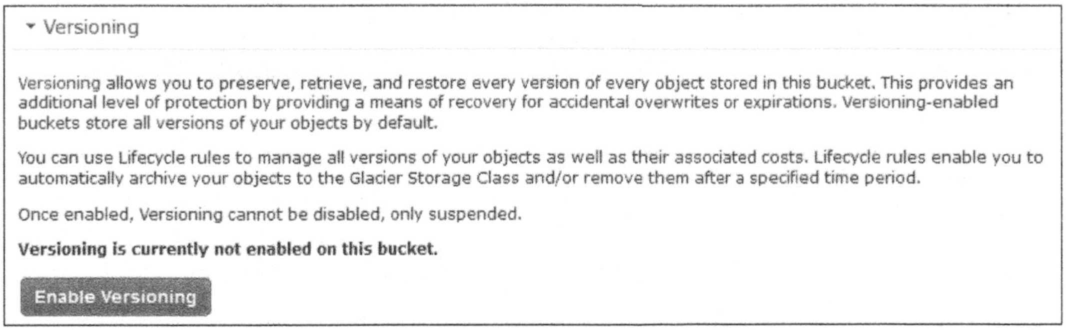

▾ Versioning

Versioning allows you to preserve, retrieve, and restore every version of every object stored in this bucket. This provides an additional level of protection by providing a means of recovery for accidental overwrites or expirations. Versioning-enabled buckets store all versions of your objects by default.

You can use Lifecycle rules to manage all versions of your objects as well as their associated costs. Lifecycle rules enable you to automatically archive your objects to the Glacier Storage Class and/or remove them after a specified time period.

Once enabled, Versioning cannot be disabled, only suspended.

Versioning is currently not enabled on this bucket.

Enable Versioning

By default, versioning is disabled on all buckets, so you will have to explicitly enable versioning on the ones that require it. Once enabled, all newly uploaded objects will receive a unique version ID. Older objects stored in the bucket prior to enabling versioning also contain a version ID parameter, but the value of that is set to null. However, once versioning is enabled on the bucket, it applies to all the objects contained in the bucket, so all objects uploaded henceforth, new or old, will obtain version IDs. An important point to remember here is that once you have enabled versioning on a bucket, there is no way you can disable it. You can, however, suspend it by selecting the **Suspend Versioning** option.

> Each object version that you upload is an entire object in itself and hence each version upload you do will be charged the normal S3 rates for storage as well as data transfers.

So how do you upload versions of your objects to a bucket? Well, the process remains absolutely the same for any object that you upload into S3. The only difference now is that with each new version of the object that you upload, S3 will assign it a unique version ID and store it in the same bucket as its originator. To list the different versions of an object, all you need to do is toggle between the Hide and Show versions buttons as shown in the following screenshot.

Selecting the **Show** versions will display all the uploaded versions of that object including the object's creation date, version ID, and size. You can then download any of the versioned objects that you want by simply selecting it from the dashboard and, from the **Actions** drop-down menu, select the **Download** option. In case the download request is issued on the main object, then S3 will simply fetch the latest uploaded version of that object and download it for you:

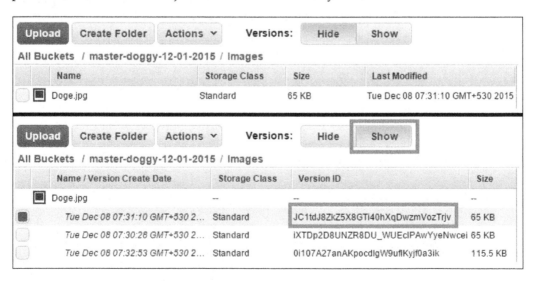

Versioning also comes in real handy when you want to protect your data from any accidental deletions or overwrites. How? Well, to put in simple words, when you try to DELETE an object that is versioned in S3, you actually don't wipe it from existence immediately. In fact, S3 will insert something called as a delete marker in the bucket and that marker becomes the current version of the object with a new version ID. When you try to GET an object whose current version is a delete marker, Amazon S3 behaves as though the object has been deleted and returns a 404 error even though that object is not physically deleted from the bucket. To permanently wipe out the object, you will need to use the DELETE object along with its version ID. Want to try it out? Then go ahead and delete a main object from your versioned S3 bucket. You will notice that although the main object is successfully deleted and not visible from the S3 dashboard, its versions are still pretty much intact. So even if this was an accidental DELETE operation, you can still retrieve the main image from the version ID! Amazing, isn't it!

Another sweet part of enabling versioning on a bucket is that you can specify an object's transition or lifecycle as well. This feature comes in real handy when you want the objects stored in your bucket to get auto-archived to, let's say, Amazon Glacier after a long period of storage in S3, or wish to transition the storage class of an object from Standard to Standard_IA for infrequent access. Logs are a classic example of where this feature comes in really handy. Your bucket can store the logs for up to a week's duration using standard storage and then post that you transition the logs to either Glacier for archiving or even delete them permanently. To enable lifecycle management, you will need to select your bucket from the S3 Dashboard and from the **Properties** panel, select the **Lifecycle** drop-down menu, as shown:

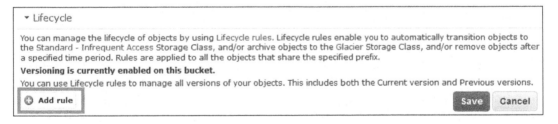

Next, select the **Add rule** option to create a lifecycle rule for your bucket. This will pop up the **Lifecycle Rules** wizard using which you can configure as well as choose the target objects for which you wish to enable the lifecycle management. The first page of the wizard is **Choose Rule Target**, where you can specify either a prefix or the entire bucket to which the lifecycle rules shall apply. A prefix is more or less like a folder name that you can specify, for example, in my case I provided the prefix **Videos/**, which is an actual directory inside my bucket. Select **Configure Rule** to move on to the next page of the wizard.

You can use lifecycle rules to manage all versions of your objects; both current as well as previously created.

In the **Action** on **Current Version** page, you get to choose and specify the type of action you wish to perform over your selected objects. For example, you can enable an object's transition to the Standard - Infrequent Access Storage class 30 days after the object's creation date, which is the ideal time to set for an object, or you can even enable Archiving to the Glacier Storage Class post 60 days your object's creation, and so on. There are a few rules that you have to keep in mind, however, when performing transition actions:

- You cannot transition from Standard-IA to Standard or reduced redundancy

- You cannot transition from Glacier to any other storage class

- You cannot transition from any storage class to reduced redundancy

The following screenshot shows the lifecycle configuration:

Action on Current Version

☑ **Transition to the Standard - Infrequent Access Storage Class**   30 ⬍ Days after the object's creation date

Standard - Infrequent Access has a 30-day minimum retention period and a 128KB minimum object size. Lifecycle policy will not transition objects that are less than 128KB. Refer here to learn more about Standard - Infrequent Access.

☑ **Archive to the Glacier Storage Class**   60 ⬍ Days after the object's creation date

This rule could reduce your storage costs. Refer here to learn more about Glacier pricing. Note that objects archived to the Glacier Storage Class are not immediately accessible.

☑ **Expire**   425 ⬍ Days after the object's creation date

Versioning is enabled on this bucket and Expiring Current Version will generate new versions. If you wish to permanently delete all versions of your objects, you can combine the **Expire** current version action here with the **Permanently Delete** previous versions action below.

If you are happy with your lifecycle configuration, click on **Review** to complete the process. In the **Review** and **Name** pages, you can specify an optional name for this particular transition rule as well. Make sure you review your rules correctly before selecting the **Create** and **Activate Rule** options. Post your rules creation. You can further edit or even delete them from the same **Lifecycle** drop-down menu found in the **Properties** panel of the S3 dashboard. To know more about lifecycle management and how you can leverage it for your objects and buckets, check `http://docs.aws.amazon.com/AmazonS3/latest/UG/LifecycleConfiguration.html`.

Cross-Region Replication

Versioning in S3 also provides us with yet another easy to use feature, which is called Cross-Region Replication. As the name suggests, this feature enables you to copy the contents of your bucket or the bucket itself asynchronously to a bucket present in some different AWS region. The copy process will basically copy all aspects of your source bucket and objects, including their creation date and time, version IDs, metadata, and so on, over to the destination bucket.

To enable Cross-Region Replication on a bucket, all you need to do is first make sure that the bucket has versioning enabled. Next, from the **Properties** panel, select the option **Cross-Region Replication**, as shown here:

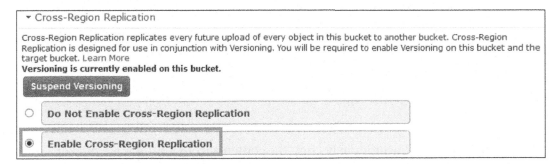

Click on **Enable Cross-Region Replication** to get things started. You can either select the entire bucket as the **Source** or even specify a prefix in the bucket, for example, **Images/**. Next, select an appropriate **Destination Region** for your bucket replication. In my case, I opted for the **Northern California** region. Select the **Destination Bucket** of your choice as well. This destination bucket is not auto created by S3, so it's your responsibility to go ahead and create one in the destination region of your choice:

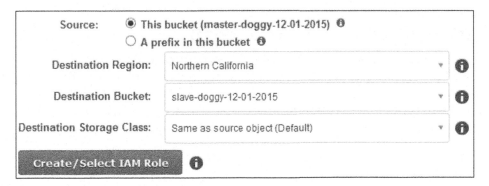

You can optionally change the **Destination Storage Class** of your replicated objects as well. For example, if you wish to minimize your costs of replication, you can instruct S3 to store all replicated objects in the destination bucket using the Standard-IA storage class. Finally, you will also need to setup an IAM Role to grant S3 permission to replicate objects on your behalf. Click on **Create/ Select IAM Role** to bring up the IAM Dashboard. There, select the **Roles** option from the navigation pane and attach the following role policy:

```
{
"Version":"2012-10-17",
"Statement":[
        {
"Effect":"Allow",
"Principal":{
"Service":"s3.amazonaws.com"
            },
"Action":"sts:AssumeRole"
        }
    ]
}
```

Once done, S3 will asynchronously copy the contents from your source bucket over to the destination bucket. This includes any new objects that you add to the source bucket as well. An important point to note here is that using Cross-Region Replication, S3 will only replicate your actions over to the destination bucket, such as adding, copying, and deleting objects. Lifecycle configuration actions, such as transitioning objects from Standard to Standard-IA or to Glacier are not replicated. You can however, configure the same lifecycle configurations as your source bucket over to your destination buckets manually.

Planning your next steps

There are plenty of amazing things that you can configure and try on S3 besides the steps we have covered in this chapter. For example, you can leverage the encryption functionality provided by S3 to encrypt data in transit as well as at rest. Amazon S3 supports two types of encryption technique especially for this purpose: client-side encryption and server-side encryption.

Client-side encryption comes in really handy when you as an end user want to manage the encryption process, the encryption keys, tools, and so on. Generally, this encryption process is performed on the object before it gets uploaded to S3. You can also protect your data in transit using client-side encryption facilities such as SSL. Server-side encryption is where Amazon S3 encrypts and decrypts your data for you before it is stored within its data centers. Server-side encryption can be leveraged along with AWS **Key Management Service** (**KMS**) as well as with Amazon S3 managed keys. You can read about both in depth using this link `http://docs.aws.amazon.com/AmazonS3/latest/dev/UsingEncryption.html`.

Another feature worth trying out in S3 is the presigned URLs. These URLs are used to provide temporary access for downloading any particular object from S3. Each URL comes with its own expiry date and time, which denies access to the object once it expires. S3 provides SDKs in Java and .NET using which you can create your own pre-signed URLs. To read more about presigned URLs and how to generate them for your own objects, go to `http://docs.aws.amazon.com/AmazonS3/latest/dev/ShareObjectPreSignedURL.html`.

Recommendations and best practices

Here are some key best practices and recommendations that you ought to keep in mind when working with Amazon S3:

- Before creating your buckets, plan and choose a region that has closer proximity to your users. You may also want to consider any legal or regulatory compliance before selecting a particular region.

- Leverage S3's versioning and lifecycle management for automatically archiving or cleaning up of your buckets and objects. This will help you save a lot on storage costs as well.

- Employ server-side encryption for encrypting your data at rest. Although all objects and buckets in S3 are private by default, you can still enforce additional security by encrypting them using either AWSKMS or using S3 Managed Keys.

- Design and use bucket policies for restricting delete operations on buckets. You can even enable **Multi-factor authentication** (**MFA**) for certain users who will be required to provide additional authentication to perform a change in an object's version ID or even delete it.

- Leverage multi-part upload when it comes to uploading large objects into Amazon S3. Using multi-part uploads, you can even resume your upload process in case it was abruptly stopped or failed.

- You can optionally enable Amazon CloudFront to speed up your static website's performance as well by caching your HTML code, photos, and videos. To know more about how you can leverage CloudFront for your S3 buckets, go to `http://docs.aws.amazon.com/gettingstarted/latest/swh/getting-started-create-cfdist.html`.

Summary

So yet another chapter and yet another awesome AWS Service walkthrough comes to an end! Let's take a quick flashback into the things we've learned so far.

First off, we started by learning what exactly Amazon S3 is, along with the various storage class options provided with it. Next, we saw how easy and effortless it is to create buckets, upload objects into them, and view them. We even tried out a simple CLI tool called as S3CMD for syncing log files from your instances over to an S3 bucket. Toward the end, you even learned how to host static websites on S3 and enable lifecycle management on objects as well.

In the next and final chapter, you will be learning a bit more about a few key AWS services, such as Route53 and CloudFront, along with a quick look at some of the newer AWS service offerings, such as Amazon EFS and ECS, so stay tuned!

10
Extended AWS Services for Your Applications

In the previous chapter, you learned a lot about how you can leverage S3 to store your objects and even perform some pretty interesting and useful lifecycle operations on them.

In this final chapter, we will be exploring a few additional AWS services that you can leverage to enhance your application's overall performance as well as availability. The two services that I'm going to cover are Amazon Route53 and Amazon CloudFront. After this, we will also take a quick look at some of the recently launched AWS services and products and how you can leverage them for your own environments, along with a final word on how to get going with AWS; so without further ado, let's get busy!

Introducing Amazon Route53

Amazon Route53 is a highly available and scalable authoritative **Domain Name Service (DNS)**, which is responsible for routing users to internet-based applications. How does it do that? Well, Route53 works like any other DNS but on a much larger scale. It translates names such as www.all-about-dogs.com to either an instance's IP address, such as 192.168.0.15, or even to an elastic load balancer's or Amazon S3's endpoints. But that's not all! The real power of Route53 comes with its ability to route traffic intelligently, which is achieved with the use of health checks and route-based traffic flows that route traffic based on latencies and geographies, and in a weighted round robin fashion. Recently, Route53 has also launched its very own domain registration service, using which you can register your very own custom domain names with AWS at absolutely nominal rates.

In this section, we will be exploring a few of these features along with some simple to follow examples and use cases that you can use to extend the functionality and availability of your applications.

Working with Route53

Getting started with Route53 is a very simple and straightforward process. From the AWS Management Console, select the **Route53** option from the **Networking** group, as shown here:

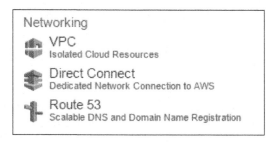

This will bring up the Route53 Management Console for the first time. Using this console, you can create and configure your very own custom domain names as well as configure health checks and traffic routing policies as per your requirements. First up, let's go ahead and create a simple hosted zone for our demo application `all-about-dogs.com`.

A hosted zone is nothing more than a logical container that holds information on how you wish to route traffic for your application. You create a hosted zone for your custom domain (`all-about-dogs.com`) and then create one or more resource record sets to tell the DNS service how you want traffic to be routed for that domain. If your Hosted Zone routes traffic over the Internet, then it is called a **public hosted zone**, and conversely if you are routing within an Amazon VPC, it is called a **private hosted zone**. Once your hosted zone is created, Route 53 will automatically create a **Name Server (NS)** record and a **Start Of Authority (SOA)** record for that zone. The NS record identifies the four name servers that Route53 creates for you. You can then provide these four NS records to a registrar or your DNS service provider, such as `https://in.godaddy.com/`, so that your application's DNS queries are routed to Amazon Route53's name servers.

 You can create more than one hosted zone with the same name and add different resources to it.

Here is a pictorial representation of how things actually work out. In this case, our demo application's domain name is already registered with `http://www.godaddy.com/`; however, you can alternatively use any other domain provider of your choice, or Route53's newly launched domain registrar service as well:

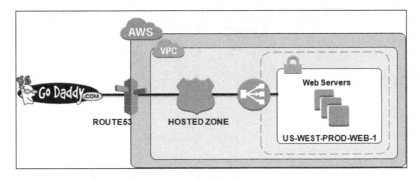

Creating hosted zones

To create your very own hosted zone, select the **Create Hosted Zone** option from the Route53 dashboard. This will bring up the **Create Hosted Zone** panel, as shown in the following screenshot. Provide a suitable **Domain Name** (in this case, I have provided our demo application's name `all-about-dogs.com`) and an optional **Comment** as well. Next, from the **Type** drop-down menu, select the option **Public Hosted Zone**, as shown. Click on **Create** once all the required fields are filled in:

You should get two record sets created as shown. The first record set is your hosted zone's NS record set that contains the four name servers, and the second record set is the SOA record set. Each new hosted zone that you create will contain its own unique NS and SOA record sets:

Once your hosted zone is created, the next step is where you create a new resource record set. A resource record set basically tells the DNS how the traffic should be routed for that particular domain. For example, you may want to route all Internet traffic for your domain name **all-about-dogs.com** to a specific IP address of an instance or an ELB, or you may even want all your e-mails to be routed to a specific mail server with the domain name mail.**all-about-dogs.com** and so on.

Each resource record set that you create will include the name of your domain, a record type, and other miscellaneous information applicable to that particular record type, such as **Time To Live (TTL)**, routing policies, and health checks. Here are some of the commonly used record set types provided by Route53:

- **A record**: A simple IP address in the form `192.168.0.15`. You can provide the IP address of an EC2 instance in this set.

- **AAAA record**: A simple IPv6 IP address in the form `2001:0db8:85a3:0000:0000:8a2e:0370:7334`.

- **CNAME records**: A **Canonical Name (CNAME)** is basically a record set that acts as an alias, pointing one domain name to another. For example, you can route all internet traffic from your domain name `all-about-dogs.com` to an ELBal's DNS name.

- **MX records**: MX records are used to specify the priority and domain name of a mail server, for example, `10 mail.all-about-dogs.com`; here, 10 specifies the priority of the MX record.

To create your own record set, simply select the **Create Record Set** option from the hosted zone dashboard. This will bring up the **Create Record Set** panel as shown in the following screenshot. Now in my case, I want to route all of my incoming application traffic on the ELB, which is hosted in us-west-2, via a domain name of **www.all-about-dogs.com**. In this case, I provided the value **www** in the record set **Name** field. Alternatively, you can provide any meaningful value there as per your requirements. Next, from the **Type** drop-down menu, select the **CNAME - Canonical Name** option. We will be using CNAME because the ELB is provided by a default DNS name, which you can obtain by selecting your ELB from the **EC2 Management Dashboard** and noting down its DNS name, which is generally of the following format: **US-WEST-PROD-LB-01-1582564436.us-west-2.elb.amazonaws.com**. Once done, paste the ELB's DNS name in the **Value** field. You can optionally edit the TTL (seconds) value; however, I have chosen to stick with the default of 300 seconds.

Next, select an appropriate routing policy based on your requirements. There are five routing policies provided, using which you can decide the best mechanism to route your queries to Route53. They are as follows:

- **Simple routing**: This is used when you only have a single source where you want your queries to be routed to, such as a single web server or a standalone server connected to Route53.

- **Weighted routing**: As the name suggests, here each record set is provided with some definite numeric value or weight that Route53 uses to proportionately divide traffic into. As a result, you can now associate more than one resource with a single DNS name using this approach. For example, a single DNS name, such as **all-about-dogs.com**, routes traffic to five web server instances, out of which three are assigned the weight 1, whereas the rest of the two are assigned the weight 2. Then, on average, Route53 will select each of the first three resource record sets 1/7th of the time (*1+1+1+2+2=7*) and the rest of the two record sets 2/7th of the time.

- **Latency-based routing**: Perhaps one of the most commonly used modes of routing, latency-based routing comes in really handy when you have your application's instances spread across multiple EC2 regions. In this case, Route53 determines the origin of the request made to your application and routes the traffic to the instances where the latency is at its minimum. For example, consider your application is spread across the us-west (Oregon) and a European region (Frankfurt) and a user request originates from, let's say, Texas; then, Route53 will route that particular request to the us-west region as the latency between Texas and Frankfurt is far greater than the latency between Texas and Oregon.

 Latency-based routing is based on latency measurements performed over a period of time and can change as a result of improved network connectivity and routing.

- **Geolocation routing**: Geolocation works on a similar principle as latency-based routing with the difference that here you can choose the resources that serve your application's traffic, based on the geographical location of your users. For example, you can route all traffic that originates from India and send it to a particular instance or an ELB. This method of routing has numerous applications, such as restricting distribution of content to only a few geographies, routing users to the same endpoint, and so on. You can specify geographical locations by either continent or by country or even by state in the United States.

- **Failover routing**: Failover routing policy is yet another simple routing technique that you can use to route traffic from one downed region to an active region. Failover routing only works if your hosted zone is Public and can only be configured for an active-passive failover scenario.

Coming back to our record set, for this particular scenario I opted to go for the latency-based routing for my application. Select the **Latency** option from the **Routing Policy** drop-down list. This will provide you with an option to select an associated region to route your traffic to. In this case, I selected the **us-west-2** region where my ELB is currently present. The final step is to provide a meaningful and unique **Set ID** or description for this particular record set. Once done, complete the record set creation process by selecting the **Create** option, as shown:

Once your record set is created, it will be displayed along the NS and the SOA records that were created by Route53 when the hosted zone was first deployed. You can create additional record sets for your hosted zone using the same steps as mentioned.

Getting started with traffic flow

It's all ok to create individual record sets using the previously described method, but what if you had multiple resources present across multiple locations and each resource required a different routing policy and configuration? This can become a real pain point when you look at it from a management point of view and that is precisely the reason why AWS recently launched an interactive visual tool called **traffic flow**.

Traffic flow basically provides you with an easy to use interface using which you can create and manage complex traffic policies, all within a fraction of the time. Using the tool is a fairly simple and straightforward process. You start off by creating one or more traffic policies, each containing multiple routing and configuration options in the form of policy records. You can even create multiple versions of the same traffic policy and use different versions to roll out or roll back configuration changes as you see fit.

To create your first traffic policy, select the **Traffic policies** option from the Route53 Management dashboard. Next, select the **Create traffic policy** option to get started. Provide a suitable **Policy name** and **Version description** as required. Click on **Next** to continue. This will bring up the **Create traffic policy** page where you can use the **Start Point** and the **Connect to** options to create child rules and endpoints. To delete any child rule, simply select close (marked by **x**) in the upper-right corner of each rule box.

The **Start Point** actually is where you choose the DNS type that you want Route 53 to assign to all of the resource record sets. Use the following DNS types if you wish to route traffic to the following AWS resources:

- **ELB**: You can provide either an **A** record (IP Address) or an **AAAA** Record (IPv6 Address) here.

- **Amazon S3 bucket**: Provide an **A** record of your S3 bucket. Note that this is only going to work if your bucket is configured as a static website container.

- **CloudFront distribution**: Provide an **A** record for your CloudFront distribution here.

Once you have defined the **Start Point** value, you can use the **Connect to** option to select an applicable rule or endpoint based on the design for your configuration. The rules can be anything from **Weighted rules** to **Failover**, **Geolocation**, and even **Latency-based** rules. Once done, click on the **Create traffic policy** option to complete the traffic policy's creation:

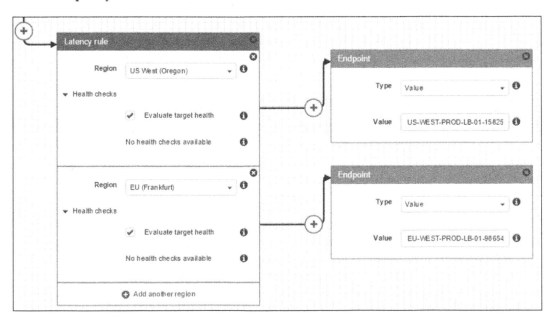

Do note that once your traffic policy is created, each edit of it will end up creating a new version of it. The previous versions of the policy are retained unless you choose to delete them explicitly. You can even create a new Traffic policy by importing a JSON-based document that describes all of the endpoints and rules that you want to include in the policy. To know more about traffic policy document format and how you can use them for your own scenarios, go to `http://docs.aws.amazon.com/Route53/latest/APIReference/api-policies-traffic-policy-document-format.html`.

Configuring health checks

Route53 also provides a mechanism using which you can effectively monitor the health and performance of your web application as well as other resources using the health check facility provided. Health checks can be configured to periodically monitor the health of your application in a very similar way that ELB does. All you need to do is provide your application's URL or endpoint and configure the notification alarm. That's it! The rest is completely taken care of by Route53.

To create your very own health check, select the **Health checks** option from the Route53 dashboard. Next, click on the **Create health check** option to get started. This will bring up the **Configure health check** page. The first thing you need to do is provide a suitable name for your health check using the **Name** field. Next, select for what you wish to configure this health check. There are two options available: you can either monitor an **Endpoint**, such as an instance or an ELB or even your application's endpoint, or you can select to monitor the **Status of other health checks** as well:

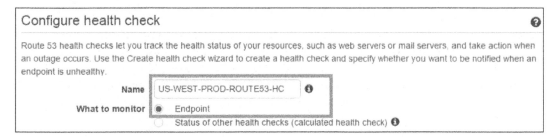

For this example, I opted to go for **Endpoint** monitoring. Next, configure the details to monitor your endpoint in the **Monitor an endpoint** section. Here, too, you have the flexibility to select between having an **IP address** or a **Domain name** as an endpoint.

 You cannot change the **Specify endpoint by** option once the health check is created.

From the **Protocol** drop-down list, select the appropriate protocol you want Route53 to use to check the health of your endpoint. Currently, the valid values provided are HTTP, HTTPS and TCP. For this particular scenario, I opted for the HTTP protocol as shown. In this case, Route 53 will try to establish a connection with the application using the HTTP protocol. If the connection is successful, Route 53 will submit an HTTP request and wait for an HTTP response in the form of a status code of 200 or greater but less than 400.

In the **Domain name** field, provide the domain name of the endpoint that you wish Route53 to monitor and also provide the **Port** on which Route53 will communicate. By default, port 80 is selected for your HTTP protocol and so port 443 is selected, in case you have selected HTTPS as the protocol. The final field left now is the **Path** field, which specifies the path that you wish Route53 to request when performing health checks. Do note that this field is only valid for HTTP and HTTPS protocols. If no value is provided here, then Route53 will automatically start requesting the **Domain name** itself:

Once done, you can optionally edit the **Request Interval** and **Failure threshold** levels from the **Advanced configuration** section, as shown in the following screenshot. Do remember that changing the request interval from **Standard (30 seconds)** to **Fast (10 seconds)** results in an additional payment. To know more about how Route53 is priced, check `http://aws.amazon.com/route53/pricing/#Health_Checks`:

With these settings configured, you can now proceed to the final step of the configuration where you can create or reuse an SNS notification to notify you in case a health check fails. Click on **Next** to continue with the health check creation process.

You can specify health checks to provide you with SNS notifications using the final configuration page as shown here. Select **Yes** to create an alarm and choose either **Existing SNS topic** or **New SNS topic** to send notifications to. Once you are happy with your settings, click on **Create health check** to complete the process:

Health checks also help you to design and configure DNS failover scenarios. For example, if your web application is running ten EC2 instances in the backend, five present in one region and the other five in another, then you can configure Route53 to check the health of those instances and respond only to the servers that are healthy. Using this mechanism, you can configure active-active or even active-passive failover scenarios and maintain the uptime of your applications. For a complete overview and guidance on how you can leverage DNS failover for your applications, refer to Route53's developer's guide: `http://docs.aws.amazon.com/Route53/latest/DeveloperGuide/dns-failover-configuring.html`.

Content delivery using Amazon CloudFront

Moving on, Route53 is yet another awesome service provided by AWS that is specially designed for distributing and delivering content across the globe and it is called **Amazon CloudFront**. For some reason, CloudFront is not one of the most commonly used services in the AWS service family; nevertheless, it is still a good alternative to S3 when it comes to distributing content geographically. How does it all work? Well, it's quite simple actually! To begin with, the first thing that you need to do is configure an Origin Server. An Origin Server is nothing more than a place from where CloudFront retrieves the files or content for distribution. Origin Servers can be anything from an S3 bucket to even an EC2 instance running in a VPC. Once an Origin is defined, the next step involves the upload of objects to your Origin Server. Objects can be anything from images, media files, to even web pages! Yes, you heard it right! Web pages as well! Anything and everything that can be served over the HTTP protocol or a supported version of the **Real Time Messaging protocol (RTMP)**. Refer to the following diagram as an example of Origin Server:

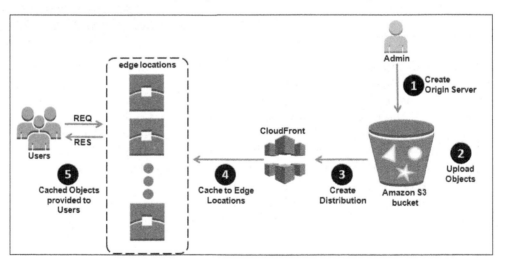

The next step is perhaps the most important one and involves the creation of a CloudFront distribution. The distribution describes which Origin Server to use when a user initiates a request to an image or a media object from your application or website. This step will provide your objects with a new CloudFront URL, which you need to substitute in your application. For example, a standard image URL may look something like this once it is referenced by CloudFront: `http://112233.cloudfront.net/myimage.jpg`. CloudFront then sends this distribution configuration to all of its specialized edge locations that are spread out across the world.

As of date, Amazon CloudFront has forty-plus edge locations spread across five continents, including North and South America, Europe, Asia, and Australia.

These edge locations are nothing more than small data centers where CloudFront caches copies of your objects and keeps them ready for distribution. When a user accesses or requests the object from your application or website, the DNS will route it to the nearest edge location. CloudFront will then check its cache for the requested file in the edge location. If the file is present in the cache, then it is returned to the user. If not, then CloudFront will request the file from the Origin Server and cache it in its edge location. This delivery method comes in really handy when you have a lot of data that gets requested or accessed by users on high frequency basis. It also improves the overall performance of your application and website as well as increasing reliability and availability.

Getting started with distributions

Now that the basic concepts are out of the way, let's look at some simple steps using which you can get your own CloudFront distribution up and running in a matter of minutes! First up, access the CloudFront option from the AWS Management Console, as shown here:

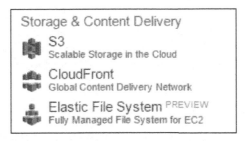

This will bring up the CloudFront Management dashboard where you will be able to create your distributions as well as perform a wide variety of monitoring and analysis tasks, such as view **Cache Statistics**, **Popular Objects** based on frequency of requests, **Usage**, alarms, and so on.

To create your first distribution, select the **Create Distribution** button. This will bring up a page where you need to select the distribution's delivery method. Currently, CloudFront supports two modes of delivering content; they are as follows:

- **Web**: Create a web distribution if you wish to distribute static as well as dynamic content in the form of HTML pages, or even CSS, PHP pages, and static images. Do remember that web distributions serve the following content over the HTTP or HTTPS protocols only. You can use either an S3 bucket or even an EC2 instance such as a web server for your web distribution.

- **RTMP**: The RTMP distribution is only meant for live streaming data and media files such as videos. This distribution only supports an S3 bucket as the origin server. The following variants of the RTMP protocol are supported by CloudFront:

  - ° **RTMP**: Adobe's Real-Time Message Protocol.
  - ° **RTMPT**: Adobe streaming tunnel over HTTP.
  - ° **RTMPE**: Adobe encrypted.
  - ° **RTMPTE**: Adobe encrypted tunnel over HTTP.

For this little demonstration, I'll be using one of the S3 buckets that we created in the previous chapter (*Chapter 9, Working with Simple Storage Service*). The bucket contains a simple video that I wish to distribute using CloudFront's edge locations, so the obvious choice for the distribution selection in this case will be RTMP. In case you do not have a bucket by now, follow the simple steps outlined in *Chapter 9, Working with Simple Storage Service*, and create a bucket, upload a video to it, and make sure that the bucket has public permissions provided to it.

Next, fill out the following details to create your very own RTMP distribution:

- **Origin Domain Name**: Provide the DNS name of the S3 bucket from which you want CloudFront to get objects for this origin. In my case, the value provided here is **master-doggy-12-01-2015.s3.amazonaws.com**.

- **Restrict Bucket Access**: CloudFront provides an added layer of security using which you can restrict end users from accessing objects using only CloudFront URLs and not using Amazon S3 URLs. This particular feature is called as **Origin Access Identity (OAI)**. For now, let's go ahead and use this feature to safeguard our bucket. Select the **Yes** option, as shown in the following image.

- **Origin Access Identity**: Once you have opted to restrict bucket access, the next step involves the creation of an OAI. Select the **Create a New Identity** option as shown and provide a meaningful name for the new identity in the **Comment** section as well:

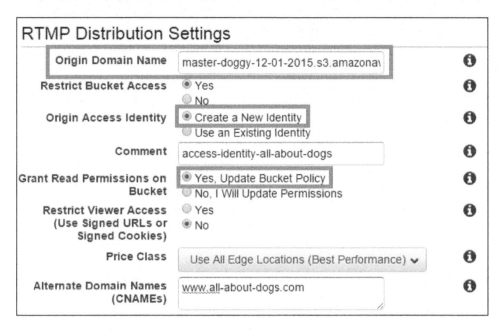

- **Grant Read Permissions on Bucket**: Select the **Yes, Update Bucket Policy** option to allow CloudFront to automatically grant the OAI the permission to read objects stored in your Amazon S3 bucket. You can choose to update the permissions manually as well.

- **Restrict Viewer Access**: Select the **Yes** option if you want to use a CloudFront-signed URL or signed cookies as a medium to provide access to objects in your Amazon S3 bucket. This is yet another advanced security feature using which you can restrict user access to your buckets. For now, I have selected **No** as the option here.

- **Price Class**: CloudFront provides three basic pricing classes that can basically help you pay lower prices based on the content you deliver out of CloudFront. The **Price Classes** field come in three variants: All, which includes all the edge locations present in AWS; Price Class 200, which includes US, Europe, a bit of Southeast Asia, and India; and finally Price Class 300, which only includes edge locations present in US and Europe. Depending on your application's reach, you can select the Price Class as per your requirements. For a complete overview of how CloudFront charges you as well as its Price Class, check http://aws.amazon.com/cloudfront/pricing/.

- **Alternate Domain Names (CNAMES)**: This is an optional field you can use if you want to replace the CloudFront URL's domain name with something a bit more customized and meaningful, such as your own domain name.

- **Logging**: You can enable logging at any time to log information about each request made to an object. Simply select the **On** option, as shown in the following screenshot, and fill out the **Bucket for Logs** option as well as **Log Prefix** values. You can optionally provide a **Comment** as well if required:

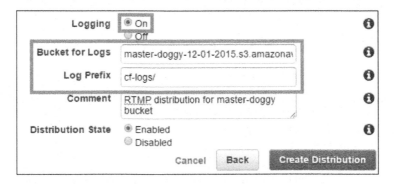

- **Distribution State**: Before you complete the distribution's creation, you need to specify whether you want the distribution to be enabled or disabled after its creation. By selecting the **Enabled** option, your users can access the CloudFront distribution immediately after its creation, whereas **Disabled** means that even though the distribution is ready for use, the end users will not be able to use it.

Once your configurations are completed, select the **Create Distribution** option. The distribution will take a couple of minutes to change from **pending** state to **enabled**. Once it's ready, you can use the CloudFront **Domain Name** to retrieve your objects from the Origin Server:

You can edit your distribution's settings anytime by simply selecting the distribution entry and clicking on **Distribution Settings** as shown. You can also **Disable** or **Delete** the state of your distribution using this dashboard. Follow the same steps and you can also configure a web distribution for your application, so give that a try as well.

CloudFront recommendations and best practices

Here are some key takeaways and best practices to keep in mind when working with CloudFront:

- Cache at every layer of your application, wherever possible.
- Use a combination of Amazon S3 and CloudFront to distribute static data. Remember that data transfer between S3 and CloudFront is free!
- Control access of data on CloudFront and S3. Make use of OAIs to ensure that there are no unwanted content leaks.
- Don't forward any headers, cookies, or query strings. Use Signed cookies instead of signed URLs.
- Use Route53 to check the health of your origin servers. In this way, you can configure Route53 to divert all traffic from the failed Origin to the healthy one.
- Use Price Classes to optimize content delivery costs.
- Make use of the alarms and notification services using Amazon CloudWatch.

What's new in AWS?

With the basic services now covered, here's a quick look at some of the newer AWS services and how you can potentially leverage them to build and host your applications and infrastructure. First up on the list is **Elastic Container Service (ECS)**.

Elastic Container Service

Before I talk about Elastic Container Service, it is essential to understand what a container is all about and why is it getting so much of importance lately.

A container is a logical entity that consists of one entire runtime environment. This environment can include an application, its dependencies, all of its libraries, and configuration files needed to run it, all packed into one small package. But wait a minute! Doesn't this all seem a bit familiar? Well to be honest, containers are nothing like virtualization, in fact I see them replacing virtualization very soon. If you see a virtual machine today, it basically comprises an entire OS plus the application hosted on top of it. You can have one or more such VMs running on top of a virtualization layer in the form of a hypervisor, which again has its own set of memory and CPU requirements. In contrast to VMs, a server running three containers runs on top of a single OS, and each container shares the OS kernel with the other containers. This means that the containers are much leaner and lightweight and use far fewer resources than conventional virtual machines, as depicted in the image here:

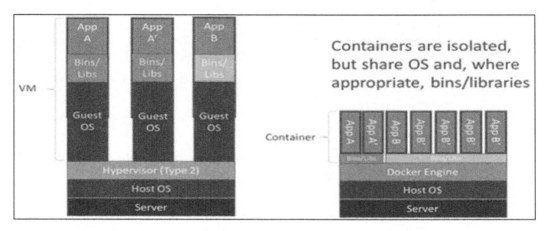

Containers are a potent solution to the problem of porting one application from one environment to the other. These environments can be anything from a simple laptop to virtualized environments to public clouds. That's where ECS comes into picture. ECS is a highly scalable container management service using which you can create, run, manage, and scale Docker-based containers. Here are a few key benefits and features of using ECS:

- **Automated Clustering**: One of the key advantages of ECS is that it can automatically manage clusters of containers. ECS can maintain the state of your clusters as well as help you to scale past thousands of containers, all with relative ease.

- **Container Scheduling**: ECS also provides you with an in-built scheduling functionality using which you can maintain the availability as well as the scalability of your containers across your clusters.

- **Portability and extensibility**: Containers that run on your ECS environment can be made to run on any other Docker-based environment without any changes made at all. This feature can come in really handy when you don't want to get tied down with a particular cloud provider and wish to have the flexibility to move your workloads anytime anywhere you want.

- **AWS integration**: You can leverage ECS containers to work with other AWS services as well, such as CloudWatch, VPC, S3, **Elastic File System** (**EFS**), ELBs, and so on.

ECS was made generally available for use in the mid of 2015, and ever since then, AWS has continued to make further improvements and enhancements to it. I would really recommend trying out ECS and containers just because they are so cool to work with! There are plenty of starter guides available out there, so go ahead and try to deploy a simple web application on containers using ECS. Here is the Getting Started with ECS guide provided by AWS: `http://docs.aws.amazon.com/ AmazonECS/latest/developerguide/ECS_GetStarted.html`.

Elastic File System

Elastic File System or EFS is also newly launched, still in preview service provided by AWS that provides scalable file storage services for your EC2 instances. This of EFS as a highly scalable and available NFS server that multiple EC2 instances can use at the same time as a common data source for your applications, a central repository, and so on. The best part of working with EFS is that it is designed to scale up and down automatically, so the more data that you put in, the larger it grows, and vice versa. It is also based on the pay-per-use model, which means that you only have to pay for the storage used by your filesystem and not a penny more!

How does it work? Well, it's just like any other NFS server that you would create in an on-premises environment. You can start off by simply creating an EFS, mounting it to your EC2 instances and using it just as any NFS mount point would. You can even use EFS along with your VPC environments as well, but with a minor change. In the case of VPC, you end up creating one or more special mount points called as mount targets, and you mount your filesystem to the EC2 instances using these mount targets. A pictorial representation of mount targets is shown here:

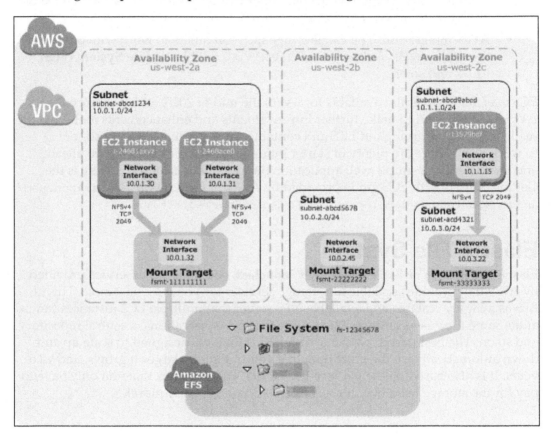

Courtesy: Amazon Web Services.

Database migration made easy with Database Migration Service

Yet another newly launched service by AWS, Database Migration Service provides customers with an easy to use and secure way to migrate their on-premises databases to AWS. The databases can be anything from propriety ones, such as Microsoft SQL and Oracle, to open source ones such as MySQL as well. Once a database migration is initiated using the Database Migration Service, AWS manages all the complexities of the migration process. It also makes sure that any data changes made in the source database are automatically replicated to the target database during the migration process.

The Database Migration Service also comes equipped with a Schema Conversion Tool that makes heterogeneous database migrations a real ease. This is made possible by converting the entire schema of the source database to a format compatible with that of the target database. If any schema code is not converted during the process automatically, it is clearly marked by the Schema Conversion Tool so that it can be converted manually at a later time.

To know more about the Database Migration Service and how you can sign up for the preview, go to `https://aws.amazon.com/dms/`.

Go serverless with AWS Lambda

Imagine if you had the power of running and scaling your code dynamically based on certain events getting triggered! That's precisely what AWS Lambda is all about. AWS Lambda is basically a compute service very similar to EC2 or Elastic Beanstalk where you upload your code to Lambda and the service runs the code on your behalf using the underlying AWS infrastructure. Once your code is uploaded, you need to create some custom functions called as **Lambda functions**. These functions take care of provisioning and managing the underlying instances that you use to run the code. But how is this so different from your EC2 service? Well in the case of Lambda, all the heavy lifting and complex tasks such as server management and provisioning, OS patching, code monitoring, logging, and so on, are managed by Lambda itself. All you need to do is upload your code and voila! The rest is all taken care of by Lambda itself.

 As of date, AWS Lambda supports Node.js, Java, and Python as the languages for your application's code.

So when and where is Lambda useful? Well if you have any real-time log processing or analyzing a stream of data for pattern analysis, social media analysis, or even if you want to build scalable backend services for your mobile or web applications, then Lambda is the right choice for you. To know more about Lambda and how it works, check `http://docs.aws.amazon.com/lambda/latest/dg/lambda-introduction.html`.

Resources, recommendations, and best practices

There are a ton of resources present on the web and on AWS's website itself where you can find good content, guides, how-to tutorials, and much more:

- For anyone just starting off with AWS, I would really recommend reading the Getting Started with AWS guides. These are some well written and to the point guides covering topics such as hosting static websites, deploying web apps, analyzing Big Data, and so on. Go to `https://aws.amazon.com/documentation/gettingstarted/` to know more.

- Next, the holy grail of all AWS services and a must to read if you are planning to work with AWS — the AWS documentations page. This page is a one stop shop for all your AWS service user guides, CLI and API references as well. Refer to `https://aws.amazon.com/documentation/` for more information.

- Although not mandatory, the AWS case studies page is yet another important place where you can read about how and what customers are using AWS for. You can filter case studies based on their use cases, all provided at `https://aws.amazon.com/solutions/case-studies/`.

- Make sure you also have a look at the pricing for each of the AWS services that you use by following this link: `https://aws.amazon.com/pricing/services/`.

- Here are some best practice guides provided by AWS as well, which are a must read if you are planning to use AWS as a production environment:
  - General AWS Cloud Best Practices to follow: `http://media.amazonwebservices.com/AWS_Cloud_Best_Practices.pdf`.
  - How to build fault tolerant application on AWS: `http://media.amazonwebservices.com/AWS_Building_Fault_Tolerant_Applications.pdf`.

- ° A few design considerations and best practices to keep in mind when designing DR solutions on AWS: `http://media.amazonwebservices.com/AWS_Disaster_Recovery.pdf`.

- ° AWS Security Best Practices guide: `http://media.amazonwebservices.com/AWS_Security_Best_Practices.pdf`.

Summary

Well it has really been a wonderful journey writing this book! You started off with learning the basics of Cloud Computing and slowly, but gradually, covered so much. From compute (EC2) to networks (VPC) to storage (S3), identity and access management (IAM), databases (RDS), DNS (Route53), and content delivery services (CloudFront).

Although this book may seem a lot to read and grasp, trust me, this is all just a drop in the ocean. AWS is a rapidly expanding and highly innovative public cloud that, if used correctly, can bring your business and organization a lot of benefits such as scalability, flexibility, and cost savings. The principle, however, remains the same—plan out your way before you start, make sure you have designed for failure, and continuously monitor and automate your infrastructure. Remember these and you should be just fine!

Index

Thank you for buying
AWS Administration – The Definitive Guide

About Packt Publishing

Packt, pronounced 'packed', published its first book, *Mastering phpMyAdmin for Effective MySQL Management*, in April 2004, and subsequently continued to specialize in publishing highly focused books on specific technologies and solutions.

Our books and publications share the experiences of your fellow IT professionals in adapting and customizing today's systems, applications, and frameworks. Our solution-based books give you the knowledge and power to customize the software and technologies you're using to get the job done. Packt books are more specific and less general than the IT books you have seen in the past. Our unique business model allows us to bring you more focused information, giving you more of what you need to know, and less of what you don't.

Packt is a modern yet unique publishing company that focuses on producing quality, cutting-edge books for communities of developers, administrators, and newbies alike. For more information, please visit our website at www.packtpub.com.

About Packt Enterprise

In 2010, Packt launched two new brands, Packt Enterprise and Packt Open Source, in order to continue its focus on specialization. This book is part of the Packt Enterprise brand, home to books published on enterprise software – software created by major vendors, including (but not limited to) IBM, Microsoft, and Oracle, often for use in other corporations. Its titles will offer information relevant to a range of users of this software, including administrators, developers, architects, and end users.

Writing for Packt

We welcome all inquiries from people who are interested in authoring. Book proposals should be sent to author@packtpub.com. If your book idea is still at an early stage and you would like to discuss it first before writing a formal book proposal, then please contact us; one of our commissioning editors will get in touch with you.

We're not just looking for published authors; if you have strong technical skills but no writing experience, our experienced editors can help you develop a writing career, or simply get some additional reward for your expertise.

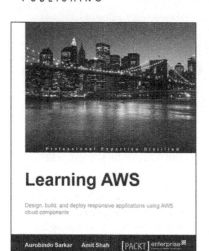

Learning AWS

ISBN: 978-1-78439-463-9   Paperback: 236 pages

Design, build, and deploy responsive applications
using AWS cloud components

1. Build scalable and highly available real-time
    applications.

2. Make cost-effective architectural decisions by
    implementing your product's functional and
    non-functional requirements.

3. Develop your skills with hands-on exercises
    using a three-tiered service oriented application
    as an example.

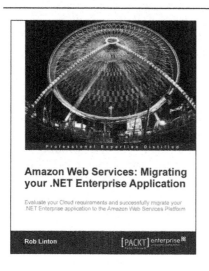

Amazon Web Services: Migrating your .NET Enterprise Application

ISBN: 978-1-84968-194-0   Paperback: 336 pages

Evaluate your Cloud requirements and successfully
migrate your .NET Enterprise Application to the
Amazon Web Services Platform

1. Get to grips with Amazon Web Services from a
    Microsoft Enterprise .NET viewpoint.

2. Fully understand all of the AWS products
    including EC2, EBS, and S3.

3. Quickly set up your account and manage
    application security.

4. Learn through an easy-to-follow sample
    application with step-by-step instructions.

Please check **www.PacktPub.com** for information on our titles

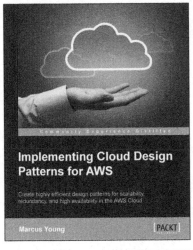

Implementing Cloud Design Patterns for AWS

ISBN: 978-1-78217-734-0   Paperback: 228 pages

Create highly efficient design patterns for scalability, redundancy, and high availability in the AWS Cloud

1. Create highly robust systems using cloud infrastructure.

2. Make web applications resilient against scheduled and accidental down-time.

3. Explore and apply Amazon-provided services in unique ways to solve common problems.

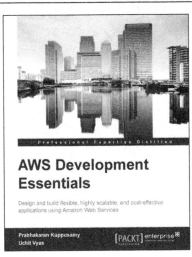

AWS Development Essentials

ISBN: 978-1-78217-361-8   Paperback: 226 pages

Design and build flexible, highly scalable, and cost-effective applications using Amazon Web Services

1. Integrate and use AWS services in an application.

2. Reduce the development time and billing cost using the AWS billing and management console.

3. This is a fast-paced tutorial that will cover application deployment using various tools along with best practices for working with AWS services.

Please check **www.PacktPub.com** for information on our titles

CPSIA information can be obtained
at www.ICGtesting.com
Printed in the USA
BVOW09s1430110617

486583BV00003B/33/P